MAYA SAINTS AND SOULS IN A CHANGING WORLD

Maya Saints and Souls in a Changing World

by
John M. Watanabe

UNIVERSITY OF TEXAS PRESS, AUSTIN

First Edition, 1992

Requests for permission to reproduce material from this work
should be sent to Permissions, University of Texas Press, Box 7819,
Austin, Texas 78713-7819.

⊗ The paper used in this publication meets the minimum
requirements of American National Standard for Information
Sciences—Permanence of Paper for Printed Library Materials,
ANSI Z39.48-1984.

Library of Congress Cataloging-in-Publication Data
Watanabe, John, 1952–
    Maya saints and souls in a changing world / by John Watanabe. —
1st ed.
        p.   cm.
    Includes bibliographical references and index.
    ISBN 0-292-75137-0 (cloth). — ISBN 0-292-75141-9 (pbk.)
    1. Mam Indians—Social conditions.   2. Mam Indians—
Economic conditions.   3. Coffee plantation workers—
Guatemala—Santiago Chimaltenango—Social conditions.
4. Wages—Coffee plantation workers—Guatemala—Santiago
Chimaltenango.   5. Coffee trade—Guatemala—Santiago
Chimaltenango.   6. Santiago Chimaltenango (Guatemala)—Social
conditions.   7. Santiago Chimaltenango (Guatemala)—Economic
conditions.   I. Title.
F1465.2.M3W38   1992
972.81'004974—dc20   91-25313
                                                              CIP

✛ *Contents* ✛

Illustrations

Photos

Figures

Tables

✣ *Preface* ✣

THIS BOOK concerns the interplay of identity, history, and experience in a Mam-speaking Maya town in the western highlands of Guatemala. In it I take up several long-standing problems in anthropology: the nature of community; the dynamics of social, cultural, and economic change; and the question of authenticity in cultural traditions. That it involves the town of Santiago Chimaltenango reflects my serendipitous journey there and back, the inspiration of three gifted teachers and anthropologists, and the allure as well as tragedy of that "land of eternal spring"—and, as Jean-Marie Simon (1987) has noted, of eternal tyranny.

Regarding the problem of community, the tendency has been to project onto the Maya much the same kind of "life-style enclave" that Robert Bellah and his colleagues (1985) have found in American middle-class notions of community. Cultural distinctiveness, social exclusivity, and internal homogeneity came to define Maya communities, and arguments then centered on the origins, functions, and fate of these characteristics. In contrast, I take community as a more problematic locus of contingent social cooperation involving diverse—at times divergent—individual interests. Given this perspective, those familiar with Guatemala may remark on the apparent neglect of local conflict and violence in the following pages. This stems in part from my concern with the shared conventions of "act and artifact," as Robert Redfield put it, with which people enact their community. It also reflects, despite the generalized militarization and repression in Guatemala, the relative absence of violence in the town during my stays there. As in any small town, disputes and animosities abounded, yet these remained largely of personal rather than political import. Even during the worst months of the Guatemalan army's counterinsurgency campaign in 1982–1983, the town refused to succumb to the self-serving recriminations, power-mongering, and murder that infected all its neighbors. Why this should have been evades any simple answer; I have written this book to understand it more clearly.

In traversing nearly five centuries of change in Maya life, I essay the perilous course between political economy and what Richard Shweder has referred to as the latest anthropological fashions from Paris. I firmly believe that there is a reality "out there" amenable to analysis and explanation, predicated on such undeniables as power and control, privilege and property, life and death. At the same time, individuals imbue this reality with an indeterminacy that often subverts "ultimately determinant" political, cultural, historical, or personal imperatives. Rather than choose which is more essential, I have tried to relate the historical to the personal, the meaningful to the institutional, by analyzing the cultural conventions of community that mediate them. In this regard, some readers may take exception to the lack of "real individuals" in these pages. I have chosen deliberately not to portray them because, as a cultural anthropologist, I remain primarily concerned with the patterns of understanding, organization, and action that link individuals to each other and make events possible, not with persons or events per se. Also, to take as fathomable the reality of Guatemalan society makes it all the more undeniable: in these volatile, violent times, "real individuals," whether as themselves or thinly disguised by pseudonyms, remain too vulnerable to unforeseen retribution. I have purposefully opted for a more conventional—in both senses of the term—mode of description and analysis.

The question of authenticity in cultural traditions I see as more anthropology's problem than other peoples'. Too often we tacitly attach greatest cultural authenticity to those traditions that have endured "since time immemorial"—or at least since colonial powers arrived on the scene. Instead, I have attributed to people the possibility of changing and yet retaining an abiding sense of who they are, what they are doing, and where they are going. Their authenticity inheres in what they make of themselves and the things around them, not in some primordial or immutable nature of people or things. At the same time, no people ever self-consciously encompass the totality of what they are about. They exist within a changing universe of possibilities that they themselves may not directly perceive but which nonetheless constrains as well as motivates their actions. How they respond to these conditions in the here and now constitutes as vital a part of their cultural authenticity as any enduring tradition inherited from the past. I have tried to situate the people of Santiago Chimaltenango between the immediacies of their actions and the reality of their circumstances in hopes of authenticating their historically derived yet culturally emergent identity.

To carry out this study, I traveled what seemed to me at first an impossible distance. Upon eventually arriving, I tried to listen as closely as I could to the people I encountered there. Although I occasionally resorted to formal interviews, I partook as best I could in the natural conversations that people had with one another, following them from hearth to field and back again. I pursued the art of casual questioning when topics of particular interest or significance arose, seeking verification through subsequent conversations or interviews—an inefficient, unscientific way of doing research, but I could neither bring myself to intrude more peremptorily on my hosts nor presume that I always knew the most important questions to ask. I have no illusions that such talk gave me a rounded view of the community, limited as I was to the people who would talk to me. Women proved especially unapproachable in a place where "talking to" unrelated women is a local euphemism for illicit affairs. I could only distantly appreciate women's importance from the families that I came to know best. Just once a mother confided in me her near-fatal sadness at the death of her teenage son and how her husband had thwarted the devil who came beckoning for her enfeebled soul. Chimalteco women live an intense and vital life that goes well beyond the compass of these pages. That it does reflects my inadequacy, not my intent.

Cultural anthropologists often work alone, but they seldom toil in isolation, and I am no exception. Without the guidance of three noted anthropologists, I would have never undertaken this study. Gary H. Gossen introduced me to the Maya long ago in an undergraduate seminar at the University of California, Santa Cruz. His teachings grew on me in ways that neither of us imagined at the time.

In 1937 Charles Wagley first visited Santiago Chimaltenango, and but for him I would have never learned of that special place, nor spent the last twelve years of my life trying to understand it better. During my time in Santiago Chimaltenango, his humanity, not merely his careful scholarship, became apparent. Even after forty years, many townspeople still warmly remembered *don Carlos*, and perhaps their initial acceptance of a new stranger into their midst came in part out of regard for that other gringo who had proved himself a friend so many years before. Having such a near-mythic predecessor in the field made my task incalculably easier, providing a basis for my own inquiries, a ready explanation for my presence, and much-needed inspiration during the early days of fieldwork when I had yet to gain Chimaltecos' acceptance as he so obviously had. Charles Wagley has more than once told me how honored he was to have someone return to Santiago Chimaltenango to evaluate his research. He set an admirable standard to follow, and contrary to his protestations, the honor to do so has been all mine.

My greatest debt falls to Evon Z. Vogt, Jr. Throughout the years, he has been a patient adviser, a tolerant critic, a demanding mentor, and a gracious senior colleague. Beyond sharing freely with me his vast knowledge of the Maya, he also profoundly influenced my intellectual and personal growth. During the time that I studied and taught with him, he exemplified to me the generosity of spirit and the keen enthusiasm for ideas that being both a scholar and a teacher demands.

Since first meeting Nora C. England in Guatemala in the summer of 1979, I have gleaned most of what I know of Mam linguistics from her. Without her meticulous scholarship and generous tutelage, my formal understanding of Mam, if not my practical ability to speak it, would be primeval. Similarly, W. George Lovell has given freely of his enthusiastic expertise on the history of the Cuchumatán Highlands, in addition to sharing with me his warm friendship and love of things *cuchumatenses.* Through the years, Christopher H. Lutz has generously made available to me the resources of the Centro de Investigaciones Regionales de Mesoamérica (CIRMA) in Antigua, Guatemala, and more recently in South Woodstock, Vermont. He once spent an entire afternoon with the late Bill Swezcy helping me track down information on the colonial history of Santiago Chimaltenango. Chris's generosity to me personally and to Mesoamerican studies publicly long ago convinced me that philanthropy is not dead.

At various points along the way, Robert M. Carmack, Norman E. Whitten, Jr., Edward M. Brunner, and Richard N. Adams offered kind words and impatient encouragement to "get the book done." Equally gratifying, and even more instructive, John P. Hawkins has been the most gracious and courtly adversary that I could hope to encounter in the all-too vituperative arena of scholarly debate. Carol A. Smith's masterful writings on Guatemalan political economy and history have helped me see the sense in my own work more clearly. Finally, although I have never studied formally with either of them, Roy A. Rappaport, through his brilliant but neglected essays, "The Obvious Aspects of Ritual" and "Sanctity and Lies in Evolution," and Roy Wagner, in his book *The Invention of Culture,* have fundamentally

informed the theoretical approach underlying this book. If their influence remains obscure or their arguments distorted, the fault is
mine, not theirs.

I carried out initial field research while holding a traveling fellow-
ship from the Frederick Sheldon Fund of Harvard University. In the
years since, I have gratefully benefited from a postdoctoral fellow-
ship with the Michigan Society of Fellows and a Walter Burke Research Initiation Award from Dartmouth College. I thank all these
organizations for their largess and faith in my work.

In Guatemala, I incurred many other debts. Roberto and Maryanne
Jiménez opened their home and their hearts to me, providing a haven
from the rigors of fieldwork and a sanctuary from the bureaucratic
frustrations of Guatemala City. Members of the Proyecto Lingüístico
Francisco Marroquín provided friendship and support, especially
Narciso Cojti, the late Juan Maldonado, Tricia Caffrey, and Joe Sieger;
Linda Munson first introduced me to the Maya linguists of the Pro-
yecto and gave me my first intimidating glimpse of Mam phonology.
Until his untimely death in 1989, William R. Swezey, codirector of
CIRMA in Antigua, always welcomed me with a ready smile and lively
conversation; Antigua will never be the same. Father Robert M.
Crohan, M.M., allowed me access to parish records in San Pedro
Necta and generously gave of his hospitality and knowledge of the
recent religious history of Santiago Chimaltenango. His love for the
town and the people of Santiago Chimaltenango goes beyond his
pastoral work there.

For indispensable aid in securing permission to remain continuously in Guatemala during my fieldwork in 1978–1980, Dr. José
Casteñeda Medinilla of the Instituto Indigenista Nacional and Lic.
Flavio Rojas Lima of the Seminario de Integración Social Guatemalteca have my deepest thanks.

In addition to those already mentioned, many good friends over
the years provided support when work demanded, companionship
when work was laid aside, and mutual understanding when research,
writing, and scholarship threatened to overwhelm me. I wish to
thank especially Peter and Pippi and Sam and Silas Ellison (and
Emma), Alisa Harrigan, Mike and Nitaya Polioudakis, Lars Rodseth,
and Barbara Smuts. Those at the beginning and the end of this road
deserve special mention. During seemingly interminable lunch conversations many years ago, Jim Ito-Adler helped me see questions
and think out ideas perhaps more than he knows. My wife, Deborah
Nichols, has witnessed mostly my waning gumption over a seemingly interminable project, but her faith in the integrity of its incep-
tion and its outcome—to say nothing of its author—has warmed my

efforts immeasurably. Incisive editorial assistance on the book came from Deborah Hodges at Dartmouth College; she helped me closer to the pithy tome that we would all write if we only had the time.

Anthropological convention and historical necessity demand anonymity of those Chimaltecos who, through their greatness of heart, chose to have me as their friend and to teach me about their life and language. Perhaps this is only fitting: my debt to them remains all the more irredeemable.

✠ Note on the Pronunciation ✠ of Mam Words

The orthography for Mam words used in this study follows that devised by Kaufman (1976: 89, 92–93) and used with slight modifications by England (1983: 24). Mam phonemes include:

Consonants

	Bilabial	Alveolar	Alveo-fricated	Alveopalatal	Retroflexed	Palatal	Velar	Uvular	Glottal
Occlusive	p	t	tz	ch	tx	ky	k	q	ʔ
Glottalized	b'	t'	tz'	ch'	tx'	ky'	k'	q'	
Fricative		s		xh	x			j	
Nasal		m	n						
Flap		r							
Resonant	w	l				y			
Spanish Loans	b	d					g		

Vowels	front		back			front		back
	i		u	high		ii		uu
	e		o			ee		oo
		a		low			aa	
		short					long	

Consonants are pronounced much as they are in Spanish, except for *q*, which is articulated farther back in the throat than the *k* in either English or Spanish. *Tz, ch, tx,* and *ky* represent single sounds:

tz resembles the consonant cluster *ts* in the English *bats*, and *ch* is equivalent to the English *ch*. *Tx* is a retroflexed *ch*, that is, pronounced with the tip of the tongue curled up as if to make an "er" sound in English. *Ky* is like the English *k* in *key* but articulated farther forward with the blade of the tongue arched against the soft palate of the roof of the mouth. *Xh* is the same as *sh* in English and *x* is its retroflexed equivalent. Glottalized consonants, except for *b'* and *q'*, are like normal consonants except the breath is held rather than expelled as the sound is released. Both *b'* and *q'*, however, are imploded—that is, made by drawing in air rather than by expelling it.

Mam vowels resemble those in Spanish, with long vowels tending to be slightly higher than their short counterparts: *i* as in the English *beet*; *e* as in *bet*; *a* as in *father*; *u* as in *boot*; *o* as in *boat*. A double vowel indicates vowel length, not separately articulated sounds. Stress falls on the syllable with a long vowel or, if the word has no long vowel, on the vowel before the final glottal stop in the word; if no long vowel or glottal stop occurs, the vowel before the last consonant in the root is stressed (England 1983: 37).

In normal Mam speech, short, unstressed vowels often disappear, resulting in the intimidating clusters of consonants so characteristic of the language. When next to a glottal stop or glottalized consonant, vowels acquire considerable vocal fry, or "creaky voice," another distinctive quality of Mam. In rapid speech, glottalized consonants often reduce to glottal stops, further complicating the intricacies of colloquial Mam pronunciation. Although tone carries no phonemic value in the language, Mam speech also demands prescribed variations in pitch and pacing for full expression. Together, these features endow Mam with a unique sound and style that once apprehended can seldom be mistaken for any other Maya tongue.

✙ *Part One* ✙

Past and Present

1

✤ Introduction ✤

Qejo oto?ya tzaluu?, "We who are here . . ." So Mam Maya shaman-diviners of the western highlands of Guatemala once intoned to begin their divinations and curing rituals. The invocation served to embrace all mortal participants as well as the Catholic saints in the local church, the spirit guardians of the sacred *Mundo* ("World") and nearby mountains, and the twenty sacred days of the traditional Maya calendar. In most Mam communities today, these old Maya and colonial Catholic deities wane before the incessant encroachments of a global age, before the return of a more orthodox Christian God heralded by Catholic as well as evangelical missionaries, and most recently, before the malignant political violence that desecrates their mountain abodes. This book concerns the significance of such happenings for inhabitants of one Maya community named Santiago Chimaltenango, a Mam-speaking town in the southern Cuchumatán Highlands of Huehuetenango, Guatemala.

It aptly reflects the existential irony shared by all Maya peoples today that the very name of this town should be foreign—"Santiago," the Saint James of the Spanish *conquistadores;* "Chimaltenango," a Nahuatl word from central Mexico meaning "place of the shields," perhaps a reference to the town's location on the northern marches of the old pre-Hispanic Mam kingdom (William Swezey, personal communication, June 1981, San Cristóbal de las Casas, Mexico). This irony, more than anything else, lies at the heart of the present inquiry: despite nearly five centuries of conquest, colonialism, and Christianization, the inhabitants of Santiago Chimaltenango still see themselves as a people apart, distinct from the descendants of their Spanish conquerors and from other Maya. Yet much of the distinctiveness now claimed by Chimaltecos originated in the very political and religious institutions imposed upon them by Spanish colonial rule. These two, seemingly contradictory, facts underscore a long-standing debate in the anthropology of Meso-

america: does the persistence of Maya peoples in Mexico and Guatemala reflect the survival of some primordial, if increasingly ineffable, Maya culture—an assumption rooted in ethnographies of the
1930s and 1940s informed by notions of acculturation—or does it
constitute the false consciousness of a colonialized rural proletariat
wracked by persistent forms of oppression and exploitation—a position taken more recently by Marxist scholars?

Stated in such bald terms, the extremes of this debate reveal its
fundamental inadequacy. While unquestionably conditioned by received heritage and contemporary circumstances, the Maya exist today, and have always existed, as more than cultural anachronisms or
passive victims of enduring iniquities. This study attempts to mod-
ify the terms of debate by asking two questions of one particular
Maya community. First, what is the nature of enduring ethnic distinctiveness in Santiago Chimaltenango: what exactly do Chimaltecos mean by calling themselves "Chimalteco"? Second, what is the
relationship between this ongoing Chimalteco identity and its ever-
changing context: how, and why, do Chimaltecos experience—at
times purposefully instigate—apparently sweeping changes in their
lives and yet remain Chimalteco? Answering these questions demands close attention to the nature of both Chimalteco culture and
the community where Chimaltecos live. By this I mean Chimalteco
culture not as an expression of some primordial or essential Mayanness but as the shared understandings of a living community. Similarly, I choose to regard the community of Santiago Chimaltenango
not simply as an institutional locus of colonialist domination or
peasant resistance but as a problematic social nexus in its own right,
contingent on the interests and commitments of Chimaltecos as
these are conditioned by their interactions with each other and with
the world beyond their town. Although clearly particularistic, this
approach seeks to temper, not deny, more global culturalist and historicist explanations by focusing on how Chimaltecos engage larger
realities through the local immediacies of their ongoing lives.

In attempting to plumb this question of Chimalteco identity and
its metamorphic continuity through time, I turn first to certain cultural conventions—predispositions regarding the world that "every
good Chimalteco should know"—that serve to circumscribe community boundaries. Rather than seek to capture some intrinsic essence of Chimalteco-ness, I focus on how Chimaltecos engage, and
thus identify, one another through local conventions of place, morality, and mutual obligation. I also draw on Charles Wagley's excellent 1937 study of this same town (Wagley 1941; 1949) to assess the
dynamics of change in Santiago Chimaltenango since earlier in this

century. Here again, I intend not simply to weigh the relative continuities and transformations in Chimalteco life as a measure of some
abstract cultural persistence or community solidarity. Instead, I
treat Chimalteco culture and community as experiential landscapes
that constitute strategic orientations in an ongoing present, not immutable dictates from a primordial past.

By combining cultural analysis with ethnographically informed
historical comparison, the following chapters thus reveal something
about how the Maya of Santiago Chimaltenango live their lives as
more than just cultural or proletarian automatons. Despite ever-
changing issues and interlocutors, the old Mam shaman-diviners'
invocation perhaps still best characterizes the sense that these people
have of themselves—*qejo oto?ya tzaluu?*, "we who are here"—for
it is precisely such mutual inclusion within an enduring here and
now that humanizes Chimalteco experience and continues to shape
Chimalteco, and thus Guatemalan, society and history.

Essentialism and Historicism in Maya Ethnology

The idea of culturally distinct Maya communities has long pervaded
the anthropology of Mesoamerica, and with good reason. Even today, the Maya of different Guatemalan towns still speak their own
local dialect in one of over twenty distinct Maya languages spoken
in the country; women especially continue to dress in handwoven
garments unique to each town; and socially these communities remain highly endogamous. Distinctive speech, dress, and custom
also serve to differentiate Mayas from Ladinos, Spanish-speaking
Guatemalans who wear Western-style clothing, live mainly in larger
towns and cities, and dominate the Maya political and socially, if not
always economically. Scholarly explanations of this cultural diversity have generally divided into two schools, which I would characterize as the "cultural essentialists" and the "colonial historicists."

Sol Tax first described the "local nature" of Maya cultures in two
classic articles (1937; 1941). He situated Maya distinctiveness not in
"tribes" or language groups but in *municipios*, the territorial and administrative jurisdictions of Guatemalan townships. The local community, not some larger entity, represented the relevant unit of
Maya social identity and cultural differentiation. He suggested that
this pattern went "back to pre-Hispanic times, and . . . developed
with the money economy and widespread system of trade, and the
wide formal political institutions, that existed in Guatemala before
the Spanish conquest" (Tax 1941: 35). In an equally classic paper,
Eric Wolf (1957) later deemed these Maya towns "closed, corporate

peasant communities" that had developed primarily in response to colonial and later capitalist economic conditions, not from direct survivals of pre-Hispanic Maya traditions. Marked by corporate institutions of communal land tenure and ritually sanctioned "levelling mechanisms," the closed, corporate peasant community ensured a cohesive "shared poverty" that served locally "to equalize the life chances and life risks of its members" while globally subordinating a "native peasantry" to a "dominant entrepreneurial sector" (Wolf 1957: 2–5, 8, 12).

Despite their obvious differences in intent and interpretation, both these approaches shared a common essentialist conception of Maya culture and community. Tax described local Maya cultures as inventories of traits, styles, and techniques ascribed to specific community places by a "primitive," as opposed to "civilized," Maya worldview—a "mental apprehension of reality" that remained highly localized and "clouded with animism" (1941: 37–38). Wolf in turn equated Mayanness with a "closed corporate" institutional structure dictated by the conditions of a "dualized" capitalist society: the "persistence of 'Indian' culture content seems to have depended primarily on maintenance of this structure. Where the structure collapsed, traditional cultural forms quickly gave way to new alternatives of outside derivation" (Wolf 1955: 456). Whether defined mentalistically or institutionally, an essential "Indianness" infused these outward cultural and social forms.

Ironically, the more clearly that anthropologists defined this Indianness in terms of essential traits or institutions, the more vulnerable the Maya seemingly became to the ongoing changes that so obviously shaped their lives. Tax (1941: 41) assumed that acculturation, particularly education and mastery of Spanish, would eventually undermine the "primitive" Maya worldview, resulting in a loss of cultural traits and assimilation to the Ladino world. Similarly, Wolf (1957: 13–14) predicted that local population growth and increasing differences in wealth and power would ultimately leave the closed corporate community a "hollow shell," vitiated by the wider, market-dominated, class-stratified society.[1] Richard Adams (1956) further identified this process of change as "ladinization." By this he meant the ethnic mobility of individual Mayas as well as the "transculturation" of entire Maya communities. Like Tax and Wolf, Adams identified the most essential aspect of ethnic Mayanness as a social insularity sustained by clearly defined community obligations. He argued that cultural change occurred in Maya life either when individual Maya left their natal communities and sought acceptance in the Ladino world by adopting Ladino dress, speech, and livelihood, or when the traditional social organization of Maya communities itself succumbed to overpopulation, land shortages, plantation demands for labor, the spread of national party politics, and the work of Catholic as well as evangelical missionaries. Whatever the case, while distinct communities might endure, their Indianness inevitably eroded.[2]

In contrast to the cultural essentialists, colonial historicists—most notably Latin American and Marxist—took what they considered to be a more critical stance toward such obvious asymmetries. They came increasingly to treat the Maya not simply as cultural enclaves within Mesoamerican society but as an oppressed class of peasant tributaries or low-paid seasonal laborers who occupied an indispensable—yet purposively marginalized—place in colonial and later capitalist regimes. The Guatemalan historian Severo Martínez Peláez (1979) took a particularly extreme stance, going so far as to equate the colonial term *Indian* with nothing less than the wholesale creation of Maya culture and community by the colonial order itself.

> Examination of the conditions that the conquest and the mechanisms of colonial exploitation imposed on the Indians led us directly to the conclusion that the Indian was the historical result of colonial oppression: *oppression created the Indian.* . . . The diminution or total disappearance of oppression will necessarily bring with it the abandonment of this colonial cultural complex. . . . Pedro de Alvarado [Cortés's lieutenant who led the conquest of Guatemala in 1524] never saw an Indian; he died [in 1541] when there were still no Indians. Everywhere he saw natives, including natives subjected to slavery. He never saw workers of the weekly *repartimiento* [forced labor], nor Indian *pueblos* [towns], nor communal lands, nor Indians with hats and jackets, nor *cofradías* [religious brotherhoods], nor *alcaldes* [local Indian officials], because none of these had yet been formed by the colonial regime when he died. . . . What he called *indios* [Indians] and more commonly *naturales* [natives] was not yet the human and social reality that later was going to be created by colonialism and called by those same names. (Martínez Peláez 1979: 594, 615; original emphasis, my translation)

Less outspokenly—but no less polemically—Rudolfo Stavenhagen (1968) equated "Indian" and "Ladino" with class distinctions between subservient laborer and capitalist entrepreneur, peasant producer and market-wise opportunist. Unlike Martínez Peláez, he acknowledged the intrinsic power of ethnic discriminations. "Even though relations of production will be determinant of future trans-formations in the region, ethnic consciousness may weigh heavier than class consciousness. Thus, exploited or poor as a Ladino may be, he feels privilged as compared to the Indians, even those who may have a standard of living higher than his own. Indians, on the other hand, tend to attribute all of their misfortunes to the Ladinos as such, . . . an attitude which contributes to the concealment of ob-jective relationships between the classes" (Stavenhagen 1968: 58).

Judith Friedlander (1975) echoed this perspective ethnographically by asserting that Indian culture in central Mexico consisted of noth-ing more than spurious castoffs from the dominant culture. Indian-ness therefore represented another expression of peasant socioeco-nomic marginality. Similarly, in attempting to identify an ideological component to Martínez Peláez's Marxist analysis, John Hawkins (1984) characterized the Maya of Guatemala as "inverse images" of their Ladino neighbors. He argued that a single culture shared by Maya and Ladino alike—not a multiplicity of ethnic cultures—dic-tated a "compulsive marginality" and "restricted atomism" for Maya compelled by Hispanic hegemony to be what Ladinos were not.

Polemics aside, these essentialist and historicist approaches more often than not complemented each other in their insights as well as their errors. Cultural essentialists correctly stressed the importance of ongoing differences in interpersonal relations, attitudes, and val-ues in shaping distinct Maya communities, but they tended to as-sume a static view of Maya culture itself: distinguished by dress, language, livelihood, place of residence, economic status, and local institutions, the Maya themselves would disappear as they accultu-rated to Ladino ways. Conversely, historicists rightfully perceived the colonial trappings and dialectical nature of the opposition be-tween Indian and Ladino, but they often reduced this opposition strictly to an artifact of colonialist domination: Maya culture and community became, at best, empty tokens of ideological resistance; at worst, blind, ultimately pernicious, self-deception or false con-sciousness. Implicitly or explicitly, both approaches portrayed the Maya as fundamentally passive—either the stoic survivors of a fad-ing past or the hapless victims of an unjust present. In the end, whether through acculturation, proletarianization, or even revolu-tion, the Maya would inevitably succumb to the Ladino world.

Subsequent studies of ethnicity and social change in Maya com-munities belied such simple assessments. In their analysis of Guate-mala as a "plural society," Benjamin Colby and Pierre van den Berghe (1969) argued that persistent ethnic differences between Ladinos and the Ixil Maya of the north-central highlands rested on their respective positions in shared as well as exclusive social networks and institutions, not on their retention of distinctive cultural traits. Colby and van den Berghe attempted to shift attention from culturally totalized ethnic groupings to the interactions of individual "culture users" by emphasizing the importance of subjective perceptions in defining ethnic affiliations (1969: 22–24, 182). These perceptions in turn informed contrasting cultural models of ethnic differentiation in Guatemala: for Ladinos, a hierarchical, almost castelike dualism separated them from "Indians," whom they saw as lower on the social, if not always economic, scale. For Maya, horizontal, concentric distinctions between the peoples of different places divided the world into a multiplicity of localized ethnic communities (Colby and van den Berghe 1969: 179–180). Ethnic boundaries thus persisted despite acculturative change for two reasons: culturally, an individual's subjective perceptions and appropriate behavior mattered more than retention or rejection of specific cultural traits; sociologically, the local community as an ongoing network of social relations most immediately conditioned what that individual's subjective ethnic attachments became.

Although often critical of Colby and van den Berghe's formulation as static or idealist,[3] other ethnographers confirmed patterns of obvious transformations yet enduring continuities in Maya communities of western Guatemala. Douglas Brintnall's (1979) study of Aguacatán in the southeastern corner of the department of Huehuetenango likened the disintegration of the community's traditional religious and political organization to a "revolt against the dead." Local reforms renounced the ancestors who had formerly sanctioned participation in the town's rotating civil and religious offices. Although such an act could have also easily repudiated the ancestry that conventionalized local Maya groups as "social races" (Brintnall 1979: 21–22), "modernization" in Aguacatán did not lead automatically to "Ladinoization." Indeed, Brintnall concluded, "The major and unifying theme in the institutional innovations . . . [remained] the [Awakatek Mayas'] struggle against Ladino domination" (1979: 168, 180). Similarly, in his study of several Maya towns in the department of San Marcos, Waldemar Smith (1977: 124, 126–132, 176) attested to the persistence of local ethnic attachments and identities, which endured regardless of Maya immiseration or prosperity—this despite his own stated preference for purely economic explanations of Guatemalan ethnicity.

In the central highlands of Guatemala, Sheldon Annis (1987) found that the rise of Protestantism in San Antonio Aguas Calientes resulted from the growing economic inadequacy of the traditional, largely Catholic-centered ethic of *milpa* production and ritual communalism. While substantiating a marked Protestant individualism, however, his findings also showed that Protestants did not entirely sever relations with the community but retained their local language, dress, and evidently something of their local identity as well: despite the schism between Catholic and Protestant, the community continued to evince a "strong Indian identity," and social and economical success required "facility in both Indian and non-Indian spheres" (Annis 1987: 28). Kay Warren (1978) deftly summed up these studies of contending Maya opportunism and ethnic conservatism when she dubbed "Indianness" in San Andrés Semetabaj "the symbolism of subordination." She argued that traditional Maya identity in this Kaqchikel town involved an ethnic separatism that buffered local Maya from Ladino intrusions but marginalized them from Guatemalan society, thus insuring Ladino domination.

These studies all demonstrated that substantial changes in Guatemalan Maya communities could occur without resulting automatically in acculturation or Maya obeisance to Ladino will. As Warren's phrase, "the symbolism of subordination," suggests, however, historicist predilections led these revisionist community studies to attribute Indianness to enduring oppression and exploitation. Persistent but ever-changing, Maya culture and community remained the artifact, if not the direct instrument, of more global colonial and capitalist iniquities.[4]

While clearly recognizing the importance of this global context, Carol Smith (1978; 1984b; 1987) argued for a more dialectical interaction in western Guatemala between global and local factors, material conditions, and ideology. She effectively challenged any easy presumptions of absolute global determinism in the region's economic history (Smith 1978) and social structure (Smith 1984b), then analyzed Maya culture and community as a "language of class" in Guatemala (Smith 1987). In this last regard, she noted that although Mayas split into self-ascribed ethnic enclaves, all Maya communities opposed the same Ladino-controlled state—equated with Ladino discrimination in general—in a de facto struggle against proletarianization. At the same time, the Guatemalan state tended to disregard distinctions between Maya communities and lump all Indians together as a source of potential—if intractable—labor. This totalization of each ethnic group by the other served to reaffirm subjective ethnic animosities while objectively articulating a "class struggle without class" (Smith 1987: 208–209; 214). In contrast to previous analyses, Smith stressed the relational rather than substantive nature of "ethnic classes" and acknowledged cultural differences as intentional, strategic oppositions in formulating these relations.

As the Maya have thus begun to emerge as purposive rather than passive social actors in Guatemalan history (cf. Smith 1990b), the question remains: what continues to make local communities so essential to Maya social action? Why, in the face of often transformative changes in their lives, should the Maya preserve communities as a locus of enduring ethnic identity, let alone as the strategic basis for "class struggle"? Ironically, most recent ethnographies of highland Guatemala have neglected this question, precisely because they take Maya communities as historically, ideologically, or materially given. They tend to ignore how, given their circumstances, the Maya themselves continue to find it appropriate to sustain a sense of community and retain their local Mayanness—often despite decisive pressures to the contrary. In other words, attention must be paid not only to how global circumstances encompass local realities but also to why these circumstances, both local and global, prompt the Maya to engage the world in ways not entirely dictated by global intents. Such an inquiry entails looking at culture in its meaningful rather than typological aspects, at history as a contextual rather than deterministic reality, and at community as an emergent social nexus in its own right rather than as some externally motivated refuge or restraint. The difficulty remains how to consider a more relativized, strategic Maya sense of community without succumbing to either the static essentialism or the global historicism of past formulations.

Culture and Community

To articulate a more flexible conception of Maya culture and community, I return to Robert Redfield's insight that the characteristics of so-called folk societies owe more to the inherent qualities of small-scale village life than to their specific cultural content or historical origins. Redfield noted that, far from an arbitrary miscellany of traits, a people's culture consisted of "an organization of conventional understandings [about the world] manifest in act and artifact" (1941: 132–133). Such understandings reflected the social patterns of "intercommunication" that articulated them in the first place. In the relatively circumscribed confines of a "little community," lifelong associations between individuals tended to produce conventional understandings that were tacit, widely shared, highly personalized, and densely interwoven (Redfield 1962a). That is, intimate familiarity with a local place and with the particular individuals who lived there engendered abiding personal attachments directly associated with compelling presuppositions about how properly to live in that place.

Rather than reify this insight into some insular, ideal type "folk society," however, I draw from Redfield the more modest proposition that places such as Maya communities constitute their own "existential sovereignties" rooted essentially—but never exclusively—in the immediacies of local sustenance and sociality. By existential sovereignty, I mean the conjunction of place, as an ongoing here and now, with individuals committed to the emergent possibilities and conditions of that place. Together, place and people precipitate commonly held conventional premises about how to get along in that place with those people. Far from some exclusive essentialist typology or enduring historicist residue, I take the resulting community to represent the emergent, relatively bounded sociality of individuals who, by virtue of continuity in time and contiguity in space, come to recognize common commitments and concerns as well as conventional ways of dealing with those concerns, regardless of how they change through time. I choose to situate community contingently within such existential relations because a focus on the conjunction of place, people, and premise enables—indeed demands—concern for what motivates individuals and groups to live in communities in the first place. It also requires careful attention to how global situations are actually realized in local contexts.

Within this existential sovereignty of place, people, and premise, a stress on pragmatic commitments and concerns of "sustenance and sociality" implies neither simple environmental determinism nor materialist reductionism. Instead, it suggests that local attachments inhere most strongly in individuals' everyday activities and interactions, not necessarily in disembodied cultural patterns or specific institutional arrangements. The exigencies of local existence, in and of themselves, can often engender community defined and redefined by the mutual interactions of self-interested—if by no means always selfish or calculating—individuals. The "neighborliness," as Henry Glassie (1982) calls it, of such a community lies in individuals' commitments not necessarily to agree with or to conform to others but to engage those nearest at hand in the immediacies of life and so turn mere existence into meaningful human experience. The perceived circumstances of place simply inform the interests of people living there, and these then motivate the conventional premises of local commitments and concerns that give shape and sense to the community.

At the same time, such premises represent more than the artifact of other abiding circumstances or concerns: they serve in their own right to transform physical propinquity and practical activity into more consciously affirmed—and affirmable—social affinities. In one sense, individual recognition and understanding of such shared premises substantiate common presumptions as well as validate the propriety inherent in common expectations. At the same time, shared premises also help to establish the familiarity that differentiates community members from outsiders. Together these premises of place and people—and the propriety presupposed in both—constitute the basis of the community's culture. Culture in this sense refers not so much to conscious ethnic ideologies (cf. Warren 1978) or, even less, to inferred propositions about the "deep structure" of ethnic oppositions (cf. Hawkins 1984). Instead, I take culture to represent the conceptual and behavioral premises embodied in conventional forms of "act and artifact" that make the world recognizable to those who share and practice them.

Just as community emerges out of the pragmatic activities of its members, the culture that such community presupposes exists not as a disembodied system of symbols and meanings but as a multiplicity of conventions. By convention I mean acts of communication through the use of symbols that entail both the context of articulation—that is, the motivation behind the symbol's use—and those doing the articulating, the interlocutors. Far more than merely the mechanical application of symbols to specific situations, the motivation and articulation of conventions demand that interlocutors improvise symbolic usages that particularize given symbols in reference to ongoing events while also conventionalizing the particulars of such events to make them recognizable (cf. Wagner 1981). Conventions are not strictly traits to be catalogued, logical codes to be deciphered, symbolic texts to be read, or cultural otherness to be contemplated. Instead, they represent those regularities in interactions between individuals that give rise to mutual recognitions of intent and understanding.

Such recognition need not always precipitate readily defined—or definable—cultural meanings, precisely because meaning depends on the triadic tension between conventions, the experiential contexts that conventional usages inform, and the emergent intentions and responses that interlocutors impart through such usage. That is, meaning only exists as meaning *to* someone. It abides in the intentions of the addresser and the recognition of such intentions by the addressee. Both actions remain private to the interlocutors involved rather than inherent in the objective patterns of language or behavior used to convey the message (cf. Cherry 1966: 266, 299, 307). Consequently, no convention's meaning ever finds complete articulation within any single occasion of expression, nor do all the conventions of a culture ever occur all at once. To interlocutors familiar with the culture, however, use of a convention always evokes its potential usage in other contexts as well as its association with conventions that might have been used instead, whether properly or not. Familiarity with such possibilities circumscribes the meaningfulness—if not the specific meaning—of conventions. Culture constitutes the sum of these conventional usages, motivations, and associations, and as such, it remains largely tacit to the interlocutors themselves. What to cultural insiders passes as self-evident conventions embedded in everyday experience, anthropological analysis self-consciously reconstitutes as culture by articulating these tacit associations between conventions and their contexts of usage.

Contingent on the personal experiences, intentions, and eloquence of interlocutors, cultural conventions thus remain relative rather than absolute determinants of thought and action. Nonetheless, conventionality still exerts two kinds of constraints in relation to usage and meaning, the first communicative and largely formal, the second constitutive and largely historical. First, because human social communication rests on mutual consent rather than on genetic constitution, it necessitates some minimal acquiescence to the shared forms of expression, implication, and intention that make intelligibility between individuals possible. Conventions thus presuppose morality because they rest on the continuing obligation of interlocutors to conform to standards of conduct beyond their personal volition. This intrinsic obligation imbues conventions with an apparent coercive force that itself remains purely conventional to the extent that overly idiosyncratic use, misuse, or disregard for conventions constitutes its own sanction of unintelligibility. No one can arbitrarily make up new conventions or attribute new meanings to old ones without risking the ability to make sense of, or to be sensible to, others. The greater the real or perceived need for communication and for the social interdependency this implies, the more powerful such purely conventional communicative constraints become.

The second constitutive constraint exerted by conventions involves their relationship to the contexts in which they are used. On one hand, conventions tend to preserve the significations of past situations and articulations, if only because intelligibility demands that they be expressed in experientially familiar terms. Similarly, the ongoing existential and historical situations in which conventions find articulation constrain the potential arbitrariness of conventions and their meanings: within broad limits, conventional meanings must ultimately conform to physical as well as cognitive realities. On the other hand, past articulations never completely determine how conventions will be used in future contexts because the actions of interlocutors and the meanings that result from them remain essentially inventive and therefore continuously emergent (cf. Wagner 1981).

Whatever the case, in using conventions, rather than merely applying them to situations, interlocutors not only communicate with one another but also often intentionally affirm more enduring social affinities based on the mutual recognition that such encounters engender. Fredrik Barth (1969: 14, 24–25) thus notes that "value orientations" as well as self-validating ethnic "performances" often serve to bound—and thus identify—the social group that holds them. Simply through their usage, such conventions precipitate an experience of common identity, differentiating a palpable "we" from a "they" who neither understands nor acknowledges the conventions being used. This power to sustain contexts of usage and the need to accommodate physical and historical realities form the constitutive constraints intrinsic to the use of conventions. Together with the more formal communicative constraints of symbolic communication, these situational realities anchor, but by no means reduce, conventions to the immediacies of time, place, and history.

Maya Community, Change, and Identity

The approach to culture and community sketched above suggests three clarifying assumptions concerning persistent Maya communities and social change in Guatemala. First, as meaningfully bounded social places, rather than institutionally delimited structures, Maya communities involve relative participation in local contexts of conventional discourse, commitment to and investment in the concerns of that discourse, and the knowledge, experience, and interpersonal familiarity needed to intuit events and individuals within such discourse. Because interlocutors never experience their culture or their community all at once, membership in the community remains relative rather than absolute, contingent on the recognition and use of conventions within ongoing contexts and events. The meaningful continuity engendered by such usage—not necessarily the specific institutional patterns that such usage often precipitates—thus constitutes the most enduring index of local, and therefore often ethnic, affinities. Material or behavioral changes in the community need not jeopardize this identity, since the actual experience of culture and community means that change normally involves cumulative instances of innovation within particular contexts, rather than abrupt, wholesale social transformations. The approach to culture and community taken here thus obviates the paradox of ethnic persistence in the face of social change by particularizing meaningful social interactions into conventions and acts of articulation instead of totalizing them into such monolithic analytical abstractions as culture, ethnicity, or class.

Second, a focus on Maya communities as the conjunction of place, people, and premise clarifies their nature as a nexus of diverse individual commitments and concerns. Rather than represent some primordial cultural pattern or historically dictated enclave, Maya communities emerge contingently from the ongoing personal pursuits and perceptions of their members, as well as from the possibilities informed by the larger world around them. Community in this sense does not constitute a kind of "life style enclave" that aims solely at social homogeneity or conformity (cf. Bellah et al. 1985: 72). Instead, it lies closer to the ecological sense of community as an interrelation of diverse life-forms—in this case, diverse individual abilities, ambitions, and histories—within the circumscribed possibilities of certain places. In integrating abiding differences, human communities obviously involve more than some impersonal ecological equilibrium of complementary differentiation or functional interdependence. The willful exercise of power often decisively shapes diversity within and between them. Nonetheless, Maya communities do embody a multiplicity of interrelated parameters—both local and global, physical and social, historical and institutional—that makes them at once theoretically more problematic but also more concretely analyzable as ongoing negotiations of actors' contextually motivated interests, conventionally established options, and perceived existential circumstances.

The third assumption resulting from a focus on cultural conventions of community suggests that Mayas' localized engagements with the world constitute the core of their ethnic identity. This reflects Tax's (1941) emphasis on worldview as an essential aspect of Maya identity, but it defines worldview in conventional rather than purely cognitive terms. The worldview embedded in the Maya conventions of community discussed above implies that being Maya involves not just viewing the world in particularly Maya ways but doing so from particular Maya places in the company of particularly Maya neighbors. Affinities of place and people imbue the resulting sense of identity with the moral force intrinsic to the conventions that convey it. At the same time, because cultural conventions can sanctify pernicious as well as adaptive states of affairs (cf. Rappaport 1979b), the conventions of Maya community and identity also ultimately reflect the relative power of individuals and groups to affirm, assert, or impose on others their own conceptions of reality. Thus, lest this concern for cultural convention and ethnic community be mistaken for a retreat into cultural obscurantism, such inquiry directly addresses the nature of what Carol Smith (1987: 207) has called "communities of interest"—that is, the ethnically distinct local sociality that defines and organizes Maya struggles for physical survival and moral legitimacy, especially against the Guatemalan state. "The Indian language of social division is based on the particularity of specific communities, not on abstract, general oppositions. . . . Understanding the nature, meaning and specificity of community, therefore, is basic to understanding the potential for revolutionary change in Guatemala" (Smith 1987: 205).

The Study

As with most anthropological studies, the intellectual concerns discussed above result from a twofold project engendered by the nature of ethnographic fieldwork: the present work attempts to understand what it might mean to belong to a Guatemalan Maya community, but it also reflects how I came to this understanding. Consequently, the study takes its shape from my initial preconceptions about Guatemala, from what I actually encountered there, and finally, from rationalizations of the whole experience after I came back. Outlining this process of presumption, encounter, and reflection will perhaps help to explain—without exculpating—the resulting intellectual biases and personal motivations behind my analysis.

My original fieldwork, begun in November 1978 and lasting until September 1980, consisted of twenty-two months' residence in Santiago Chimaltenango, a Mam-speaking community on the southern fringe of the Cuchumatán Highlands in the department of Huehuetenango, Guatemala. I have since visited the town twice, in the summer of 1981 and then in January 1988, for a total of about four weeks. After a preliminary field trip to Huehuetenango during the summer of 1977, I returned to Guatemala in September 1978 in hopes of studying Maya beliefs about illness and curing. Because curing represented a central aspect of Maya folk Catholicism, I intended to use this study to gain insight into broader patterns of social and religious change within a particular Maya community. I chose Santiago Chimaltenango for three reasons. First, Charles Wagley's research there in 1937 (Wagley 1941; 1949) provided a rare anthropological opportunity for detailed historical comparison. Second, the town remained relatively isolated, one of the few municipios, "townships,"

in Huehuetenango still lacking regular bus service in 1978. Demo-
graphically, Santiago Chimaltenango also remained small, its 1973
population of 3,269 being almost entirely (99 percent) Maya (DGE
1977). More importantly, two-thirds of its inhabitants lived in the
town center itself. I hoped that the community's isolation had safe-
guarded much of traditional Chimalteco culture and that its small,
compact population would facilitate research. The third reason for
choosing Santiago Chimaltenango was entirely practical, and perhaps the most compelling. I had been given the name of a Chimalteco who had once worked with a Catholic missionary linguist and
had had experience teaching his language to foreigners. His assistance, I felt, would—and did—prove invaluable, especially given the
intricacies of Mam and the marked variation in dialects between
communities.

Although I intended to study social change, the assumptions underlying my proposed research originated more from essentialist
rather than historicist concerns. A desire to collect information
comparable to Wagley's placed me within the compass of his earlier
research, but in general, I already subscribed to the essentialist view
of culture present in his monographs. I regarded the *municipio* as
the relevant focus of cultural analysis and assumed that cultural
change basically involved the slow erosion of Chimalteco beliefs
and practices. Culture itself could be defined and measured only indirectly through its immediate manifestations, such as concepts of
illness and curing. I supposed Chimalteco culture to be more than
the sum of its parts, and I set out to find that essence.

Such grandiose ambitions, of course, were soon dashed.

As the following chapters demonstrate, Santiago Chimaltenango
had changed remarkably since Wagley's 1937 visit. Despite the differences, however, my first impression of the town, mired in the aftermath of a late afternoon cloudburst, left me ruefully wondering
how much tougher anthropologists must have been in Wagley's
time. Prospects for research hardly appeared any more encouraging
by light of day: the shaman-diviners of the traditional religion whom
I hoped to consult had fallen into disrepute; the flotsam and jetsam
of modernity lay everywhere; and Chimaltecos proved more worldly
than I had expected. A specific study of surviving Chimalteco concepts of illness and curing, which I later carried out in part (Watanabe 1981b), became less pressing than an explanation for the wholesale cultural transformation that appeared to confront me.

I only slowly came to realize that this metamorphosis remained far
from complete. What I had automatically interpreted as acculturation to Ladino ways evidently meant nothing of the sort to Chimal-

tecos, for despite the changes, they considered themselves no less Chimalteco than their parents and grandparents had in Wagley's time. This distinctiveness lay as much in the pride that they took in local progress as it did in their assumed moral superiority to outsiders, Maya and Ladino alike (cf. Bricker 1973: 161–166). As one Chimalteco put it, "*Puuro moos nxb'aalni, pero xiinaq qiini* [My clothes are all Ladino, but I am a man]," expressing not the bravado of machismo but his worthiness as a person and a good Chimalteco. In contrast, Maya of other *municipios* could be less "civilized," shameless thieves, crafty hagglers, or simply, as another local put it, "*medio listo* [half bright]."

Disapprobation fell on Ladinos as well. In contrast to many *municipios*, the two Ladino families native to Santiago Chimaltenango held little economic or political power, being neither large landowners nor active merchants. The prerogatives they commanded derived largely from their status as Ladinos rather than from any substantive dominance in the community. Although never overtly antagonistic, Mayas and Ladinos regarded each other with wary ambivalence and seldom mixed. Older Chimaltecos would recount how Ladino officials had formerly made free demands on local food and assistance and how Chimaltecos had endured forced labor on government road gangs and Ladino plantations. Two events during my stay showed why such memories stayed fresh in Chimalteco minds: after being vouched for by a native Ladino of the town, a local Ladino school teacher absconded with Q500.00 loaned to him by various Chimaltecos.[5] Several months later, an itinerant Ladino repairman set up shop in the town, ostensibly to fix radios and watches. He stayed long enough to attract customers and then left, supposedly to work a fiesta in a neighboring town. When he failed to return, Chimaltecos discovered that he had stolen the articles they had given him to repair. Such encounters inspired little love for Ladino strangers and reinforced local stereotypes of Ladinos as selfish, immoral, and dangerous. Ironically, such suspicions often did not extend to distant plantation owners or to city shopkeepers, who sometimes exploited Chimaltecos more fundamentally but dealt with them more straightforwardly. Chimaltecos assured me that not all Ladinos were bad, but as strangers who appeared unheralded in their community, they were not to be trusted.

I began to understand that what distinguished Chimaltecos in their own eyes lay precisely in this surety of long-standing interpersonal relationships and local reputation. Familiarity with their neighbors, not steadfast allegiance to old ways, most immediately rendered to their community its sense of moral integrity. Indeed, when speaking of lost traditions, Chimaltecos often characterized change as improvements in local life, not as the decay of some traditional ideal. As I learned more about the community, I discovered a subtler sense of enduring traditionalism, rooted at least in part in the fact that many of the changes since Wagley's time had affected women much less than men. Chimalteco women still wore the traditional dress unique to the town, remained largely monolingual in Mam, and had the least contact with the outside world. This difference in acculturation clearly made Chimalteco women the conservators of local language, culture, and worldview. As the primary socializers of the young, they tacitly imparted to children an orientation to family, household, and neighbors around which their lives revolved. Experientially, then, external influences and local innovations fitted into an already established "existential sovereignty," modifying instead of transforming the perceived Chimalteco-ness of community life. But what exactly was changing? What continued to make Chimaltecos distinctive? My quest for the essence of Chimalteco culture, it seemed, was on once again.

Upon arriving in Santiago Chimaltenango, I saw "culture" everywhere. Local life assaulted me in a kaleidoscope of successive happenings, each new event blotting out the last in an insistent demand for my soon exhausted attention. The language, observed social interactions, my own personal encounters—all were obviously meaningful, yet often they remained frustratingly enigmatic. Such strangeness, however, cut both ways. Because of my Japanese ancestry, Chimaltecos initially mistook me for a Ladino, although my peculiar Spanish accent led them to suspect that I came from somewhere else in Central America. Protestations that I was indeed a gringo only prompted skeptical questions of why I did not look like the tall, blond Mormon missionaries or the Peace Corps volunteers they had known. My journal entries came to reflect the frustration of overcoming this ethnic misidentification. Given the mutual antipathy between Chimaltecos and Ladinos, I feared that becoming known as a Ladino would doom my efforts to build rapport—that essential but elusive ingredient of successful fieldwork.

As I walked diffidently around the town, children called out, *"Ke tii moos!* [Look out for the Ladino!]" *"Nya? moos qiini* [I'm not a Ladino]," I responded, using one of the first Mam phrases that I had learned. The children would laugh and run away, shaking their heads knowingly, while nearby adults smiled and turned away as I approached. At first I was proud of these brief exchanges in a language that I had just begun to learn, but I soon found them increasingly aggravating—and not merely because they signaled a hindrance to my research. Compelled to affirm my own ethnic identity, I fought the more fundamental threat of self-dissolution that culture shock induced. Feeling ever more ghostly, I realized that my own identity depended more on the perceptions and acceptance of those around me than on some self-evident or self-professed personal worth. Townspeople had no reason to trust me, nor had I any way of reassuring them of my good intentions. In my anxiety to correct misapprehensions of my ethnic origins, I succumbed to the initial otherness of Chimaltecos to me, even as I internalized my otherness to them. I had truly become a stranger.

In this regard, Vincent Crapanzano (1980: 137) has observed: "The ethnographer's entry into the field is always a separation from his world of primary reference—the world through which he obtains, and maintains, his sense of self and his sense of reality. He is suddenly confronted with the possibility of Otherness, and his immediate response to this Otherness is to seek both the security of the similar and the distance and objectivity of the dissimilar." True to form, I sought the security of the similar by trying "to be myself" and thus evoke familiar responses from those around me. In particular, I tried, perhaps overzealously, to avoid any hint of the presumptuousness of a Ladino-like *patrón*. I decided to get to know my neighbors rather than merely hire them as informants. Conversely, like a good anthropologist, I rationalized the undeniable distance and dissimilarity between myself and Chimaltecos by objectifying such differences as Chimalteco culture.

Eventually, however, the strangeness diminished, and I came to engage—if clumsily and incidentally—in the affairs of everyday life, working and visiting with people who became my friends. I learned more than I had expected to about farming: how to hoe corn uphill, to plant in even rows, to wrap bean stalks around the growing corn, which coffee berries to pick and which to leave until the next pass, and how to load a mule without getting kicked or bitten—or losing the load halfway home. Eating in Chimalteco kitchens on low stools near smoky fires, I learned to relish the stacks of yellow tortillas and even the bland but somehow satisfying *q'ootj*, "corn gruel." In addition to work and food, talk also sustained me: Chimaltecos had as many questions about my life as I had about theirs, and I found, at times to my surprise, that some individuals enjoyed talking with me because they could express hopes, opinions, and ambitions that might otherwise prompt censure or jealousy from their neighbors. In the end, Chimaltecos realized that I was a different sort of stranger, just as I discovered that we were not as different as I had first imagined. Indeed, having heard my account of how my grandparents had emigrated to the United States, at least one Chimalteco concluded that my predilection for Chimalteco life must have originated in my ancestral roots as an "Indian" from a faraway place called Japón.

Paradoxically, as individual Chimaltecos became more familiar to me, and I to them, the linguistic and cultural conventions that enabled us to interact became increasingly opaque. What initially had been fragments of culture that needed interpretation slowly became everyday life that involved living. Once-burning insights about Chimalteco culture set down in my journal and fieldnotes evaporated into seemingly empty generalizations and self-evident truisms. "Real life" in its endless routine of unique events emerged to garner my attention, and I eventually found it difficult to sustain the curiosity and constant questioning of assumptions that productive fieldwork demanded. Behind this complacency lay an equally real reluctance to jeopardize my newfound personal security by delving into new areas of Chimalteco experience or by making new acquaintances, which might provoke resentment or jealousy among the friends I already had.

I had finally "arrived" in Santiago Chimaltenango, but the essence of Chimalteco culture still eluded me. Indeed, I became plagued by the uncertainty of knowing when I had acquired an authentic piece of cultural information. When did a hunch become an ethnographic fact? Was a Chimalteco's statement necessarily more privileged than my own insight into the matter? More importantly, did I need such a statement to validate my intuitions? In short, I became increasingly unsure at what point my own familiarity with Chimalteco life metamorphosed into a legitimate fact of Chimalteco culture. Direct questioning of friends seldom helped. They often appealed to custom or referred to specific situations when explaining their culture to me; most often they met my questions with quizzical looks and well-meant attempts to salvage a derailed conversation. As an ethnographer, I sought those generalities in local life that remained most implicit to Chimaltecos themselves, whether the gloss of a word or explication of someone's behavior. This apparent obtuseness, coupled with my own insecurities, drove me to attend ever more closely to the subtleties of Mam words and grammar, to the intricacies of village life, and to the economics and logistics of corn and coffee farming, all in hopes that such details would crystallize into Chimalteco culture. I left Santiago Chimaltenango after twenty-two months with the sense that whatever insight I had gained into Chimalteco life I had largely fabricated myself.

In a very real sense this was true, but only in writing this ethnography has the nature and the necessity of this fabrication become clearer to me. My quest for the essence of Chimalteco culture proved illusory precisely because doing ethnography necessarily involved learning Chimalteco culture rather than merely observing it. The inherently social nature of doing ethnography demanded that I find a common ground on which to engage Chimaltecos and not simply catalog the objective differences that separated us. My socialization into the community occurred neither by rote nor by mastery of cultural rules that Chimalteco reticence tried to hide from me. Like Chimaltecos themselves, I learned their culture by assuming the meaningfulness of others' behavior, then attempting to recognize and use these conventional patterns in accord with the responses they evoked in others. In the process, I learned that Chimalteco culture was not something more than the sum of its parts, something monolithic and determinant. Instead, it was something less: my own conceptual shorthand for those interactions that conveyed the meaningfulness of individual experience against a common background of time, place, and circumstance.

In learning Chimalteco culture—in doing my ethnography—my concerns resembled those of Chimaltecos themselves, engaged as we were in common interactions motivated by the same human needs of recognition, reassurance, and understanding. My interest in their sense of identity and community echoed my own preoccupation with identity and belonging that arose while I lived in Santiago Chimaltenango. Conversely, in writing this book, in recounting my ethnography, my concerns and motivations have diverged from theirs. Regardless of all that I learned about being Chimalteco, I did not become a Chimalteco. However much my friends and I may have shared, I never truly lived in their world. What separated us was not some insurmountable barrier of cultural "otherness" but the Chimaltecos' embeddedness in their own time and place. I was only an interloper, a stranger who arrived, a friend who would leave and perhaps not return. They aspired wholly to live in their world; I strove instead to think about it, in the end coming to an understanding that might never matter to them. In acknowledgment of their trust and friendship, I must begin with their concerns—but in the telling not pass off my cultural fabrication as an unadulterated reflection of their culture. By this I mean that I tried to hear Chimaltecos talk to each other—not just to record what they said to me— but in trying to make sense of that talk, the meanings in this book must ultimately remain idiosyncratically mine, not authoritatively theirs.

The following chapters, then, represent my fabrication of Chimalteco culture, but it grew from close observation and learning, not from arbitrary fantasy. The work consists of three parts. Part 1 describes the ethnographic and historical background of the study and captures as best I can the round of contemporary Chimalteco life, then discusses the historical bases for its ethnic distinctiveness. Such an examination suggests why Maya identity inheres so closely to the local community and how this accounts for the dialectical nature of Guatemalan ethnicity. Part 2 analyzes what I see as essential cultural conventions that Chimaltecos use to communicate their sense of common identity: chapter 3 deals with Chimalteco definitions of the physical, social, and conceptual boundaries of their community; chapter 4 discusses the conventions of Chimalteco morality and their relationship to local ethnic identity; and chapter 5 focuses on the articulation of this morality through participation in local political and religious organizations. Finally, Part 3 relates these Chimalteco cultural conventions to changes that have occurred in the community since Wagley's work there in 1937: chapter 6 involves inquiry into local economic changes, while chapter 7 pertains to transformations in local politics; lastly, chapter 8 investigates the impact of Catholic and evangelical missionaries on Chimalteco religion. In the Conclusion, I return to the broader implications of this analysis for an understanding of enduring Maya ethnic identity in Guatemala.

A Chimalteco friend and I sat together one day. The breadth of his knowledge and awareness of his own culture and language belied his three years of formal schooling. At a loss for questions, I casually asked him, "If you were to write a book about Santiago Chimaltenango, what would be the most important thing that you would write about?"

He thought briefly and answered, "I would write about Indians and Ladinos." He proceeded to draw an elaborate diagram consisting of two columns, one labeled "Ladino," the other "Indian." In the Ladino column he wrote: Wealth, Exploiter, Literacy, Religious Faith, Medical Curing, Self-Improvement. In the Indian column he penned: Poverty, Ignorance, Illiteracy, Traditional Beliefs, Magical Curing, Alcoholism. He then drew an arrow from the Indian column to the Ladino one, indicating that this was the desirable direction of change.

Struck by the asymmetries between his columns, I asked, "When all these changes have taken place, will there still be Indians in Santiago Chimaltenango?"

He thought for only a moment before replying, "Yes."

"Why?" I countered.

Again a brief pause. "Because of the *ambiente,* the environs of this place, because of the things that it provides us, the food that we eat and the land that we work," he answered.

I still struggle to discern all that he meant and all that I thought I understood in that simple assertion.

2

✝ *Santiago Chimaltenango* ✝

The Place

Seen from the south, the Cuchumatán Highlands of western Guatemala loom like a wall above the plain surrounding the provincial capital of Huehuetenango. The highest nonvolcanic mountain range in Central America, this is a steep, broken land of fast-flowing streams and lofty peaks alternately framed by white clouds against a cobalt blue sky or swathed in gray, forbidding mists. Its highest reaches once gave birth to glaciers; in its lowest valleys oranges now flourish. Despite a population of over half a million Mayas speaking eight distinct languages, the land gives the impression of solitude. Green, steep-sided valleys patched with corn fields and the random scatter of red tile roofs testify to human habitation, but all else argues for its insignificance. The mountains teach patience, the rugged slopes and deep valleys dwarfing human endeavors, demanding not achievement but endurance (see fig. 1).

Not until the 1950s did a paved highway penetrate the region, and then only to skirt the southern face of the Cuchumatán Highlands, following the banks of the Rio Selegua down to the Mexican border. Along this twisting, two-lane road, ramshackle buses ply between the outlying *municipios* and Huehuetenango, the major market town and administrative center of the region. About an hour's ride west of Huehuetenango, the highway plunges through a spectacular gorge. At the bottom, an unpaved side road veers east across a new concrete bridge spanning the river and then snakes up the cliff in a series of jolting, breathtaking switchbacks. At the top, the opposite side of the gorge still towers far above, over a mile high from its peak to the highway far below. Turning from the precipice, the road descends gently into the town of San Pedro Necta, nestled in a rich, green valley. There the dirt road ends, and a narrow track winds southeastward, climbing more than 2,000 feet in less than two miles. Once out of the valley, the track twists along a ridge, a dirty orange

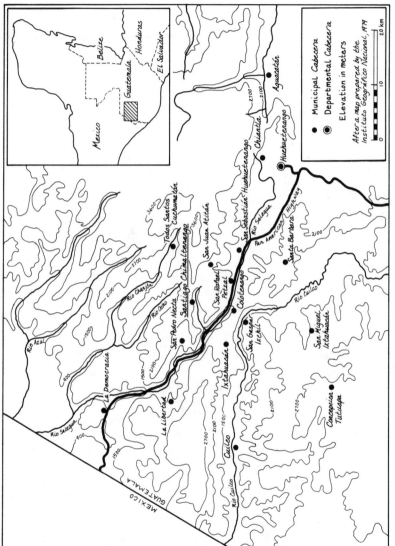

Figure 1. The northern Mam region of western Guatemala.

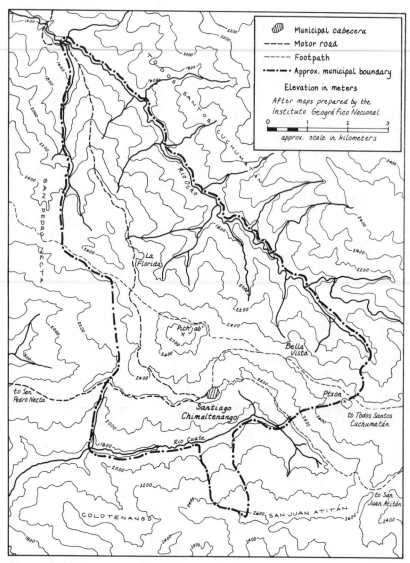

Figure 2. The *municipio* of Santiago Chimaltenango.

The town of Santiago Chimaltenango (*center left*) halfway between the mountain peak of Pich'jab' to the north and the valley of Río Cuate to the south, March 1979.

streak against dark trees and underbrush. A mile farther on it skirts another mountain, and where the valley widens into a cul-de-sac it enters the town of Santiago Chimaltenango, halfway between the mountain peak to the north and a steep valley to the south (see fig. 2). At an altitude of nearly 7,400 feet (2,246 m), the town typifies *tierra fría* with a climate euphemistically described as "cold and healthy" (Recinos 1954: 315).[1] The Maya who live here speak Mam, one of more than twenty Maya languages spoken in Guatemala; their ancestors probably arrived in this region some fifteen centuries ago (Kaufman 1974).

I first saw Chimbal, as Maya inhabitants call their town, after an exhausting hike up the mountain from San Pedro. In the lowering twilight of a late September rainstorm, the place seemed hardly changed from Charles Wagley's 1937 description of it. Even the yellowish street lamps veiled in mist did little to dispel the impression that time had stood still during the intervening forty-one years. The town still clung to the mountainside, hunched on either side of the

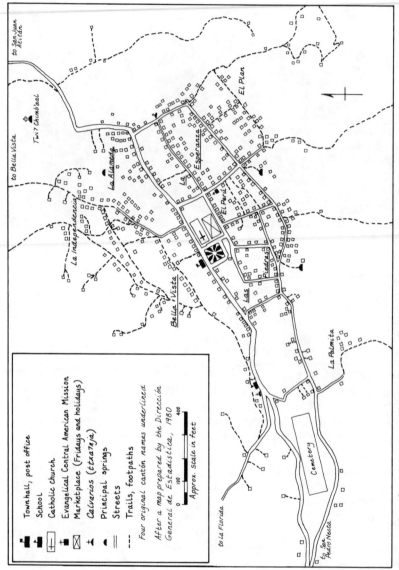

Legend

- ◼─◼ Townhall, post office
- ◼─◼ School
- ⊞ Catholic church
- ◼─◼ Evangelical Central American Mission
- ⊠ Marketplace (Fridays and holidays)
- ✦ Calvarios (ɛtxaʔŋja)
- ● Principal springs
- ═ Streets
- --- Trails, footpaths

Four original cantón names underlined.

After a map prepared by the Dirección
General de Estadística, 1980

Approx. scale in feet
0   100   400

Figure 3. The *cabecera* of Santiago Chimaltenango.

road, while the church dominated the uneven cluster of tile roofs around it like a huge ship majestically aloof to the smaller craft in its lee. Whitewashed and fronted with a turquoise facade flanked by two squat towers, it remained, as Wagley had observed, "the most imposing edifice in the village" (1941: 10).

Chimaltecos point to the great size of their church's adobe bricks and to the height and thickness of its massive walls, marveling at their forebears' strength and ingenuity. The church is *tjaa dyoos*, "the house of God," or more specifically, *tjaa Santiyaawo*, "the house of Santiago," the municipal patron saint. It stands as mute proof of an ineffable past, a familiar abode in an increasingly uncertain world.

Unlike most Guatemalan Maya, Chimaltecos dwell in a town. Over two-thirds of the *municipio*'s thirty-five hundred inhabitants live in the *pueblo*, or town center; the remaining population resides primarily in the two largest *aldeas*, "hamlets," of Bella Vista and La Florida. Officially, the pueblo is the *cabecera*, or head town, of the *municipio*, which covers about thirty-five square kilometers (fig. 2). The town that Wagley once described as "remarkably compact" (1941: 9) has become positively cramped. Houses crowd one another, some dug into the steep slope, while others perch precariously on narrow ledges above and below the main street (see fig. 3). Often the porch of one house overlooks the roof of the house below. Paths and streets follow the steep contours of the land, dodging in and out among the houses, and the few that are paved with rough stones become treacherously slick in the rain. The heavy cloudbursts of June and September turn many streets into rushing torrents, which leave cobblestones eroded and weathered houses looking as if they grew from the mountain itself. During the rainless months of March and April, these same streets lie dusty and yellow, unshaded by any tree.

Chimbal has grown in recent years, encroaching on the surrounding *milpas*, or corn fields, wherever level ground permits. Within the town itself, Chimaltecos have built houses in what were formerly the garden plots of older houses, blurring the boundaries between the house compounds of different family groups (cf. Wagley 1949: 12–13). Similarly, the pueblo's four wards, or *cantones*, once named after their patron saints (Wagley 1941: 11), have expanded to eight—Bella Vista, La Alameda, La Esperanza, Las Piedras, La Independencia, El Perú, El Plan, and La Palmita—the first four being the original subdivisions. *Cantones* still serve minor administrative and ceremonial functions, although they have lost their associations with the lesser saints in the town church. They hold little impor-

The church, plaza, and town hall (*center right*) in Chimbal with the peak of Ptxon in the background, spring 1979.

tance in day-to-day affairs, and many Chimaltecos do not even know their exact boundaries.

The fountain that once dominated the plaza in front of the church has given way to a small garden bordered by pink and turquoise cement benches. When the Guatemalan army occupied the town in 1983 during its campaign against leftist guerrillas, soldiers built a two-storied cement gazebo at the center of the plaza as part of a "civic betterment" program. The town hall, a municipal salon, and the post office—all boasting corrugated sheet metal roofs—surround the plaza. The classrooms once housed in these buildings have been moved to a new school on the western edge of town. Chimaltecos built it during the mid-1980s with donated labor, and twelve Ladino teachers presently staff it; five more teachers conduct classes in the *aldeas*.

A marketplace adjoins the plaza on the south side of the church. In 1980, it too received a metal roof to shield weekly vendors from rainy-season downpours. A potable water system installed in 1954 means that Chimalteco women no longer rely on the springs below the town (cf. Wagley 1941: 11) but draw water from cement *pilas,* or public sinks, spaced along the streets. In 1977, electricity reached Chimbal, but even now only about a quarter of the houses in the pueblo have electric lights. The rest of the town and all those who live in outlying hamlets still use the kerosene lamps and pine pitch *ocote* torches of former times.

Most Chimalteco houses are one-room affairs with adobe walls, earthen floors, and tile roofs, although more prosperous individuals own multiroom houses with cement floors and corrugated metal roofs. The town also boasts several two-storied houses made of cement block, and at least two have the metal *zaguán* doors typical of larger Ladino houses in the city. The wattle-and-daub, thatched-roofed houses of the past have disappeared completely. When I showed Chimaltecos pictures that Wagley had taken in 1937, younger townspeople marveled that such houses had ever existed in Chimbal. Some Chimaltecos brighten their houses with glass windows or skylights of translucent corrugated plastic fitted among the roof tiles. Usually, however, the interiors of Chimalteco houses are dark, windowless, and smoky from the hearth fire that smolders on the floor all day long. Furnishings consist of low stools near the fire, planks on sawhorses for beds, an occasional table, and a few chairs. A wooden chest or box hung from the wall holds possessions, and a board shelf supports the ubiquitous battery-powered radio. Tools and cooking utensils hang from spikes driven into the walls and from hooks dangling from the rafters. Rough-hewn boards laid over the roof beams make a loft for storing dried corn, and a wide front porch provides a place for firewood and extra tools.

When I first arrived in Chimbal, the most obvious changes in the town immediately garnered my attention. I was disappointed that Chimaltecos seemed less exotic than in Wagley's time, yet I was also relieved, believing that this might make them somehow more accessible. Most Chimalteco men had given up their traditional dress of white pants and shirt, red sash, and black woolen jacket; local shaman-diviners no longer performed sacrifices or prayed at the surrounding mountain shrines; radios blared from nearly every house; and Chimaltecos had become truck owners, storekeepers, school teachers, and commercial coffee growers.

I only slowly began to perceive the quiet persistence of an older way of life. Chimalteco women still wore the traditional red *huipil* and navy blue skirt and tied their hair up elaborately with a long red band. Despite their change in dress, the men too were not really different—the dark eyes in weathered faces, the calloused hands like rough-hewn boards, the stocky build that could not be disguised by brightly colored polyester shirts and pants or cheap plastic shoes. The faces that I saw on the street in front of my house were the same as those that peered out at me from forty-year-old photographs. In the tall green corn and black pungent earth, in the people's pride and resourcefulness that came from working the land, in their wariness of a capricious world that always demanded and seldom gave, I came to recognize a deep continuity with the past that Wagley had known and captured so faithfully in his monographs.

The Daily Routine

The day begins early in Chimbal. Long before the sun rises over the three-pronged peak of Ptxon, the tallest mountain to the east of the town, women begin their morning tasks. Spigots splash water noisily into the cement basins of the public *pilas* as women exchange quiet greetings and draw water for the day's use. The sky lightens, and the pungent smell of wood smoke fills the air. The rest of the family slowly unwraps from the heavy wool blankets that fend off the damp night chill. Radios begin shouting staccato Spanish and mariachi music into the early morning air; the sun's first glare throws the mountains into flat relief against the white morning sky; and the tile roofs steam with evaporation and smoke, veiling everything in a misty haze.

A quick meal of tortillas, beans, and coffee, a short consultation about the work to be done that day, and fathers and sons set out for their fields, hoes over their shoulders and machetes dangling casually from their fingers. Generations of inheritance have scattered Chimalteco farms, so men often work several scattered plots, some over an hour's walk from the pueblo. By eight o'clock, the town has been left to the women and infants, the infirm and the ill. Streets remain nearly deserted from morning until midafternoon, only occasionally disturbed by the sound of rooting pigs and gobbling turkeys. Children sporadically attend school in the town from January to November, but the demands of work at home and in the fields come first.

Women's tasks—cooking, washing, weaving, caring for the children—are year-round occupations. Constant childbearing, in addition to their daily labors, causes Chimalteco women to age much faster than their menfolk. Women often spend part of the morning at one of several springs, washing clothes and hair, and exchanging the latest news. They spend a good part of the day preparing tortillas, the staple of the Chimalteco diet, stripping the dried corn from the cob and boiling it in lime overnight. The resulting hominy then has to be rinsed and ground into a dough. At mealtimes, women pat this dough into thin cakes and toast them on a clay griddle. Adult Chimaltecos easily consume ten large tortillas at a meal, so the supply must be plentiful. In recent years, corn mills and tortilla presses have eased this task, although the rhythmic slap of tortillas being patted out remains as evocative of Chimalteco mealtimes as the wood smoke of cooking fires.

Lunchtime comes by eleven o'clock. If men are working close to the pueblo, wives or daughters take them their food. After lunch with their menfolk, women often stop to gather a load of firewood or fodder before returning home. When working in more remote fields, men carry their food with them, taking time out at lunch to make a fire to heat their tortillas. Work in the fields and at home resumes until three or four o'clock. Before trudging back to town, men often gather a load of firewood themselves or survey their next day's work. In the late afternoon, the main road into Chimbal streams with men, axes and hoes slung over their shoulders, machetes cradled in their arms. They call out jokingly to friends, exchange gossip, or arrange help for some upcoming project. Once home, men invariably relax with a cup of coffee or *q'ootj*, a thin gruel made of corn dough and water. By five o'clock Chimbal has come alive again: radios air Mexican mariachi tunes and Guatemalan marimba music, children play and laugh, youths visit in the streets, men relax in doorways, mothers busily prepare the evening meal. The smoke of cookfires filtering up through nearly every roof makes the town appear from afar almost as if it were on fire.

By nightfall, supper has been eaten, and almost everyone is home to stay. As in all highland regions, the air turns cool as soon as the sun sets, further discouraging excursions outside. If there is enough firewood, and especially if work has been heavy and grueling, Chimaltecos heat up their sweatbath, or *chuuj*, as Mam-speakers call it. The *chuuj*, a low adobe structure resembling a large oven, adjoins nearly every house in Chimbal. To prepare the bath, a fire is built under a rack holding a number of large stones. After the fire burns down, the bather closes the entrance with a heavy blanket, then sits on a low platform against the back wall. Drops of water thrown on the hot stones produce a saunalike vapor. Once the bather has worked up a copious sweat, he or she gets out, rinses off with warm water, and wraps up in clean clothes. Fathers and mothers usually bathe first with the youngest children; other members of the household follow rapidly before the bath cools. As Wagley (1941:10) once noted, "Chimaltecos are a clean people," bathing as often as scarce supplies of firewood permit. After the sweatbath, everyone gathers around the hearth to enjoy a final cup of *q'ootj* before retiring. One by one the children nod off to sleep, and the fire dies down to glowing red coals.

Electric lights have encouraged some Chimaltecos to visit more at night, but few stay up late. By eight o'clock the streets are nearly empty. Only the occasional bobbing wink of a flashlight or the crunch of quick footsteps in the street betrays a stray Chimalteco hurrying home through the deserted town. By nine o'clock Chimbal is asleep, leaving its streets to barking dogs, the trickle of dripping water, and the lonely spirits and demons that townspeople say haunt the empty hours between sunset and dawn.

Chimaltecos measure time by the sun's passage across the sky. The weekly market each Friday punctuates the quotidian routine with a morning's respite of noisy buying and selling, visiting, and occasional drinking. Vendors as well as buyers come from the neighboring towns of San Juan Atitán, Colotenango, and San Pedro Necta to stroll up and down the narrow aisles where they can find everything from produce and chickens to flashlights, plastic goods, clothing, and tape recorders. In recent years Chimaltecos have become more active merchants, but the high cost of transportation, local competition for a limited market, and narrow profit margins prevent anyone from becoming a full-time *comerciante* (see chapter 6).

The market ends by noon, but it always leaves in its wake a number of *k'alq'e?n*, "drunks," victims of a style of drinking that appears to demand consumption of sugarcane rum or beer as fast as possible before succumbing to the inevitable stupor. A Chimalteco in his cups will wail his misery or loudly proclaim his manhood and wealth, depending on his mood. He readily vents feelings he would never express when sober. Because of this, drunks are seldom taken seriously or even overtly scorned; they are sent home if possible or persuaded good-naturedly to leave. The only fights a drunk ever gets into are with other drunks and sometimes with his wife. Most Chimaltecos, men and women alike, confine their drinking to holiday celebrations, some to weekly market-day binges. A few indulge daily, abetted in their affliction by the three *cantinas*, "bars," in the town. The aggressive nature of drinking, the desire to belong or at least not to offend by refusing a drink, and the lack of other diversions make alcoholism an abiding problem in places like Chimbal. Chronic drinkers eventually incur the disapprobation of their neighbors, not necessarily on moral grounds, but on the practical grounds of wasting too much money.

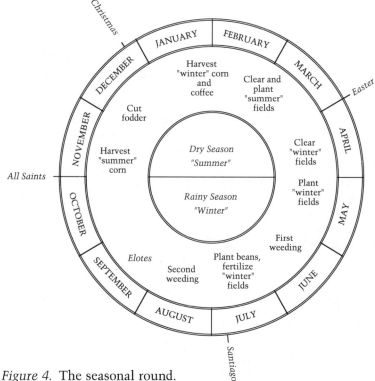

Figure 4. The seasonal round.

The Seasonal Round

The surest gauge of time lies in the seasonal round. Chimaltecos, like most agriculturalists, live according to the seasons, if only because of the different tasks that each demands (see fig. 4). Over the years, these tasks have changed with modifications in farming techniques, but the length of the agricultural cycle remains the same. The growing population of the town has made land increasingly scarce in recent times, and most Chimalteco households plant only about one and a half to two acres of corn each year. While this is less than half the average acreage planted in 1937 (cf. Wagley 1941: 73), the introduction of chemical fertilizers has enabled Chimaltecos to grow enough food for themselves on these smaller plots of land. Land productivity has doubled during the last fifty years, but so has the population, obviating any real economic gains. Furthermore, the need to purchase fertilizers has made Chimaltecos ever more dependent on Guatemala's cash economy. Most of this income comes from migratory wage labor on the coffee and cotton plantations of Guatemala's Pacific coast and from local cash-cropping in coffee (see chapter 6).

The agricultural cycle begins in February and March at the height of the dry-season "summer."[2] After the last heavy rains in late October, the mountainsides turn progressively browner, shading the few remaining stands of trees a darker green against the golden patchwork of drying corn fields and yellowing brush. Under the dusty February sky, Chimaltecos begin to turn under the stalks of their old fields and to clear new ones. Smoke from burning scrub smudges the landscape, and often at dusk, orange flames wink on a distant slope as a farmer fires a new field. By day the singed earth contrasts sharply with the surrounding bush. High on the ridges above the pueblo, Chimaltecos plant their "summer" fields in March, long before the rainy-season "winter" begins. Because crops grow much more slowly at these colder altitudes, few Chimaltecos bother to fertilize their higher fields, and the meager November harvest only supplements shrinking reserves of corn before the main harvest in January. Chimaltecos concentrate their efforts on fields that lie on the more temperate valley slopes below the pueblo, clearing them in April to await the beginning of the rains in May. Here, with the aid of fertilizers and insecticides, Chimaltecos grow the bulk of their corn.

There is nothing subtle about the beginning of the rainy season. Starting in April, late morning clouds creep over the mountains from the north and east, and by midafternoon huge thunderheads dwarf the tallest peaks. Thunder echoes down the high valleys, and then comes the rain—curtains of water blown on the wind that turn the sky a milky white. Rain blots out the landscape and roars in deafening torrents on the tile roofs. The welcome dampness soon turns to a chill as the swirling clouds engulf the town. After the rain passes, the conspicuous silence is broken only by the gurgle of the runoff and then by voices that slowly put the misty world back on a human scale once again.

The rains turn the earth a muddy black and make the fields ready for planting. Each day, distant figures dot the steep mountainsides, seeding the corn in even rows: the jab and twist of an iron-tipped planting stick, four kernels dropped into each hollow, a scoop of damp earth—so goes the sower's rhythm. By mid-May the crop is in the ground; the weather has settled into a round of cleanly washed mornings followed by dreary afternoons that seem to last forever; and the smell of mildew permeates anything left untouched by the morning sun.

Newly cleared summer *milpas* on the flanks of Ptxon, February 1979.

The fields quickly begin to turn green with newly sprouted corn—and with weeds that threaten to strangle the young crop. A few Chimaltecos use herbicides to clean their plots, but most still rely on hoes. The backbreaking labor of the first weeding goes on under the rainy June sky. Working alone or in small groups, men toil up the slope of their fields, leaving behind the bright green stalks of young corn and the black expanse of tilled earth. Chimaltecos take great pride in their gardens, and a well-tended field attests to a man's maturity and ability. "My fields are like children," one Chimalteco observes. "If they are well fed and well clothed, they will grow healthy and strong."

The heavy rains of June taper off into the *canículas*, a brief dry spell during July. High overhead, the bright sun casts sharp blue shadows on the verdant mountains, making this one of the most beautiful times of the year. This is the time when Chimaltecos plant beans and squash alongside the young stalks of corn and fertilize the fields. At the end of July, the four-day fiesta of Santiago, the town's patron saint, provides a welcome respite from the drudgery of farm work; then the rains begin again in August, gradually building to a peak in September. Orangish red scars gape on the green mountainsides where the rain-soaked earth gives way to landslides.

The corn must now be weeded and fertilized a second time and the bean stalks carefully entwined around supporting sticks. By late August, most of the heavy work in the fields is over, and Chimaltecos can leave their *milpas* to ripen on their own. The rhythm of social life in Chimbal slows as many families leave for the coffee and cotton harvests on Guatemala's Pacific coast plantations. Houses are closed up, weekly market crowds dwindle, and the streets at midday become even more deserted than usual. Nearly two-thirds of the households in the town send at least one member to the plantations each year. Often the entire family goes, but most Chimalteco migrants, unlike many other highland Maya, stay for two months or less (see chapter 6). Chimaltecos left in the town cultivate their small coffee groves, tend their *milpas*, cut firewood, and gather fodder for their mules. But most of September and October they spend listening to the rain falling on the roof every afternoon. Roasted *elotes*, ears of newly ripened corn, provide small consolation to the damp chill.

As the rainy season drizzles to an end, migrant Chimaltecos return from the coastal plantations to commemorate the dead on November 1, All Saints' Day. A few days before, men scythe away the weeds in the cemetery, and on the morning of the fiesta Chimaltecos hurry out to decorate the graves of their relatives. A low arch of pine boughs and a scatter of bright flower petals adorn humble wooden crosses and stucco sepulchers alike. Here and there a cup of coffee and a few tortillas stand as polite offerings to the returning souls, and marimbas provide music for their enjoyment. Three, sometimes four, men play each marimba, or *chnab'* in Mam, a large wooden xylophone with resonators below each bar. It remains the instrument of choice at all public celebrations, and Chimbal is renowned for its virtuoso companies. The lively liquid rhythms of the traditional *son*, "melodies," sound at once lighthearted and lonely.

At dusk, flickering candles at the gravesides appear to float in the soft halo of a late rainy-season mist. In this community where so many infants and children die and where even the middle-aged seem old, everyone has someone to remember. The inevitable *aguardiente*, the raw sugarcane rum of rural Guatemala, soon loosens the stoicism of everyday life. A Chimalteco cries beside the grave of a young niece. "I'm crying because of the sadness, not because I'm drunk," he insists. "I was the one who gave her her name." It is hard not to sense how little separates the living from the dead.

The cemetery falls silent once again, disturbed only by young children at play, the occasional drunk, and the not infrequent funeral. The ensuing November days grow short. It is the season of sunshine and winds, and little boys delight in kites made from twigs and the plastic sheeting recently used for rain ponchos. Tall cornstalks rattle in the wind, green and gold as they dry under the southing sun. A few workers depart once more for the coffee plantations, but most have returned to stay, and the afternoon streets come alive again. At the Friday market, vendors sell new wares to Chimaltecos with a bit of money in their pockets from stints on the coast. The bright days and brisk nights and the dearth of heavy work leave the dreariness of September almost forgotten.

Christmas brings the installation of town officials for the coming year. On the day before Christmas, two youths, one dressed as a man, the other as a woman, run through the town "capturing" the new officials. In the plaza, the outgoing officials drink and dance to the music of a marimba, celebrating their imminent freedom. The clear weather, the excitement of the ceremony, and the holiday market that accompanies it ensure a lively, *muy alegre* occasion. The music and the colorful dress of Chimaltecos and other visiting Maya all in their best clothes bring the pueblo to life in a way unseen since the fiesta of Santiago, half a year before.

January continues fresh and dry. Nights and early mornings are sometimes chill, but the sun soon penetrates into all but the shadiest groves and the dark interiors of the houses. Before the cornstalks dry completely, farmers trim the tops for animal fodder, leaving the ears of corn on the naked stalks to parch under the cloudless sky. Ten-foot-tall bundles of cornstalks grow legs and rustle along the trails as Chimaltecos lug their leafy cargo home on tumplines. Chimaltecos harvest beans next, and then in late January the corn harvest begins. Everyone lends a hand at this hectic but happy time. Dried rock hard by the sun, the ears of corn are stripped from the stalks, husked, and hauled to town by mule or, where roads permit, by pickup truck. Chimaltecos save the best ears for seed corn, then hoist the rest into the loft above the rafters. After safely storing the last load of corn, a Chimalteco kneels momentarily in the cramped space under the roof and offers a simple prayer of thanksgiving—acknowledgment that no one, no matter how diligent, alone ensures the certainty of this harvest upon which life for the next year depends.

For some Chimaltecos, this ends the seasonal round, and they turn once more to preparing fields for the next crop. Others take advantage of the clear, dry weather to build a new house or repair a leaky roof. For those who own land temperate enough for small groves of coffee, much work still awaits. In the cool highlands, coffee ripens more slowly than on the tropical coastal plains, and the coffee harvest in Chimbal does not begin until February. The ripe berries must be picked and hulled, and then the ivory beans left to dry in the hot sun. Chimaltecos remain at the mercy of the international coffee market and the grasping Ladino middlemen whom they dub "coyotes," but most manage to eke out a profit from their marginal groves through long hours and self-sacrifice. Coffee has become the Chimaltecos' principal cash crop, as crucial to their economic livelihood as corn is to their daily sustenance (see chapter 6).

The yearly agricultural cycle is finally complete. By mid-March the coffee is harvested and sold, debts can be paid off, new purchases made, and plans for the coming year devised. The four-day Easter celebration of Holy Week sanctifies this secular passage from completion to rebirth, from sustenance to regeneration (see chapter 5). But the future remains fragile in Chimbal. Heavy rains can rot the corn crop or wash away fields. Inflation and falling coffee prices can dash the hopes of an aspiring entrepreneur. Sickness in the family can wipe out the year's savings in expensive consultations with city doctors and endless prescriptions of medicine. And death can come, swift and irrevocable, in an accident on the overloaded buses that rattle up and down the mountainous countryside or in the politically inspired massacres that spread across the highlands like the plagues once brought by the Spanish *conquistadores*.

But the turning of the seasons pays no heed to human afflictions. Chimaltecos face the inexorable passage of time, knowing they survive only through ceaseless perseverance. "Such is the life of a farmer," they say, some with pride, others with deprecation. "Day after day, and there's never enough time. We struggle all our lives, and for what? Just to feed ourselves. Who knows why God left this as our lot in life?" Others respond, "Yes, we struggle, but for ourselves, for our food. What we have is ours."

The Past

The town of Chimbal has existed at least since the Spanish conquest. Chimaltecos have no abiding memory of the conquest and subjugation of their ancestors by Gonzalo de Alvarado in 1525 (Fuentes y Guzmán, cited in Recinos 1954: 475–498) and only the vaguest notion of when the first Chimaltecos arrived and built the church at the center of town. In a sense they are right: before the Spanish conquest, Indians as such did not exist, only autochthonous lords, commoners, and slaves fragmented into warring kingdoms (cf. Recinos

1954: 471–474; Fox 1978; Carmack 1981). Nonetheless, while much of what now passes as "Indian" in contemporary Guatemala originated in colonial times (cf. Martínez Peláez 1979: 615), this attests neither to the Hispanic conquerors' triumph over a passive native peasantry nor to the conquered Mayas' "false consciousness" of willing conversion to the conquerors' ways. Instead, I would argue that the transformation of Chimaltecos from native Maya to colonialized "Indians" reflects centuries of grudging acquiescence as well as opportunistic accommodation to a colonial society that coerced but could never mold them entirely to its will.

Chimbal first appears in the historical record in 1530 as part of a disputed *encomienda* held by a Spaniard named Juan de Espinar. *Encomiendas* were grants awarded to individual *conquistadores* giving them rights to the tribute and initially to the labor of natives from a specified town or towns. In return, *encomenderos* were charged with the often neglected responsibility for Christianizing and civilizing their tributaries (cf. Sherman 1979: 85–128; Gibson 1966: 48–67). Pedro de Alvarado, conqueror of Guatemala, gave the town of Huehuetenango in *encomienda* to Juan de Espinar in 1525. In 1530, Espinar sought to enlarge his holdings by cajoling or intimidating the natives of half a dozen Mam towns, including Chimbal, into moving down from the mountains closer to Huehuetenango. He had the towns burned to prevent their inhabitants from returning— but evidently also to deny rival *encomenderos* access to them (Kramer et al. 1991). The ensuing litigation between Espinar, Alvarado, and other *conquistadores* over jurisdiction of these towns revealed that Chimbal had consisted of five hundred houses, two hundred in the town center and three hundred in outlying settlements. This would have made it one of the larger sixteenth-century Mam settlements outside the valley of Huehuetenango—and larger than it would be again until well into the twentieth century. Chimbal also reportedly had its own "temples and a *patio* [central plaza]," implying some degree of local sovereignty. Native testimony suggested that these towns originated as Mam refuges against K'iche' Maya invasions of the fifteenth century (Kramer et al. 1991; cf. Carmack 1981: 122, 135).

Chimaltecos eventually returned to their town, and the community reestablished itself, although in much diminished form. It subsequently became part of the *encomienda* of another *conquistador* named Francisco Zurrilla (Kramer et al. 1991) and, like other Mam towns, suffered continuing demands for tribute, food, and labor, coupled with a drastic decline in population.[3] By 1549, when Chimbal and the neighboring town of San Juan Atitán became the *enco-*

mienda of yet another Spaniard—this time the daughter of a colonial official named Leonor de Castellanos—the two towns amounted to a paltry award. On July 5, 1549, the thirty-five tributaries (married males between eighteen and fifty, see Lovell 1985: 101) in the two communities were assessed an annual tribute of four *fanegas* of maize and half a *fanega* of beans.[4] They were also required every four months to produce "fifty *mantas* [pieces of coarse cotton cloth] of the size they are usually accustomed to giving" (AGI:AG 128).[5] In accordance with the New Laws of 1542, designed to protect Indians from the worst colonial abuses, Chimaltecos did not have to provide any other goods or services outside of their pueblo. Although the New Laws were enforced at first indifferently and then only briefly (MacLeod 1973: 108–116; but cf. Sherman 1979: 186–187), Chimbal found a more abiding—if ultimately inadequate—defense in geography. The rugged and economically unpromising Cuchumatán Highlands, far from the centers of colonial power and production, meant that Chimaltecos may have suffered relatively less debt peonage and forced labor than Maya elsewhere in Guatemala, at least prior to the eighteenth century (Lovell 1985: 104–105, but cf. 117; MacLeod 1973: 326, but cf. 225).

Like most Maya in Guatemala, however, Chimaltecos fell subject to *congregación*, or resettlement, during the middle years of the sixteenth century. As imperial Spain slowly established order from the indiscriminate exploitation of the early postconquest years, colonial authorities pressured the largely dispersed highland Maya population (cf. Borhegyi 1965: 72–73) to settle into *congregaciones* or *reducciones*, nucleated settlements designed to facilitate both the conversion of the Maya to Christianity and the extraction of native tribute and labor (Lovell 1985: 78–82; MacLeod 1973: 120–122; van Oss 1986: 14–17). First proposed in 1531 by Vasco de Quiroga, the bishop of Michoacán in Mexico, *congregaciones* were intended to create "Indian cities, organized on the lines of [Thomas] More's ideal commonwealth, in which the natural virtues of the Indians would be preserved and perfected by training in the Christian religion and polity" (Keen 1971: 106). Spaniards were forbidden by law to live in them (Mörner 1967: 46).

As actually carried out in Guatemala by Bishop Francisco Marroquín and friars of the Dominican and Franciscan religious orders, *congregación* usually entailed consulting or bribing local chiefs to select a suitable site and having *milpas* planted there to feed the new town. Prospective residents were set to work building a house for the priest, a church, and a plaza in the center of town. They then laid out streets in a grid pattern radiating from the plaza, along which they built their houses. Made of wattle-and-daub walls and thatched roofs, houses reportedly could be built in four hours and an entire town in two days (Remesal 1932: 244). Each settlement also received one square league (about six and a half square miles) of *ejido*, or in-alienable common land, administered by local Maya officials for the sustenance and well-being of the community (cf. Wagley 1941: 57–60; Lovell 1985: 78).

The date of Chimbal's transition from Maya community to Span-ish *congregación* remains unknown. The town may have undergone some form of consolidation after the burnings of 1530, but Domini-can friars evidently did not begin moving into the area to found *con-gregaciones* until the late 1540s (Lovell 1985: 77–79; van Oss 1986: 34–35).[6] It is perhaps significant that the 1549 tribute assessment mentioned previously referred to the town by the Mexicanized name "Chimaltenango" rather than the Mam "Chimbal," as in Espinar's litigation of the 1530s. This suggests that resettlement, and the re-naming that often accompanied it, had taken place by mid-1549. Whatever the case, the thirty-five tributaries that Chimbal shared with San Juan Atitán clearly indicate how many of the inhabitants of the town of twenty years earlier had either died, fled, or never returned.[7]

Although these 1549 tributary figures probably reflect both a gen-eral underreporting by local native leaders and a lowering by Crown officials of the number of individuals liable for tribute (Lovell et al. 1984: 466–467), Chimbal and the *congregación* that it became at mid-century never equaled the town that it had been in the 1520s and before. Indeed, as in most other places, the artificial nature of the *congregaciones*, the lack of Spanish personnel to supervise them, and the deep attachments that Maya maintained to their old lands and communities only slowly gave way to more stable settlements at the end of the sixteenth century (Lovell 1985: 80–82; van Oss 1986: 17; Hill and Monaghan 1987). Bishop Quiroga's vision of uto-pian Indian communities never came to pass, yet even today the colonial churches that dominate the most remote towns of the Cu-chumatán Highlands stand as mute testaments to the once ubiqui-tous power of imperial Spain and to the vigor of the colonial Catho-lic church.

Perhaps the most telling blow to Mam society came from the dev-astation wrought by Old World infectious diseases on its immunolog-ically defenseless native population. In 1520, even before the Spanish arrived, epidemics of smallpox and plague brought from Mexico rav-aged the Guatemalan Highlands; "it is safe, indeed conservative, to say that a third of the Guatemalan highland population died during this holocaust" (MacLeod 1973: 41; cf. Recinos and Goetz 1953: 115–116). After the conquest, repeated outbreaks of infectious diseases, especially the pandemics of 1545–1548 and 1576–1581, probably halved and then halved again the Maya population of Guatemala (MacLeod 1973: 110, 205).[8] In the Cuchumatán Highlands, the population plummeted from an estimated high of 260,000 in 1520 to barely 16,000 a century and a half later—a decline of nearly 94 percent (Lovell 1985: 140–147). Sporadic epidemics throughout the seventeenth and eighteenth centuries impeded demographic recovery, and the Maya population of highland Guatemala may not have achieved its preconquest size again until the mid–twentieth century (Lovell 1985: 149–172).

For Chimaltecos, this periodic and precipitous loss of population undoubtedly eroded the pre-Hispanic Mam social distinctions of power and class that Spanish hegemony had already undermined (cf. MacLeod 1973: 134–142; Carmack 1981: 322–324).[9] For the Spanish, the shrinking Maya population meant reduced income from tribute and labor drafts, as well as critical food shortages. Such shortages eventually led to the growth of *haciendas*, large ranches where the Spanish raised cattle and grew indigo and food crops (Wolf 1959: 202–211). While the direct expansion of *haciendas* onto their lands undermined many Maya communities, in regions of little commercial value, communities like Chimbal managed to retain their lands and thus a precarious autonomy throughout the colonial period. Ironically, the steep decline in population also lessened pressure on local lands, enabling the survivors to maintain a viable—if impoverished—subsistence economy (cf. Lovell 1985: 118–139; MacLeod 1973: 218–231).[10]

Despite the upheavals of conquest and demographic collapse, Spanish rule in Guatemala remained far from absolute. As Nancy Farriss (1984: 285) has aptly observed for colonial Yucatán, "Spanish colonial rule was too inconsistent, too self-contradictory, to be a perfect instrument of either benevolent paternalism or oppressive exploitation." One problem involved the sheer magnitude of the native population. Even a quarter of a century after conquest, barely five hundred Spanish *vecinos* lived in Central America among a thousand times as many natives (MacLeod 1973: 218, figure 15; Sherman 1979: 4–8). The Mercedarian fathers who ministered to Chimbal and other Cuchumatán *congregaciones* numbered only four in 1542 and thirteen in 1572–1574, with many of them staffing their convent in the capital of Santiago de Guatemala (van Oss 1986: 14, 32, 62). The Spanish may have triumphed militarily, but for much of the colonial period, Crown and Church in Guatemala administered the Maya more by visitation than by enduring presence.

Spaniards themselves divided into factions of Crown, Church, and colonists. The Crown had relied heavily on private adventurers to pacify Central America and consequently had to reward them with the spoils of conquest or risk revolt or abandonment of the colony by disgruntled *conquistadores*. In search of easy wealth that might return them to Spain rich men (cf. MacLeod 1973: 46–47), the *conquistadores* argued that native idolatry and human sacrifice justified their enslavement of these "subhuman" natives (cf. Pagden 1986: 166n3). Too free a hand in such matters, however, dangerously challenged an already tenuous imperial sovereignty, while also diverting potential royal revenues from native tribute into private hands (cf. Elliot 1986). The Crown chose to curtail the power of aspiring colonists by instituting *congregación*, in effect placing the Maya directly under royal and ecclesiastical authority. At the same time, however, by restricting the amount of land granted to each community, the Crown forced the Maya to perform tribute-producing labor for both sovereign and colony. In this manner, it was hoped, the demands of empire could be met without unduly provoking the colonists (cf. Wolf 1957: 9; Sherman 1979; 156–159; Martínez Peláez 1979: 63–69).

Within this regime, however, the Church, and in particular its religious orders, soon acquired power and vested interests that made them more than cat's-paws of the Crown against the colonists. As the only bodies capable of undertaking the massive task of missionizing and acculturating the Maya, Franciscan, Dominican, and Mercedarian friars received royal permission to leave their monasteries and evangelize Guatemala. They were charged with converting the Maya while protecting them from the baser influences of Christian society. Once parishes were established, however, they were supposed to turn them over to the secular clergy. Strategically placed as "defenders of the Indians" against colonial abuses and as primary interpreters of the royal will to their native charges, the missionary friars quickly became too accustomed to worldly power to return immediately to their cloisters. Long after the initial evangelization of the Maya had ceased to justify their presence, the friars continued to insist that their charges remained too Indian to be ceded to the secular clergy. Thus, in seeking to instill in the Maya proper Christian humility and Spanish civility, the religious orders succumbed to their own economic and ecclesiastical self-interests, embracing the Indianness of Maya communities precisely so that they could continue to administer them. At the same time, for most Maya—and thus for much of Guatemala—the colonial order became the Catholic church itself, but a local church inextricably bound to particular friars who ministered to specific towns (cf. van Oss 1982; 1986: 50–58, 69–78, 153–158, 179–188). Ironically, these highly localized "republics" of friars and Indians ensured the survival of Maya communities in Guatemala's western highlands.

Within this nexus of contending natural and human forces, the Maya too acted as more than passive tokens. True, *encomienda* and subsequent forms of economic exploitation such as *repartimiento* (labor drafts), *derramas* (forced buying and selling of goods at fixed prices disadvantageous to Indians), and *composición* (sanctioning the illegal seizure of Maya lands through payment of a fee to the Crown)—to say nothing of the constant exactions of the friars for services rendered—all ensured Spanish domination (MacLeod 1973: 206–209, 223–224, 316; van Oss 1986: 85–96). Nonetheless, *congregación* granted to the Maya legally recognized jurisdiction over their lands and internal political affairs. It also gave them recourse to the judicial system as wards of the Spanish Crown (cf. Taylor 1979: 17). Consequently, the second half of the sixteenth century saw a marked increase in Maya litigation against encroachments by land-hungry *encomenderos* (Sherman 1979: 187). This meant, of course, that local Maya authorities had to adapt to Spanish legal niceties, making them ever more dependent on, and invested in, the very order that threatened their few remaining prerogatives. Not surprisingly, this emerging stratum of Maya *caciques*, or political bosses, appears to have been no more averse to abusing their fellows than were their Spanish overlords (cf. Sherman 1979: 301–303; García Añoveras 1980: 168–170).[11]

The Guatemalan chronicler Francisco Antonio de Fuentes y Guzmán came to know one such Chimalteco *cacique* during his term as *corregidor*, "magistrate," of Huehuetenango in 1672–1673 (Recinos 1954: 227). When he visited Chimbal, Fuentes y Guzmán was impressed by the town's fine church and well-constructed houses. He found the Chimaltecos "so rational and intelligent that they are known generally as the *políticos* [politicians] of Chimaltenango" (1972: 24). One of them,

> don Pedro Hernández, a native of Chimaltenango . . . was a man noble by blood, but more so by his revered habits. . . . He never accepted public office, although many times he was elected to the post of *alcalde ordinario* [mayor] and chosen by *corregidores* for governor; but he prudently refused them all, yet even without

those offices he was always feared and respected. . . . He was a great friend of the church, . . . he always performed the sacraments faithfully; and in raising his children he was careful and vigilant in the instruction of Catholic dogma . . . [and] in his life he never knew another woman but his own wife. But this excellent and exemplary Indian citizen also lived attentive to mercy and the common good, making sure that everyone lived productively and worked to support themselves from their fields, crops, and pastures: each year at the fiesta of San Juan [on June 24], the Indian justices of his pueblo reported to him the account of tributes collected and the persons who had yet to pay them, and visiting their houses, he himself would ascertain the cause of these unmet obligations; but finding them to be widows, cripples, or invalids, he paid their tribute out of his own pocket. He was foremost at the visits and salutations of the priests and *corregidor,* contriving to attend them with great veneration and respect. (Fuentes y Guzmán 1972: 24–25; my translation)

This account of don Pedro Hernández suggests two things. First, even after a century and a half of colonial domination, a fair degree of economic, and perhaps even social, differentiation still existed in Chimbal. Indeed, don Pedro may well have constituted part of the hereditary Maya elite that survived well into the eighteenth century in both highland Guatemala and Yucatán (cf. Carmack 1981: 312–316, 320–324; Farriss 1984: 238). Whatever his origins, don Pedro died a rich man, able to leave five hundred pesos to the Church for masses to be said for his soul. "And he left another sum to be loaned to Indians at a rate (although bad) of one *real* on the peso, and with this interest the tribute of poor widows and sick and disabled men was to be paid, leaving another part of this interest for the salutations that *alcaldes* make to the priests and *corregidor* upon their visits (for which the justices collected taxes and molested the poor)" (Fuentes y Guzmán 1972: 25; my translation). Don Pedro's enthusiastic religiosity suggests that he may have also enjoyed the status of *reservado,* a native exempt from tribute because of service to the local church. Such exemption often accrued to men of elite status, but freedom from tribute in itself would have helped to ease *reservados* into the new elite of their communities (cf. Farriss 1984: 236–237; MacLeod 1973: 139).

The second lesson to be gleaned from don Pedro lies in the local nature of his power. Don Pedro's piety and obsequiousness certainly gained him the regard of colonial officials, but Chimaltecos also feared and respected him despite his lack of formal office. In fact, he

studiously avoided such service, perhaps to escape the liability of
local tribute collection, for which local officials were often jailed if
assessments went unmet (cf. Sherman 1979: 289; Gibson 1964:
217–218). He apparently brokered his wealth into local influence by
paying the tribute of other Chimaltecos and thus perhaps indentur-
ing them to his personal service. The collection of tribute by town
rather than by individual or household facilitated this kind of accumulation of social capital, at once stratifying yet consolidating communities like Chimbal. Poorer Maya became dependent on richer
Maya, and for those astute enough to turn the colonial regime to
their own, admittedly limited, advantage, the boundaries imposed
by *congregación* came to define a social context within which they
could exercise a personal power and authority that colonial rule denied them outside of the community.

At the same time, however, this colonialized Maya elite had to
conform to the ethnic conditions of these community boundaries in
order to enjoy the benefits derived from their social capital. Maya
communities apparently remained surprisingly permeable throughout much of the colonial period, and excessive demands by local
elites could prompt villagers to flee to other communities or even to
Spanish *haciendas,* where they became welcome laborers or tribute-
payers (cf. Farriss 1984: 200–218; Wasserstrom 1983: 89–90). Similarly, Maya *caciques* who emulated their colonial lords by affecting
Spanish language and dress soon found themselves shut out of their
towns (cf. MacLeod 1973: 328). Ironically, then, even the colonialized self-interests of Maya elites sustained the separation between
Maya and Spaniard, just as they helped to consolidate Maya life
around the very settlements intended to teach the Maya Christian
piety and Spanish manners.

As don Pedro and other Chimalteco *caciques* like don Pedro Ortiz
and don Baltasar del Castillo (Fuentes y Guzmán 1972: 25) acquired
a vested interest in the stability of their community, direct intervention by civil and religious authorities also lessened. By the seventeenth century, "Spanish employers of Indian labor noticeably tried
to move away from formal and regulated systems of labor and tribute
such as encomienda and *repartimiento.* Instead they became involved in more informal, individual, and extra-legal arrangements"
(MacLeod 1973: 224; cf. Lovell 1985: 105–107). At the same time,
the presence of religious authorities also declined. Baptismal records
from 1663 to 1766 show that priests visited Chimbal an average of
nine times a year, with a low of five in 1728 and a high of sixteen in
1749. Most priests preferred the amenities of the capital and larger
towns, evidence of a general waning of missionary zeal after the six-

teenth century (van Oss 1986: 22–23, 29–30).[12] The transfer of Chimbal from Mercedarian care to that of the secular clergy during the 1760s further enervated Church control, especially since secular priests, unlike the friars before them, seldom spoke Mam. Even if they had, they would have probably still found themselves power-less to alter long-standing local practices to any great degree (van Oss 1986: 138, table 5.2, 140–142).

Economically, however, tribute still had to be paid, and Chimalte-cos continued to suffer the demands of petty officials whose income depended in large part on what they could extort from their jurisdic-tions during their brief terms of office (cf. MacLeod 1973: 314–316, 344). More than a few Maya probably left Chimbal voluntarily, find-ing life on the *haciendas* preferable to the burdens of tribute and official abuse (MacLeod 1973: 226). Periodic outbreaks of infectious diseases also continued to debilitate the community. An unidenti-fied epidemic killed 124 Chimaltecos, mostly adults, between De-cember 1716 and June 1717. The lack of records for the rest of 1717 suggests that the death toll was undoubtedly higher, and fatalities may have amounted to one-fourth the adult population.[13] Sixty years later, the smallpox epidemic of 1780–1781 carried off 79 Chimalte-cos between April and September, over half of them children—again nearly a fifth of the town's population (Lovell 1985: 155, figure 11, 158–159, table 19).

In May 1770, Father Felix Rosel, curate of the parish of Huehuete-nango, noted that there were only 110 families in Chimbal, totaling 451 souls. Moreover, he reported that "not even a third of these families live in the pueblos [of this parish] because they are found scattered in the provinces and coasts [lowlands] in pursuit of their subsistence and necessities, and they only come to their pueblos on certain occasions, possibly two or three times a year, and staying several days, they leave again" (AGI:AG 928.2: 77; my translation). Far from the authority of church and state, these Maya reportedly succumbed to the vices of "lust and drunkenness." They also felt se-cure enough to oppose the establishment of formal schools in their pueblos because they needed the children's help in planting and tending their fields. Father Rosel reports that there were only "In-dian *maestros* who teach Christian doctrine to the girls in the after-noon and to boys in the evening," but one can only wonder how Christian the doctrine actually was. Rosel continues:

About a year ago I seized an old Indian woman kneeling with a smoking clay censer on an artificial mound raised on a small hill, and there were several eggs broken open with much chicken blood on the ground. . . . And having her seized by those who accompanied me, I asked her why she was burning [pine pitch copal] incense in the mountains, and she replied that she was asking God for her health and that all the people went there to do likewise. . . . I have gone to that place again and found the same thing, and once I asked an Indian what motive or purpose they had in doing that, and he answered that such was the method that they used to ask for the death of their enemies.

Regarding the respect that Indians have for the Holy Sacraments, I say that in my judgement they have little or none. I infer this from the tedium and repugnance with which they receive them. The experience of nine years, in which I have worked so hard to meet my yearly duties, has taught me this. [Their indifference] can also be attributed to the fact that the Indians positively do not desire salvation nor fear damnation. (AGI:AG 928.2: 78; my translation)

Maya evasion of colonial authority was becoming increasingly hostile, a threat that prompted Archbishop Cortez y Larraz to conclude, after visiting all the parishes of the diocese of Guatemala in 1774: "The Indians take the Spanish and Ladinos for foreigners and usurpers of these lands. For this reason they view them with implacable hatred, and those who obey them do so only out of pure, servile fear. . . . The Indians want nothing from the Spanish—neither religion, nor doctrine, nor customs" (cited in García Añoveras 1980: 172, my translation). Clearly, Maya conversion to Christian civility had failed.

By the nineteenth century, Maya hostility to outsiders was undisguised, no doubt encouraged by the further deterioration of centralized government control after Guatemalan Independence in 1821. John Lloyd Stephens, a noted American traveler, recoiled at what he saw as the primitive and sullen, even alien, nature of the Maya he encountered in the western highlands of Guatemala in 1840 (cf. Stephens 1969: 147–151, 168–170, 187). Passing through Todos Santos, the Mam town bordering Chimbal on the north, he writes:

As we rode through it, at the head of the street we were stopped by a drunken Indian, supported by two men hardly able to stand themselves, who, we thought, were taking him to prison; but staggering before us, they blocked up the passage, and shouted "Passeporte!" . . . Not one of the three could read the passport, and they sent for the secretary, a bareheaded Indian, habited in nothing but a ragged cotton shirt. . . . We were neither sentimental, nor philosophical, nor moralizing travelers, but it gave us pangs to see such a magnificent country in the hands of such men. (Stephens 1969: 235)

This hostile introversion of Maya communities persisted into the twentieth century, particularly in the Cuchumatán Highlands (cf. LaFarge 1947: 15−17). Only late nineteenth-century demands for land and labor from Guatemala's coffee plantations and growing overpopulation within their communities began to erode the Mayas' intractable provincialism.

Indian and Ladino

Chimbal's past reveals two fundamental but apparently paradoxical facts. First, the town can hardly be considered primordially Maya. The disruptions and disintegration of Mam society during the first half century after conquest were too radical to allow any pristine cultural preservation. On the other hand, the imposition of Spanish polity and religion—Chimbal's two enduring legacies of conquest— engendered a local community whose inhabitants continue to see themselves as a people apart from the rest of Guatemalan society. Neither purely Maya nor completely colonial, an abiding sense of Chimalteco otherness persists. Such intense provincialism centered on local communities underlies much of what has come to be called Indian in contemporary Guatemala. Some prefer to see this as purely the outcome of a postconquest Guatemalan political economy in which Indian has always carried the opprobrium of one fit only to serve (cf. Martínez Peláez 1979; Friedlander 1975; Hawkins 1984). It is equally important to note, however, that this essential otherness preceded the formation of colonial Guatemalan society and in no small part determined its development.

From the first moment of conquest, the profound racial and cultural disjunction separating Spaniard and Maya prompted in both a deep sense of alienness. To the early *conquistadores,* the Aztecs, Maya, and other native peoples were a strange new race whose cultural refinements only accentuated the barbarism of their idolatry, human sacrifice, and cannibalism (cf. Keen 1971: 55−70). For the Maya, the arrival of the fair-skinned Spaniards with horses, cannon, and steel weapons provoked equal consternation: in the words of one native Guatemalan chronicler, "In this manner the Castilians arrived of yore, oh, my sons! In truth they inspired fear when they arrived. Their faces were strange. The lords took them for gods" (Recinos and Goetz 1953: 121).[14] The ascendancy of Spanish conqueror over conquered Maya immediately imbued such phenotypic and technological distinctions with the asymmetry of political and social rank, yet the colonial regime did not simply enforce these distinctions out of convenience. Instead, a dialectic of ethnic self-ascription, attribution, and counterattribution continuously transformed yet reinforced initial oppositions between Old World and New.[15]

The Spaniards brought to the New World social values and institutions inherited from the hierarchical, estate-based society of late medieval Castile, in which different social groups held distinct legal statuses, privileges, and obligations. In the New World, however, race, and not a person's relationship to the land, came to define social and legal status. The coincidence between the *conquistadores'* apparent distinctiveness and achieved ascendancy made their "natural" superiority seemingly all the more self-evident (cf. Mörner 1967: 53–54). Nonetheless, although cultural and physical distinctions served to rationalize Spanish domination, the size and distribution of the native Maya population strongly influenced the course that Spanish domination was to take. In the heavily populated regions of Guatemala's western highlands, the early missionary friars sought to broker their monopoly in Maya languages and culture into their own worldly kingdoms (cf. van Oss 1986: 30–32, 45–49, 134–136). The availability of native labor and the vagaries of climate and commerce likewise affected entrepreneurial strategies of Spanish domination (cf. MacLeod 1973).[16]

In turn, the Mayas' colonial experience did nothing to erase their nativistic sense of distinction from their Spanish overlords. On one hand, as Spaniards came to equate Maya nativism with inferior social position, the Maya became ever more aware of their ethnic distinctiveness. The special legal rights, obligations, and restrictions imposed upon them by colonial rule only intensified differences already evident in their dress, language, heritage, and physiognomy. On the other hand, even when Maya accepted the conditions of this new social order, they clearly remained outside of it: Spanish *encomendero*, colonial official, and Catholic friar all obviously obeyed laws and lived by standards other than those dictated for Indians. Indeed, if "after baptism an Indian began to steal, swear, lie, kill, and steal women, he would say, 'I am getting to be a little like a Christian'" (Remesal, cited in Sherman 1979: 155).

Given the undeniable hegemony of conquest and subjugation, Maya nativism found its most ready expression in the cultural syncretism that came to pervade all the colonial institutions imposed upon them. When subjected to the forced acculturation of *congregación*, the Maya subverted the policy through the gradual dispersal—

or *decongregación* as Lovell (1983b: 171) aptly puts it—of many Cuchumatán Maya pueblos during the seventeenth century; the resulting communities reflected the structure but not the intent of Spanish institutions (cf. Lovell 1983b: 169–72; MacLeod 1973: 328). When given jurisdiction over town lands, the Maya often subdivided their new *ejido*, or common land, according to pre-Hispanic social groups called *calpules* or *parcialidades* by the Spanish; they also continued to cultivate their old lands in the mountains, even when these were some distance away from their new settlements (Lovell 1985: 126; cf. Hill and Monaghan 1987). When taught the Roman alphabet by Catholic friars, the Maya produced manuscripts like the *Popol Vuh* and the *Annals of the Cakchiquels*, written in their own languages to preserve pre-Hispanic cosmology, mythology, and history (cf. Edmonson 1971; Tedlock 1985; Carmack and Morales Santos 1983; Recinos and Goetz 1953). When enjoined to Catholic celebrations, the Maya used *cofradías*, religious brotherhoods charged with the veneration of particular saints, to honor their dead or to reinforce local bonds (cf. Watanabe 1990; Fuentes y Guzmán 1972: 26–27; García Añoveras 1980: 144–147; Hill 1986). Outwardly, then, Maya nativism acquired colonial form, but it continued to substantiate local communities at odds with the larger colonial order (cf. Taylor 1979: 21–23).

As the Maya came to conventionalize their distinctiveness in terms of local boundaries, their otherness was sharpened from without by another conventional primordialism of racism. Ironically, despite the fundamental importance to colonial society of the natural distinction between Spaniard and native, a dearth of Spanish women led to pervasive race mixture, which began to blur racial categories immediately following—indeed, even during—the conquest. This gave rise to a growing number of Ladinos and other so-called *castas*. The term *ladino*, meaning "sagacious, clever, cunning" in Central American Spanish, appears first to have been used in the sixteenth century as an adjective applied to acculturated Maya or to those who spoke Spanish (cf. Tax 1941: 21; Sherman 1979: 187). As miscegenation increased, the term came to refer to the offspring of Maya women and their Spanish overlords. These offspring were so often illegitimate that by the late sixteenth century the terms *ladino* and *bastard* had become nearly synonymous (Sherman 1979: 319).

At first these children were absorbed into one ethnic group or the other, depending on whether or not their Spanish fathers chose to acknowledge them. As their numbers grew during the seventeenth century, however, Ladinos came increasingly to exist on the margins of colonial society. Neither Spanish nor Maya, they held no legally

recognized status: disenfranchised, forbidden to live in Maya pueblos, yet unable to find a livelihood in the cities, many Ladinos took
to the *haciendas* or to lands abandoned by the shrinking Maya population and there lived a furtive, poverty-stricken existence (Mörner
1967: 60, 97–101; Martínez Peláez 1979: 376–387; García Añoveras
1980: 119–121; MacLeod 1973: 211–213; Sherman 1979: 319–320;
Farris 1984: 283; Wolf 1959: 233–240).[17]
   Although socially inferior to whites, Ladinos considered themselves superior to Indians. Because they spoke Spanish and often
served Spanish masters, the Maya too saw Ladinos as dangerous
agents of colonial power and authority. While mixed descent denied
Ladinos absolute dominance in colonial Guatemalan society, the purity of the Castilian blood they did possess, their freedom from tribute, and the liberty to live and work as free individuals, theoretically
made them "better" than most Indians (Mörner 1967: 60–61; Martínez Peláez 1979: 268–269). By the eighteenth century, phenotypi-
cally based distinctions between Maya and Spaniard had given way
to the equally rigid and powerful social discrimination of racism.
Initially, race had defined social status, but now the social hierarchy
sanctioned by these categories came increasingly to define racial
status: Indians were those who continued to live in Indian communities "in accordance to Hispano-Indian norms set down in the Laws
of the Indies" (Mörner 1967: 102); Ladinos were those who did not.
At the same time, Indians and Ladinos had become virtually indistinguishable, and "passing" occurred in both directions—Indians becoming Ladinos working on *haciendas*, Ladinos taking up residence
in Indian towns (Mörner 1967: 94, 97–100). This ambiguity only exacerbated Ladino disavowals of their non-Spanish heritage, for without such differentiation, they constantly risked being classed as
Indians by those above them in the social hierarchy (cf. Guzmán-
Böckler and Herbert 1970).
   The ironies here are patent: neither cultural syncretism nor race
mixture has reduced the "primordial otherness" that first divided
postconquest Guatemala. Instead, both have intensified it. Syncretism has come to substantiate an intractable Maya ethnicity, expressed in colonial rather than pre-Hispanic forms. In turn, race
mixture spawned a brutal racism predicated on a presumed purity of
blood that today finds expression in cultural, not biological, terms.
Consequently, the purely cultural practices that distinguish Indian
from Ladino continue to impute innate, mutually derogatory racial
dispositions: to Maya, Ladinos are by nature arrogant, lazy, and un-
trustworthy; to Ladinos, Indians will be forever brutish and uncivilized.[18] The dialectical contradiction here simply perpetuates the

conventional wisdom of both syncretism and racism as strategies of social survival: Maya syncretism confirms Ladino stereotypes of Indians incapable of comprehending civilized ways; the cruelties of racism, both great and small, in turn reinforce Maya withdrawal into the stoic inscrutability of their own communities.

The ethnic conventionalizations of "Indian" and "Ladino" thus result from the opportunistic responses of subordinate social groups to a society predicated on the hierarchical distinctions between conqueror and conquered, Spaniard and Maya. The colonial order, however, did not create these oppositions but instead coalesced around them. As highland Maya society disintegrated in the face of conquest and demographic collapse, the adoption of Hispanic institutions both preserved and elaborated Maya ethnic separatism, even while it ensured Maya political subjugation (cf. Warren 1978). Conversely, as race mixture blurred original definitions of colonial Guatemalan social statuses, a socially defined racism enabled Ladinos to differentiate themselves from Indians, even though their very existence repudiated any such physical distinctions at all. The contradictions inherent in both positions only intensify the antagonism between them, leading to more emphatic and rigid conventionalizations of a natural distinction between Maya and Spaniard that no longer exists.

History, Ethnicity, and Community

The patterns in Chimalteco history and quotidian routine highlight three important features of local Chimalteco identity. First, Chimaltecos are not simply passive victims of economic exploitation and colonial oppression. Neither are they noble but doomed survivors of a long-vanished civilization. Their distinctive community and way of life represent a dynamic adaptation to conquest and colonialism that turned externally imposed institutions to local ends. If nothing else, the machinations of Chimalteco *caciques* like don Pedro Hernández suggest that local economic differentiation and individual self-interest contributed as much to the formation and persistence of the community as did Spanish fiat. While the military and cultural conquest of the New World demonstrated an awesome Hispanic energy and zeal, to view the Maya past and present as purely a creation of Spanish colonialism gives the *conquistadores* too much credit: the land was too vast, the pueblos too distant, communication too slow and sporadic to enable them to mold the highland Maya entirely to their will. The myth of Indian passivity lies rooted in their historical silence, not in historical reality.

Second, Chimalteco identity is dialectical rather than essential, oppositional rather than innate. The distinctive features of Guatemalan ethnicity change through time, but the opposition between Indian and Ladino persists. This persistence entails no teleological inference of past ethnic differences from present ones because history attests to the time when a "new world" was born in the confrontation between two old ones. Nor does this dialectical opposition mean that Maya and Ladino cultures exist simply as opposed—or, as John Hawkins (1984) has argued, "inverse"—conventionalizations of each other. Indians are more than what Ladinos are not—not rich, not powerful, not political, not together—just as Ladinos are not simply non-Indians who dress in non-Indian fashion, speak a non-Indian language, and live acculturated non-Indian lives in non-Indian communities. The oppositions between them constitute the negative other for each group against which everyday life takes shape and meaning. This otherness represents the boundary, not the substance, of ethnic identity in Guatemala.

A third and final feature of Chimalteco identity involves a fundamental concern with the here and now. Chimaltecos sometimes appear to live in a timeless, if constantly changing, present bounded only by the eternal seasonal round, by the immutable mountains, and by the memories of *tiij xjaal*, "the old people." They have little sense of any pan-Indian identity. The most important distinction for them lies between *aj Chimb'aal*, "those of Chimbal," and *moos*, "Ladino, stranger, outsider," or less frequently, *gringo*, "white foreigner." Experientially, their community constitutes the center of their world. It matters little that their church, the house of Santiago, is of colonial Catholic origin. What matters is that it constitutes the physical as well as spiritual heart of their community. Understanding contemporary Chimaltecos entails understanding the nature of this community, not simply as an expression of pre-Hispanic Maya survivals or as the product of colonial and later capitalist exploitation. Instead, it represents a dynamic social reality that has adapted —and continues to adapt—to the vagaries of changing historical circumstances.

✢ *Part Two* ✢

Saints and Souls

3

✛ The Conventions of Community ✛

In describing the quotidian and historical realities that shape Chimalteco life, the previous chapter raises a fundamental question. How do Chimaltecos in their own eyes relate the seemingly "timeless present" of their everyday existence to the colonially imposed realities of ethnic status, polity, religion, and economy? If Chimalteco identity is as dynamic and dialectical as asserted, what combination of experience and history articulates and motivates the distinction between Chimaltecos and others? In this chapter, I begin to address these questions by analyzing the cultural conventions that Chimaltecos use to circumscribe the boundaries of their community. The relationship between the physical landscape, Chimalteco conventionalizations of this landscape, and the social relations entailed in both all reveal how daily routines and associations precipitate the experiential limits of the community through a continual recombination of received cultural forms and contemporary situations.

I begin with Chimalteco definitions of publicly shared space, which also involve cultural notions of time and experience. This chapter thus concerns Chimalteco cosmology and worldview—but a cosmology that must be analyzed as a "lived-in" reality as much as a "thought-of" order, and a worldview that has to do with a physical place as much as it does with abstract categories of space and causality. Daily experience and cultural conventions, plus the importance of local continuity through time, reveal that Chimalteco identity involves perceiving the world in a particularly Chimalteco way and, perhaps more importantly, viewing it from a particularly Chimalteco place.

Chimalteco Categories of Space

Although most Maya in highland Guatemala live in hamlets scattered across the countryside (Tax 1937: 431), Chimbal's nucleated settlement pattern makes the *cabecera,* "municipal seat," both the social and administrative heart of the community. Life revolves around the densely populated pueblo, and townspeople insist, as they did fifty years ago, that those forced to live in distant hamlets are "poor and sad" (cf. Wagley 1949: 11).

Topography reinforces the social centrality of the pueblo. Chimbal nestles in its own circumscribed world: the pueblo sits halfway up the northern slope of a narrow valley that runs roughly east to west for about five miles (8 km), ringed by prominent peaks to the north and east. To the south, a high ridge encloses the valley, but from the mountainside just above the pueblo, three of Guatemala's tallest volcanoes can be seen dominating the distant horizon. Only to the north, on the far side of the mountain, do municipal lands extend beyond sight of the pueblo into the valley of the Rio Ocho (fig. 2). There Chimaltecos have planted coffee to take advantage of the lower altitude and sheltered slopes. Many townspeople have built houses near their small groves, but most still maintain permanent houses in the pueblo. When they go for several days or weeks to tend their coffee in Rio Ocho, they say they are going *ti witz,* "to the mountains." There is a sense that any place outside the valley immediately surrounding the pueblo is not really Chimbal.[1]

For most Chimaltecos, space extends conceptually in concentric rings of decreasing familiarity from the pueblo to the most distant volcanoes (see fig. 5). They distinguish four broad categories of space: *jaa,* "the house"; *tnam,* "the town"; *kjoʔn,* "corn fields"; and *chk'uul,* "the wilds," or "forest." *Jaa,* along with the patio next to it, constitutes the most frequented, permanent place in Chimalteco life. There daily activities begin and end. *Tnam* refers to the clustered houses that surround the local church and central plaza. The cramped conditions of the pueblo minimize distinctions between houses as separate places, and the town as a whole constitutes the most clearly bounded local place. *Kjoʔn* encompass the permanence of house and town in a patchwork of cultivated plots interspersed with overgrown fields in fallow, thicket-choked ravines, and the ever-encroaching bush. Chimaltecos shift their fields according to the dictates of an extended bush-fallow cycle, resulting in the uneven scatter of fields (see chapter 6). Beyond the fields, *chk'uul* envelops this realm of human endeavor, in places even penetrating it where plots have lain too long in fallow. Remote, aloof, and seldom cultivated because it is too steep, too rocky, too inaccessible, *chk'uul* crowns most mountaintops, testament to a ruggedness that refuses to yield even to increasingly acute land shortages. Thus, as Chimaltecos move outward from house and town through fields to

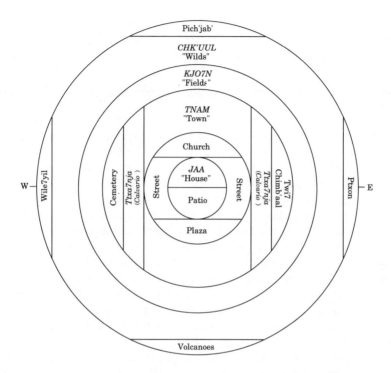

Figure 5. A schematic representation of Chimalteco categories of space.

forest, space becomes relatively less frequented, less familiar, and less settled—and potentially more unsettling as well.[2]

Nonetheless, relative placement alone fails adequately to define Chimalteco distinctions between house, town, fields, and forest. Although the physical boundaries of each category remain conceptually well marked, the cultural meaning of these spaces varies according to the time of day. In Chimbal, diurnal time—and the social activities that fill it by day and the slumber that leaves it largely unapprehended by night—relativizes the meaningfulness of these spatial categories. Quotidian routine inextricably links space and time, a property reflected at all levels of Chimalteco cosmology.[3]

Conceptually and experientially, life in Chimbal expands and contracts with the rising and setting of the sun. During the day, normal activities extend beyond the confines of house and town to the distant fields and mountainsides where Chimaltecos toil, bringing *kjo?n* and *chk'uul* within the familiar bounds of experience. Under the waning afternoon sun, however, Chimalteco life slowly contracts to the pueblo. At nightfall, as townspeople retreat to house, hearth, and bed, the local landscape fades into a world where the strange and uncanny can prowl even the familiar streets of the town, calling like a cat or owl, rattling shuttered windows or bolted door. Like the *chk'uul* on remote mountaintops, night holds unknown risk for Chimaltecos, not so much out of superstitious fear as out of unfamiliarity. Chimaltecos seldom leave town after nightfall, and few stay up late—except during fiestas, when both men and women often socialize in plaza, marketplace, and cantina long into the night. Normally, to be outside alone after dark is doubly anomalous, with questionable import for one's welfare and, more ominously, for one's intentions, since witchcraft is always performed at night (see chapter 8). Daily routines clearly temper the meaning of Chimalteco categories of space, reinforced by a general conformity to the same schedule of early to bed and early to rise.[4]

This diurnal oscillation of Chimalteco cultural space recalls the time-space principle found by Gary Gossen (1974: 29–30) in Chamula cosmology. The Chamulas, a highland Maya community in nearby Chiapas, Mexico, associate what is known—and therefore "good"—with things close in space and time, while relegating what is unknown—and therefore most likely "bad"—to distant times and places. In Chimbal, this conjunction of space and time reflects daily routines and experiences. Unlike the Chamulas, who imbue unknown places with the asocial behavior of mythological times, Chimaltecos appear to associate socially empty or unfamiliar space with distance in quotidian time—that is, with the dormant period of night—regardless of actual location or relative distance from the pueblo. For Chimaltecos, then, I would argue that diurnal time, and the human pursuits embedded in it, most immediately define spatial and temporal categories. The same time-space principle found in Chamula may still formally apply, but it remains concretely rooted in the realities of a continuing here and now rather than motivated by more abstract considerations.

The Conventionalization of Space

Chimaltecos formalize the boundaries of house, town, fields, and forest through the placement of important shrines and by conceptualizing the local landscape as domains of different conventionalized personages. At the center of *tnam* stands the Catholic church, the principal Chimalteco shrine and home of Santiago, the municipal patron saint. Townspeople often refer to the church as *tjaa Santiyaawo*, "the house of Santiago," because the saint lives inside, much as all good Chimaltecos live properly in their own houses. As early as the mid–seventeenth century, Chimbal boasted "a very well made parish church with a tile roof, and with an altarpiece and sacristy ornaments of great decency and adequate service" (Fuentes y Guzmán 1972: 24; my translation). No one knows when the present church was built, but it underwent renovation in the early 1950s, acquiring two bell towers, a new facade, and a corrugated metal roof. More recently, the faithful have added a wooden ceiling with three skylights to the interior (see chapter 8). Here Chimaltecos pray to images of Santiago, Christ, and the Virgin Mary, seeking assurance in an uncertain world.

Several shrines surround the church, marking the boundary between the town and nearby fields. Two of these shrines, called *ttxa ʔnja*—literally, "edge of the houses" in Mam—stand at the eastern and western outskirts of the pueblo. They mark the two principal entrances to the town, and Chimaltecos also refer to them as *calvarios*, "crossroads." While the main road through Chimbal in part determines the location of these entrances, other approaches to the pueblo lack any special markers. This may reflect the salience of the east-west axis in Mam cosmology, in contrast to the fourfold cosmology of the Maya of Yucatán, which dictates placing town cross shrines at the four cardinal directions (Watanabe 1983; cf. Redfield and Villa Rojas 1934: 114). The western *calvario* consists of a small house that stands next to what was once the old cemetery before it was converted into a basketball court and more recently into the site for the new school. The eastern *calvario* is simply a widening of the street adjacent to the ravine that runs behind the houses on that side of town.(fig. 3).

Another important locale called Twiʔ Chimb'aal lies just to the east of the pueblo on a low hill crowned with cypress trees. Its name can be translated either as "the head of Chimbal," perhaps in reference to its importance, or as "above Chimbal," perhaps alluding to the association in Mam cosmology of east with "up" and with the rising sun (Watanabe 1983: 718–719). Although the old stone altar and cross that once marked the shrine have now disappeared, Chimaltecos still remember the clay figurines that adorned it (Wagley 1949: 55). Another shrine, now gone, once overlooked the pueblo from the mountainside to the north, nestled in a second grove of cypress trees (cf. Wagley 1949: 55). In addition to these shrines, other places in or near the town also once held particular ritual significance—for example, a small spring on the path to Twiʔ Chimb'aal where curers took their patients to "wash away" their sickness. Finally, in opposition to Twiʔ Chimb'aal on the east, the cemetery still lies on the western edge of the pueblo, possibly reflecting the frequent association in Maya cosmologies of west with the waning heat of day, with darkness, and with death (cf. Gossen 1974: 33–35).

Chimalteco shaman-diviners formerly included many of these shrines in their prayer rounds, although the most important places to pray remained the church and the tall cross that once stood in front of it (cf. Wagley 1949: 54–55). At each stop shaman-diviners performed *costumbre,* "custom" or "tradition," which in Guatemalan Spanish denotes any native ritual involving the recitation of prayers, the burning of candles and *poom,* "pine pitch copal incense,"[5] and occasionally the sacrifice of a turkey or chicken. Appropriately located at the transition between town and fields, the shrines provided access to the "spirit owners" of the land who held sway over crops, health, and good fortune. Although Chimaltecos today no longer perform *costumbre* publicly (see chapter 8), the *ttxaʔnja* shrines on the eastern and western edges of the pueblo still serve as important stops during the processions of Lent and Holy Week and generally continue to distinguish the domesticated space of the town from the uninhabited wilds of the fields and mountains.

Beyond the confines of the town, prominent features of the landscape—especially mountains and the corn fields scattered across the mountainsides—order Chimalteco space. In Wagley's time the fields themselves constituted a kind of shrine where Chimaltecos performed frequent *costumbre* at crucial stages of the agricultural cycle (Wagley 1941: 32–44). Today most Chimaltecos forego such rituals, although they sometimes utter a simple prayer of safekeeping before beginning work in their *milpas.* Nonetheless, what Redfield once observed for Maya corn fields in Yucatán still holds true in Chimbal. "The milpa is a place the native feels to be inhabited by invisible presences, as he comes upon it, suddenly, after walking through miles of bush: the planted corn, the fence, perhaps a broken calabash. It is the feeling one of us has on entering an empty house, with the table laid and the fire set" (Redfield and Villa Rojas 1934: 114). In the final months before the harvest, farmers often leave their fields untended for long periods of time, but no matter how overgrown with beans, squash, and other plants, the orderly rows of corn still contrast with the surrounding bush, testament to the hand that first planted them. Many Chimaltecos still leave two stalks of corn standing in each field at harvest time to guard the gathered ears until they can be hauled to town. Here again, the enduring alliance between people and maize in Chimbal appears to be as much social as alimentary. While I would not say that Chimaltecos worship maize in any strict sense, they do call it *qtxuʔ kjoʔn,* "Our Mother Corn"—

which suggests their profound respect for this source of all life and livelihood.

Beyond the fields, nearby mountain peaks dominate the immediate periphery of local Chimalteco space. The names of prominent peaks allude to their "spirit owners" or "guardians," known in Mam as *taajwa witz*, "owner or master of the mountain," or simply as *witz*, "mountain." As both literal and metaphorical mountains, *witz* personify the land and all that it produces. Chimaltecos no longer conceptualize these *witz* as actual personages as they once did, but like watchful corn fields, the peaks themselves suggest an impassive, brooding presence. To the east rises the three-pronged peak of Ptxon; directly above the pueblo to the north looms Pich'jab'; to the west on the border with Colotenango stands Wile?yil. The owners of the first two mountains are male, the third female. Other geographical features that dot the countryside include Twi? Chuumb'il, a shrine noted for curing sickness of all kinds. It stands on the ridge between Chimbal and the neighboring town of San Juan Atitán. Lying to the west of Wile?yil, another *witz* called Paaxil represents the Owner of Maize—the place where Chimaltecos say that a flea brought the first grains of maize through a narrow crevice to give their ancestors corn (cf. Wagley 1941: 20).

At the farthest visible boundary of the Chimalteco world stand Guatemala's three tallest volcanoes. Like the local peaks, each has an owner. The volcano Santa Maria, called Kab'yo?k in Mam, is the home of Xwaan No?j, the most powerful of all *witz*. As *taajwa iil*, the Owner of Misfortune, he sends illness and death to insure a bountiful harvest of souls to toil inside his mountain. Less sinister is Rosnaa, the *witz* living in Tajumulco, Guatemala's tallest volcano. According to a story that Chimaltecos tell, the first coffee trees came from Rosnaa when Rufino Barrios, the nineteenth-century president and Liberal reformer of Guatemala, arranged for his son to marry the daughter of this *witz*. The bride brought with her seeds for coffee trees, and Chimaltecos say this is why the first coffee plantations in Guatemala began on the Pacific coast near Tajumulco. The third and westernmost volcano of Tacaná stands on the Mexican border. Called Tokyaan in Mam, Wagley's informants told him that it has a female *witz* (Wagley 1949: 59).[6]

The placement of shrines around the periphery of the pueblo and the anthropomorphization of the surrounding mountain peaks divide local space into the domains of two types of personages. On one hand, Catholic saints live in the church and watch over the community's welfare. On the other, *witz* personify Chimalteco fields and forest. More remote still, Xwaan No?j lurks on the fringe of Chimalteco life, ready to intrude in local affairs with dire consequences. These domains coincide with the spatial categories occasioned by daily Chimalteco movement between home, field, and forest, suggesting that the more unfamiliar and less frequented the landscape, the more potentially menacing its landlord becomes.

As in daily life, however, the realms of saint and *witz* also expand and contract diurnally, and the nightly wanderings of Chimalteco spooks and demons chart these shifting boundaries. The generic term for these anomalous beings is *siky'puul*, "spook," derived from the verb stem *siky'pu-*, "frighten." Some *siky'puul* are simply *taanma kyimni*, "souls of the dead," who wander through the wilds and haunt the deserted streets of the town. *Siky'puul* can also be poltergeists who call out to passersby on lonely paths or throw rocks at them. At other times they are disembodied sobs of inconsolable weeping. Chimaltecos learn of these spooks early in life: a young girl at a half-opened door points into the darkness outside, repeating "*Ke tii juuris!* [Look out for the monsters!]" as her little brother goes out to urinate; a man walks a young boy home through the gathering dusk to reassure—while also tacitly reaffirming—the child's unspoken uneasiness about spooks.

Encounters with a more dangerous type of *siky'puul* called *mib'inaq* invariably presage bad luck. Usually seen late at night on a deserted street, *mib'inaq* always appear as silent women dressed in Chimalteco garb with their long hair hanging loose instead of bound up neatly in the usual fashion. One man told of seeing a *mib'inaq* shortly before his mother-in-law died. After an evening of drinking with friends, another Chimalteco man followed a *mib'inaq* thinking it was an ordinary woman, and one of his *comadres* died shortly thereafter. Owls and cats also bode ill if they cry out near someone's house at night. Chimaltecos say that they are *tsam demonyo*, "emissaries of the devil," because they wander through the night.

As walking dead, as voices without bodies and bodies without voices, *siky'puul* are anomalous and therefore symbolically appropriate mediators between cultural categories—in this case, categories of space (cf. Douglas 1966: 34–40). Their presence embodies the contradictions between nearby, frequented space, which thus should be known and familiar, and the socially dormant period of night, when this space becomes deserted and consequently as unknown as the distant *chk'uul* ruled over by *witz*. The saints, like mortal Chimaltecos, apparently leave night to the unseen denizens that know it best. As these spooks and demons retire before the approaching day, however, the realm of the saints comes once again to life, reestablishing the proper correspondence between spatial categories, conceptual domains, and human experience and familiarity.

The conventionalization of town, fields, and forest as the domain of protective saints, brooding *witz*, and wandering spooks reiterates the importance of human activities in defining spatial categories. Experientially, daily routines circumscribe the normal extent of Chimalteco life and work. Conceptually, the conventions of saint and *witz* ground these routines in an immanent sociality rooted in the land itself. In other words, as conventionalized social beings bound to specific features of the landscape, saint and *witz* imbue the place where Chimaltecos live with moral rather than merely spatial import. Since Chimaltecos situate Chimbal physically and conceptually between where saint and *witz* reside, it is important to examine what Chimalteco relations with saint and *witz* reveal about the community circumscribed by these figures.

The Conventionalization of Social Relations

Saint and *witz* represent more than place markers for Chimalteco concepts of space. In the past, they constituted the most salient figures in local religious life by virtue of their presumed proximity as well as ritual accessibility. Although God and Christ received frequent mention in Chimalteco prayers, both remained somewhat vague and diffuse: God was benevolent but remote and unknowable; Christ appeared in Chimalteco myths as a local culture hero or trickster, but his feats related mostly to the distant past (cf. Wagley 1949: 51–52). More recently, the teachings of evangelical and Catholic missionaries have assailed the eminence—as well as the immanence—of saint and *witz:* evangelicals decry the godless idolatry of both, while Catholic priests remind the faithful that saints only reflect—and by no means idolatrously—the greater glory of God's grace. Despite a definite "disenchantment" of *witz* and creeping doubt about the saints, however, the immediacy of these images in everyday life makes them hard for Chimaltecos to disregard, much less disown. Just as *witz* remain the mountains and volcanoes that dominate the physical landscape, so the saints—in particular Santiago—remain tangible images that articulate the sociality linking Chimaltecos with God and Chimaltecos with Chimaltecos.

The saints live in the church at the center of town. A large wooden image of Santiago called *Santiago Patrón* dominates the chancel wall behind the altar. A much smaller figure of the saint on horseback resides in a glass-fronted niche below and to the right on the south side of the altar. Called *Santiago Chiquito,* "Little Santiago," this smaller saint sits astride a diminutive white horse with sleepy eyes and long, burrolike ears. His right arm is raised as if he once held a sword, but his empty hand now hangs harmlessly in the air. *Santiago Patrón* remains permanently in the church, whereas townspeople carry *Santiago Chiquito* in the various processions celebrated each year. Unlike the Tzotzil Maya of Zinacantán, however, Chimaltecos have apparently never explicitly linked these images into a junior-senior pair but treat them as distinct powers and pray to them separately (cf. Wagley 1949: 53; Vogt 1976: 34).

The two Santiagos share their church with a number of other images. Directly below *Santiago Patrón* hangs a large image of Christ on the cross that also never leaves the church. Across from *Santiago Chiquito* on the lefthand side of the altar, an image of Santa Ana resides in another glassed-in niche. Perhaps because her feast day closely follows Santiago's in late July, Santa Ana has become the "wife" of Santiago, and her image accompanies him in all processions. Other images occupy niches along both walls of the church: on the northern side stand a Madonna and child that Chimaltecos once called the *mujer de Cristo,* "the wife of Christ" (Wagley 1949: 54), a statue called *Paask* (from the Spanish *Pascua,* "Easter")—a wounded Christ with hand upraised that Chimaltecos carry in the Easter processions of Holy Week—an image of Christ in the tomb enclosed in a glass-covered niche, and two small female saints—one a second Madonna and child and the other a Virgin.

Opposite these images, four male saints look down from the south wall of the church. They once served as patrons of the town's four original *cantones,* or wards, but since the *cantones* no longer carry saints' names, there is some confusion over the figures. Wagley identified them as San Miguel, San Andrés, San Pedro, and Santo Domingo (or San Juan?) (Wagley 1941: 11; 1949: 54, 120). Some forty years later, however, save for San Miguel and perhaps San Pedro, the names that I elicited consisted of San Pablo, San Rafael, and San José. By 1988, San Miguel had become San Gabriel. These images evidently hold little import for Chimaltecos now—and indeed, few townspeople even claim to know them. In contrast, there is no question about Santiago's identity or his association with Chimbal, particularly regarding *Santiago Chiquito.* As in Wagley's time, "the smaller image is by far the favorite of the village people. It is described as 'very likable' and 'very pretty.' . . . Chimaltecos are quite frankly proud of their Santiago on horseback and they treat it with a familiarity not shown toward any of the other images" (Wagley 1949: 53).

Santiago Chiquito being carried in procession, June 1979. Note the white pants, red sash, and shoulder cloth of the traditional Chimalteco man's dress.

Santa Ana, the "wife" of Santiago, dressed in the traditional Chimalteco woman's *huipil*, belt, skirt, and woolen hair band, being carried in procession with Santiago following behind, July 1979. Photograph courtesy of Susan Masuoka.

Chimaltecos incorporate Santiago into the community in several ways. First, they treat him unequivocally as a fellow Chimalteco, praying to him in Mam, not Spanish. Equally important, despite his white skin, black beard, and Catholic origin, the small image of Santiago on horseback wears the traditional men's dress of blue shirt, white pants, red sash, and red embroidered kerchief. Santa Ana also wears the red *huipil*, "blouse," navy blue skirt, and woven red belt of a good Chimalteco woman. The saints of nearby *municipios* also wear the traditional dress of their towns. When the two saints from San Juan Atitán visit Santiago on his feast day and at Corpus Christi in early June, Chimaltecos invariably comment on how much the images look *"mera swaʔn"* (just like Sanjuaneros), despite their obvious European features. In Guatemala, where the Maya of different communities have long worn distinctive clothing and spoken distinctive local dialects, dress and language constitute immediate and pervasive markers of ethnic identity, and local saints reinforce this.

A second indication of Santiago's intimate association with the community lies in his embodiment of local sovereignty in both space and time. From his position overlooking the altar, *Santiago Patrón* presides over Chimaltecos when they assemble in the church, and the small image of Santiago on horseback sallies forth during religious processions to survey the boundaries of his domain. Mythologically, Chimaltecos also equate *Santiago Patrón* with the founding of Chimbal and the construction of the church. As one Chimalteco said of Santiago's origins:

I don't know when people came here for the first time. It couldn't have been more than a hundred years ago, or maybe two hundred. I don't know, but the first people were few. There weren't many who came here for the first time. The first Chimaltecos found *Santiago Patrón* at a place called Txaʔn Tzqiij Tnam, "at the edge of the dry pueblo" [an uninhabited spot half an hour's walk northwest of the pueblo on the trail to the Rio Ocho valley]. But as the name says, there was no water nearby, and the Chimaltecos couldn't build the town there. So they came to the present site of the pueblo, where the water pours from the mountainside, and here they built the church. I don't know how they built it here because there weren't many of them, the first people. But the church is well-made, with huge adobe blocks, not like the small ones that we make for our houses today. It's true that people were bigger and stronger in those days. Their blood must have been stronger for so few of them to have built the church so large.

When the church was finished, the Chimaltecos went to fetch Santiago where he waited in Txa'n Tzqiij Tnam. They carried him down the mountain and placed him in the church. But Santiago didn't like his new home, and the next morning he was gone. The people looked for him everywhere and finally found him back at Txa'n Tzqiij Tnam. They carried him back to the church, but the next morning he had disappeared again. Once more, the people found him at Txa'n Tzqiij Tnam, but this time when they tried to move him, Santiago made himself so heavy that they could hardly lift him. The people finally got fed up and beat him with whips to get him back to the church, and this is why *Santiago Patrón* has all those scratches and gouges on his back today.

Two points stand out in this narrative. First, Santiago is neither primordially Chimalteco nor the founder of Chimbal—indeed, the first Chimaltecos had to force him to take up residence in the pueblo. Second, although not the community's founder, Santiago nonetheless embodies the reality of its founding. In fact, the Chimalteco ancestors' lack of awe and reverence for him makes Santiago's recalcitrant incorporation into church and town doubly indicative of the skill and power of these first Chimaltecos. On one hand, the adobe walls built by the ancestors still house the community's patron saint; on the other, he still bears on his back the scars of their anger that finally made him behave properly. Notably lacking is any mention of the Spanish conquest or Catholic evangelization. Instead, the founding ancestors live on in the Santiago that they "domesticated" and in the place that they created for him. Saint image and "ageless" church together authenticate the past that binds contemporary Chimaltecos to their ancestors—and to each other as well.[7]

A final expression of Santiago's identification with Chimbal lies in the periodic processions that Chimaltecos celebrate during the major holidays each year, especially at Holy Week, Corpus Christi, and the fiesta of Santiago. Heralded by skyrockets and accompanied by music from drum and *chirimía*—a double-reeded woodwind instrument called *suu'* in Mam—Santiago emerges from the church on the shoulders of town officials to make a symbolic round of his domain, usually just a short turn around the church and plaza. Each Friday during Lent, Santiago and the small image of Christ also make a circuit of the two *ttxa'nja* shrines. Children run ahead, scattering a path of pine needles along which the procession moves from the church to the western *calvario* and then back to the eastern edge of town. Except for the late afternoon Lenten processions and the reenactment of Christ's progress to Calvary on Thursday night of Holy Week (see chapter 5), processions for Santiago usually occur close to noon, tacitly reinforcing associations between the realm of the saints, the centrality of town and church, and the diurnal primacy of day over night.[8]

In a certain sense, processions constitute rituals in which the saints appear as principal participants rather than merely objects of devotion. As the images float serenely above the crowd on the shoulders of their celebrants, bowing ceremoniously to each other, it is as if processions are performed by the saints, not merely in homage to them. Although no Chimalteco ever said as much, Santiago's processions parallel the traditional prayer rounds once conducted by Chimalteco shaman-diviners. Santiago still performs his *costumbre*—even if others now neglect theirs—but he can do so only when Chimaltecos carry him to the various shrines, swing the censers of copal incense for him, recite his prayers, play the music, and launch his offerings of skyrockets into the heavens.

In contrast to the saints, *witz* oppose Chimalteco sociality in their lack of ritual accessibility, putative Ladino identity, and cavalier attitudes toward Chimaltecos. Formerly, Chimaltecos conceptualized *witz* as actual personages to a much greater extent than they do today (cf. Wagley 1949: 55–62), and contemporary tales of encounters with *witz* lack the immediacy of personal experience noted by Wagley in 1937 (1949: 56). While many Chimaltecos now look at *witz* as nothing more than old-fashioned *creencias*, "beliefs," images of *witz* nonetheless remain meaningful because they continue to capture the "spirit" if not the fact of other presences that still intrude in Chimalteco experience: on one hand, the Ladino demons that haunt darkness and dreams closely recall *witz*, as does the devil of Christian scripture—a symbolic transformation under way even in Wagley's time (cf. Wagley 1949: 56n; see chapter 8). On the other hand, increased contact with the Ladino world has led Chimaltecos to transfer characteristics once ascribed to *witz* to actual—but no less dangerous—human agents, most especially Ladino strangers (see chapter 4). Although perhaps no longer taken literally, *witz* still hover ambiguously between childhood bogeyman—real enough to young Chimaltecos—and thinly veiled euphemisms for human and diabolic evil.

At least in the tales that Chimaltecos tell, *witz* still walk abroad in the world. Unlike the saints, who are fused to their images in the church, *witz* can appear anywhere and can change their appearance at will (cf. Wagley 1949: 57n). Most often they appear as *tii moos*, "imposing Ladinos," clad in European clothes and speaking Spanish. While the saints dwell near at hand, *witz* live far from the pueblo *tjaq' chk'uul*, "in [literally 'underneath'] the bush," where Chimaltecos can neither see them nor visit them at will. Instead, it is *witz* who choose the time and place of encounters, accosting Chimaltecos on lonely paths and spiriting them away to their mountain abodes. Inside their mountains, *witz* possess large plantations and huge herds of animals, along with chests full of gold coins and sumptuous clothes. There the souls of dead Chimaltecos toil for them.

Chimalteco *witz* are clearly contradictory figures. As Ladinos, *witz* cannot be trusted, yet they retain iconographic associations with snakes, clouds, and lightning—all symbols of pre-Hispanic Maya rain gods (cf. Vogt 1969: 302–303). They once controlled wild plants and animals, as well as the soil and rain that made the corn grow. Indeed, in their prayers, Chimaltecos used to refer to corn as "the hands and feet" of *witz* (Wagley 1941: 35, 36–37, 41). Like the impassive peaks that loom over the pueblo, however, *witz* remained indifferent to human appeal, since they could just as easily ruin fields by sending too little or too much rain, by loosing whirlwinds to snap the fragile cornstalks or pests to devour the crop, or worst of all, by inflicting illness or death. Sustained by their plantations and great wealth, *witz* cared little about Chimbal, and their self-sufficient autonomy underscored their unpredictable nature.[9]

Finally, in contrast to the saints, Chimaltecos formerly performed *costumbre* for *witz* whenever misfortune or illness warned that someone had incurred their wrath. *Witz* never participated in Chimalteco rituals but were the objects of fearful propitiation and placation. Furthermore, rituals directed toward *witz*, especially Xwaan No'j, occurred at night, unlike the usual daylight processions for the saints. During these rituals, shaman-diviners summoned *witz* to ascertain the cause of illness or misfortune and to negotiate the ritual "payments" needed to alleviate it. The nocturnal setting accentuated the remote, alien nature of *witz* and the precariousness of Chimalteco relations with them (see chapter 8).

Not surprisingly, the contrasts in Chimalteco conventionalizations of saint and *witz* replicate the centripetal quality of community boundaries already evident in the spatial oppositions of house, town, fields, and forest. Saints embody the diffuse sociality associated with common residence in Chimbal. Like mortal Chimaltecos, the saints are visible, familiar, and generally predictable. Santiago will watch over Chimbal as long as he receives his proper due through performance of the appropriate rituals. In turn, the saints rely heavily on Chimaltecos to clothe them, feed them, and carry them in pro-

cessions. Indeed, Chimaltecos used to say that without their offerings of candles, rum, and incense, "God"—and by implication, the
saints—"would have no *tortillas*," and they would starve (Wagley
1949: 69).

In contrast to this reciprocity, the *witz* need never depend on Chimaltecos. They remain largely unseen, willful, and always unpredictable, living in a remote world of their own, opaque to Chimalteco understanding and impervious to Chimalteco influence. *Witz*
intercede in human affairs only when it suits them, usually to en-
slave souls or to make Mephistophelian pacts with greedy or ambitious individuals. Unconstrained by local concerns or conventions, *witz* epitomize the selfish independence that results from a
lack of moral accountability. They envelop the community from
their distant abodes in a negative—or at least ambivalent—sociality
that circumscribes the limits of acceptable Chimalteco behavior.

The Conventionalization of Community

The overlapping social and spatial distinctions manifest in saint and
witz clearly reflect local perceptions and circumstances. Both images draw their substance and affective force from ethnic distinctions between Chimaltecos and Ladinos—whether actual or assumed, self-ascribed or attributed. Santiago lives in Chimbal and
behaves like a Chimalteco, whereas *witz* resemble Ladino plantation owners in dress, speech, residence, and attitudes toward Chimaltecos. The opposition between these figures graphically portrays
the perceived disparity between social realities within the community and outside of it. Nonetheless, saint and *witz* express more
than Chimalteco views on Ladino society and political economy
(cf. Taussig 1980) or local inferiority and resignation to Ladino domination (cf. Falla 1971; Hawkins 1984). While obviously shaped by
such circumstances, the juxtaposition of saint and *witz* also articulates, albeit tacitly, a more immediate sense that Chimaltecos have
of their own community.

To begin with, the opposition between saint and *witz* does not
imply that all Chimaltecos are saints or that all Ladinos are devils.
Indeed, saint and *witz* differ little in their essential natures: both are
white-skinned foreigners who originate in the mountains, and Chimaltecos even once described them as being "very close" to each
other (cf. Wagley 1949: 62). Also, despite the apparent differences
between them, the underlying dispositions of saint and *witz* reflect
a similar ambiguity. Santiago can be irritable and unresponsive as
well as protective, while *witz* provided Chimaltecos with life-giving

corn but enslaved their souls after death. In this sense, saint and *witz* constitute conventionalized social interlocutors rather than personifications of ethnic ideals or models of absolute good and evil (cf. Reina 1966: 175). Townspeople never speak of Santiago as a perfect Chimalteco; he is more like any Chimalteco rather than an ideal one. Similarly, although *witz* typify asocial behavior, townspeople gossiping about the transgressions of other Chimaltecos do not say that such reprobates have become *witz* but that they may have made a pact with one (see chapter 4).

Saint and *witz* polarize Chimalteco social perceptions, but they do not idealize them. Their actions remain morally indeterminate as the consequence of individual idiosyncracies: Santiago punishes transgressions of social norms, but he does so in regard to ritual neglect of his person rather than to enforce abstract moral standards or Christian virtues (cf. Wagley 1949: 53, 72). Similarly, *witz* inflict illness and misfortune, but they do so out of self-interest, not arbitrary wickedness. What ultimately serves to distinguish saint from *witz* lies not in their moral, immoral, or even ethnic essence but in their social relations with Chimaltecos. These relations in turn reflect the relative accessibility—and potential tractability—of each figure to Chimaltecos. Santiago's physical presence in the church enables townspeople to engage him directly, tacitly sanctioning their demands with the ritual offerings and assistance on which they take him to depend. *Witz*, on the other hand, flaunt the moral suasion of local reciprocity because their well-being requires neither enduring affiliations with Chimbal nor the approbation of its inhabitants.

This polarization of social relations finds clear expression in the ethnic transposition of saint and *witz*. Despite his Catholic origin and European appearance, Santiago dresses in Chimalteco fashion; townspeople speak to him in Mam and speak of him with warm familiarity. But Chimaltecos also say that Santiago was first discovered in the mountains—recognition of his alien origins—and only after an initial rebellion did he mend his ways and become a good Chimalteco: it would appear that Chimaltecos, including Santiago, are made, nor born.[10] That is, their Chimalteco-ness abides not immutably in some essential ancestry but rather contingently in their ongoing comportment.

Conversely, *witz* originate from autochthonous "spirit owners" probably once associated with natural cycles of exchange and regeneration (cf. Miles 1965: 285; Taussig 1980: 156–158), but they have metamorphosed into rich, avaricious Ladinos who own large plantations and exploit Maya souls. Just as Santiago's Chimalteco-ness reflects his social proximity rather than innate goodness, I

would argue that *witz* have become Ladinos, not because Chimaltecos see Ladinos as essentially evil, but because, like Ladino strangers, *witz* have little need and even less regard for enduring local
affinities. The wealth and power of *witz* further accentuate their indifference to Chimalteco importunity and affirm the lack of moral
accountability that lurks beyond community boundaries. In this
sense, the opposition between saint and *witz* articulates a local
ethic of common neighborliness as much as it reflects more global
oppositions between Chimalteco and Ladino, peasant and landlord,
Spanish conqueror and conquered Maya.

At the same time, the mutability of saint and *witz* expresses the
contingent nature of Chimalteco sociality and the ethnic affinities
and antipathies that local relations precipitate. Bad faith imperils
the community from both without and within: *witz* move freely in
the larger world—like Ladino strangers, always threatening to subvert or destroy Chimalteco ways with their arrogant self-sufficiency.
Similarly, although Santiago readily associates with Chimaltecos,
this alone does not guarantee his willing response to all appeals. The
diffuse reciprocity that binds Chimalteco to saint—and Chimalteco
to Chimalteco—only dictates social engagement, not altruism or
conformity: gift evokes eventual countergift but never ensures an
undeniable return. Santiago thus reminds Chimaltecos that the limits of local sociality lie not only in Ladino-like *witz* and *witz*-like
Ladino strangers but also in the potential *witz*-like willfulness of
fellow Chimaltecos.

In the face of such moral indeterminacy, however, Santiago does
serve two countervailing purposes. First, his enduring presence in
the town embodies the relative surety of familiarity. If not always
responsive, Santiago remains ultimately responsible. Within this
bounded but permeable social place, Santiago thus conventionalizes
the possibility of social cooperation based on common knowledge of
past interactions and regard for the future consequences of present
actions (cf. Axelrod 1984). Although inclusion within the community never insures that all neighbors will always be trustworthy, circumscribed local relations do enable Chimaltecos to discern more
readily who they can trust and how far—or who not to trust at all.

Second, Santiago's transcendent willfulness also validates the conventions that his apparent unresponsiveness sometimes threatens to
subvert. The fact that ancestral Chimaltecos mastered their imper-
ious saint and brought him to live in the community substantiates
the moral force of Chimalteco social conventions. As a conventional
embodiment of the unquestionable past, Santiago's willingness to
abide in church and town sanctifies the propriety of local social rela-

tions and legitimizes community sovereignty. By the same token, the fact that the ancestors arrived to build town and church and only then brought Santiago to live in the community establishes Chimalteco sociality as the cause, not the consequence, of local propinquity: it is appropriate Chimalteco behavior, not merely common residence, that accounts for Santiago's closeness to Chimbal and thus defines true community for all Chimaltecos. Conversely, failure to conform to local conventions engenders the social and ethnic distance epitomized by the physical remoteness of *witz* and the amoral behavior of outsiders, especially Ladinos.

Chimalteco identity, as expressed in the images of saint and *witz*, thus proves socially inclusive and spatially exclusive, defined by individual comportment and physical propinquity deeply rooted in the daily routines that transform mere space into familiar social places. It also remains dialectical rather than essential, based not on absolute moral or existential distinctions but on relative social affinities circumscribed by the antisocial presence of *witz*. Ironically, this definition of community boundaries leaves inclusion in the community problematic: if being Chimalteco primarily entails being in Chimbal and living like a Chimalteco—as Santiago's transformation implies—then individuals must constantly demonstrate their identity through proper behavior or risk losing it. The implications of this will be examined in the next chapter.

Convention, History, and Experience

Chimalteco conventions, even of their own identity, constantly change. The last fifty years attest to the passing of many practices once quintessentially Chimalteco—lost *costumbre*, forgotten shrines, elusive saints' names, "disenchanted" mountains. Despite outward appearances, however, much of the fabric of Chimalteco life that once enmeshed these practices yet endures, and Chimaltecos continuously weave new designs to take their place, no less genuine for their newness. Physically, community boundaries continue to reflect what Chimaltecos do in daily life, as well as where and when they do it—a fact demonstrated by the fluctuating diurnal meanings of local space and the nightly wanderings of spooks and demons. Conceptually, Chimaltecos still draw on images of saint and *witz* and on the antipathy between Chimalteco and Ladino, neighbor and stranger, to express the centripetal nature of their world. Socially, Chimaltecos acknowledge their common ancestry, but through the church that their ancestors built and the patron saint that they tamed, not through named ancestors themselves.

Morally, Chimaltecos wrestle, as they always have, with contradictions between willingly shared social conventions and willful self-interest—the ongoing struggle between the saint and *witz* inside us all as much as the ethnic impasse embodied by Chimalteco saint and Ladino *witz*. In the face of inexorable change, townspeople see no reason to consider themselves any less Chimalteco than their parents and grandparents did.

This, however, does not imply some primordial Chimalteco identity that transcends the vagaries of time. Like Lévi-Strauss's *bricoleur*, Chimaltecos continuously fabricate their identity out of what they have at hand—their life, their lands, their livelihood. Yet this project remains neither incidental nor trivial because it entails the very meaning of who and what they are. While the conventions that Chimaltecos create emerge from the particular place that is Chimbal and the particular past that this place possesses, the immediacies of life in the here and now shape how they use this heritage. The "timeless present" in which they live reflects the unfolding contingencies of daily life, not blind adherence to tradition. It is this emergent sense of belonging to a place, articulated by the moral alternatives of saint and *witz*, that most deeply and immediately defines what it means to be Chimalteco.

4

✤ The Conventions of Morality ✤

While Chimaltecos conventionally delimit the physical place that is Chimbal through an opposition between saint and *witz*, this opposition remains equivocal regarding the nature of Chimalteco identity. On one hand, the social relations that each epitomizes affirm a moral affinity and accountability sanctioned primarily by a contingent neighborliness. On the other, this local sociality also originates mythologically with ancestors whose mastery of their patron saint conventionalizes Chimalteco-ness as something more primordial than proper behavior in the here and now. Thus, although saint and *witz* effectively circumscribe community boundaries, they leave unclear the precise nature of the affinities that bind Chimaltecos within these boundaries.

In this chapter, I turn to how Chimaltecos articulate their Chimalteco-ness to each other through conventionalizations of morality. These conventions clarify the conjunction of identity and behavior implicit in the opposition between saint and *witz* considered in the previous chapter. I begin with the Mam word *naab'l*, perhaps best translated as someone's "way of being," but a way of being that alludes less to individual personality than to the shared—and therefore moral—proprieties of the community from which that person comes. As a nexus of personal predilections and public propriety, emergent actions and enduring morality, *naab'l* also involves Maya notions of "soul" and "soul-loss"—another link between identity and morality. By examining what Chimaltecos mean by having *naab'l*—and how they acquire and keep it—this chapter further explores the presumed constancy, as well as the moral legitimacy, of being Chimalteco in an inconstant world.

Chimalteco Sense and Sensibility

The Chimalteco concept of *naab'l* encompasses notions of both personal "sense" and social "sensibility." One Mam word list (Robertson et al. n.d.: 801) glosses *naab'l* as a person's "normality" or, more intriguingly, "beginning of conscious life." Another dictionary, based on the same town dialect, translates the word as "thought, idea, feeling" or "mentality, attitude" (Maldonado et al. 1986: 206). Both definitions suggest, on one hand, an enduring disposition—a person's "normality," "mentality," "attitude"—and on the other, a cognitive state—"conscious life," "thought," "feeling."

Linguistically, *naab'l* is derived from the transitive verb root *na-*, "feel, perceive," and the instrumental suffix *-b'il*, which indicates the instrument or place used to perform the action (cf. England 1983: 118). Taken literally, *naab'l* means "that which feels or perceives." Syntactically, *naab'l* is a noun that is always possessed, most often by human beings. Unlike other Mam nouns belonging to human beings, such as body parts, food, clothing, or kin terms, *naab'l* lacks an absolute form free of possessive pronouns, suggesting that it remains semantically more integral to its possessor than other things (cf. England 1983: 68–70). Significantly, words are the only nonhuman things possessing *naab'l, tnaab'l yool* being a word's "meaning."[1] Thus, the "normality" of *naab'l* involves not so much specific thoughts, ideas, or feelings but the general human capacity to think, imagine, and feel, or like words, to be meaningful.

At base, *naab'l* remains a fundamentally human attribute. As one Chimalteco observed, "*Ok nuul itz'j juun xhku?l, minti? txiimb'itz pero at tnaab'l* [When a baby is born, it doesn't have thoughts but it has *naab'l*]." He explained that a newborn baby will sense when its mother lays it down and wake up crying. While animals manifest a similar kind of awareness, Chimaltecos say they lack *naab'l*. The verb root *na-* confirms the uniquely human qualities of *naab'l*. In its various forms, *na-* can also mean "remember," "guess," "behave," and even "pray," indicating that *naab'l* serves to do these things as well. Furthermore, the word *naab'l* occurs in idiomatic expressions meaning "be careful," implying judgment, and "assume or suppose," implying conscious reasoning. This indicates a human knowing that goes beyond mere perception.[2] In other words, if *naab'l* means "sense," as in general sense perceptions or awareness, it also means "having sense" as in being humanly sensible to oneself and to others—including those to whom one prays.

Elaborating on this association between personal "sense" and social "sensibility," the Mam phrase *te tuul tnaab'l xjaal*—literally, "when the person's *naab'l* arrived here"—translates variously as "when the person woke up," "at the time of the person's earliest childhood memories," and "when the person recovered from an illness." All three meanings equate the "arrival" of *naab'l* with emergence from a "senseless" state: sleep, infancy, sickness. In sleep, a person is unaware and unresponsive. Chimaltecos say that the "soul"—either *aanma* in Mam or the Spanish *espíritu*—leaves the body to traverse unknown dreamscapes. Conversely, in infancy, a person is aware but neither fully articulate nor responsible. Chimaltecos recognize no formal criteria that transform an infant into a person, but the child's gradual mastery of adult behavior and responsibilities marks the growth of *naab'l* and the tacit transition into "normal" personhood. Finally, in sickness, an individual cannot interact normally with others. Conspicuously removed from the quotidian routines that give meaning to Chimalteco life and identity, the invalid is socially, if not experientially, "invalid." In all three cases, the absence of *naab'l* coincides with a lack of proper sensibilities—perhaps even sensitivity—regarding both a person's conscious state and his or her interactions with others.

Upon closer inspection, the sense and sensibility implied in having *naab'l* encompasses a threefold normality: physical, personal, and social. Physically, *naab'l* relates to perceived physiological properties of the blood, *chiky'*. Although Chimaltecos lack the elaborate system of hot and cold classification found in other Maya communities (cf. Neuenswander and Souder 1977) and in other parts of Mesoamerica (cf. Currier 1966; Ingham 1970; Tedlock 1987), hot and cold play a significant role in conceptualizing bodily states. Normally, the blood is considered "hot," evidenced by a ruddy, healthy complexion; appropriately, the Mam word *kyaq* means both "hot" and "red," perhaps an allusion to these properties of the blood. Chimaltecos say that heat in the blood accounts for the sense perception associated with having *naab'l*. The blood's natural heat can increase through physical exertion, when experiencing pain or strong emotions, or by ingesting hot substances. As the blood becomes hotter, sense perceptions become more acute until finally the blood—and by implication, *naab'l*—"dies." The person passes out, most typically when drunk.[3] Normally, a person with "strong" blood can resist, although never completely, externally induced changes. In contrast, when a person falls ill, *yaab'il*, "sickness," turns the blood cold, weak, and insensate, as evidenced by the invalid's pale, wan complexion and obvious debility—hence the absence of *naab'l*. Physically, then, all human beings possess *naab'l* as a general perspicacity normally rooted in the blood.

In terms of personal normality, *naab'l* represents more than an undifferentiated human consciousness because its quality varies from person to person. Someone whose *naab'l* is "complete," *tz'aql tnaabl'l xjaal*, is resourceful, intelligent, purposive, and self-controlled. In contrast, a person with "incomplete *naab'l*" cries or angers easily and generally lacks emotional control. *Kyuw tnaab'l*, literally "hard *naab'l*," implies a short temper, lack of patience, and stubbornness. Individuals who cannot pay attention, do not take proper notice of things, continually make mistakes, mumble to themselves, or speak nonsense all have *plooj*, "bad," *naab'l*. In other words, while *naab'l* physiologically concerns the condition of one's blood, behaviorally it pertains to the equanimity that makes interactions between individuals sensible. As such, it manifests itself in highly individual ways. Indeed, one Chimalteco went so far as to translate *naab'l* as a person's *actitud*, "attitude."

Such personal equanimity presupposes a third, social normality of *naab'l* involving the actual manner in which that equanimity finds expression. That is, *naab'l* also transcends individual idiosyncrasies by conventionalizing them in terms of more abiding, collective affinities. Chimaltecos tacitly recognize that no individual exists independently of particular times and places and that people from different places often possess different social and moral sensibilities. I repeatedly heard Chimaltecos impugn the *naab'l* of their Ladino or Maya neighbors, inferring a more enterprising, more composed, more well spoken Chimalteco *naab'l*. Over and above its individual vagaries, *naab'l* in one community cannot help but differ from that in another, immanent as it is in local habits of living, acting, and interacting.

A person's *naab'l* thus inevitably reflects his or her home community, however variously individuals within that community may evince their *naab'l*. In the context of such community-wide sensibilities, the physical associations of *naab'l* with blood and perception evoke the shared substance of local ancestral affinities, just as the personal normality of comportment and propriety substantiate the received custom of local ancestral precedents (cf. Watanabe 1989; Warren 1978: 56–57, 67–73). In its social sense, then, *naab'l* relativizes individual differences through global contrasts between communities. At the same time, it grounds emergent individualities and larger community sensibilities in the constancies of local ancestry and received tradition.

The various physical, personal, and social meanings of *naab'l* thus define general human social capacities and characteristics in reference to the conventional normality of particular communities. Comparison with other aspects of Chimalteco individuality clarifies the dialectical tension in *naab'l* between physical perception, personal sense, and shared interpersonal sensibilities.

Senses of "Self"

In addition to *naab'l,* Chimaltecos use several terms to describe individual character. The most concrete of these is *iipin,* "strength," which refers to physical capacity and endurance. Linguistically, *iipin,* like *naab'l,* is always possessed, but it can refer to inanimate or nonhuman things. Chimaltecos conceptualize *iipin* and the physical body as relatively fixed, such that once a person matures, physical characteristics should remain unchanged until old age and death. Since Chimaltecos never purposefully manipulate their physical appearance—with the notable exception of dress—changes occur most dramatically due to sickness or injury. Their conception of bodily strength as relatively fixed makes any debility all the more threatening. Individuals who lose weight during an illness worry about how—and if—they will regain the *iipin* they have lost. In contrast to the social nature of *naab'l, iipin* thus relates directly to the enduring physical presence of individuals, animals, and objects.

A second, more elusive, aspect of Chimalteco individuality is *niiky',* broadly translatable as a person's "nature" or "disposition." Most immediately, *niiky'* refers to a person's "ability, capacity, or manner [of doing something]." It includes individual astuteness as well as skillfulness, suggested in the commonly used idiomatic phrase *ne ?l tniiky' ti ?j,* literally, "[the person's] *niiky'* goes out toward it," meaning to "understand or recognize [something]." Unlike the social sensibility of *naab'l,* however, this understanding pertains to powers of intellection, not to social intelligibility between individuals. It implies a person's ability to grasp the essential idea or nature of something, to think things through and plan accordingly. The same Chimalteco who glossed *naab'l* as an individual's "attitude" translated *niiky'* as *entendimiento,* "understanding."

On a deeper level, *niiky'* expresses more than individual aptitude. To Chimaltecos, observable propensities reflect the more fundamental character of a person or object. The Mam phrase *tu ?n tniiky'* literally means "because of [its] *niiky'"* and denotes the effect that the possessor of this *niiky'* has on other things. This may be causal or intentional, depending on the agent involved.

Tu ?n tniiky' q'e ?n ma chyoon twi xjaal.
Because of [the nature of] *aguardiente* [rum], the person has gotten drunk.

Tu ?n tniiky' pwaq o che ?x xjaal tu ?j piinka
Because of [the need for] money, the people went to the plantation.

Tu'n tniiky' Yeek ma txi' nmaani tu'j tzee'.
Because [for the fault] of Diego, my father has gone to jail.

These examples imply that the outcome of the action or event stems
from the character of the things or people involved. It is the nature
of *aguardiente* to make men drunk; it is the nature of money to
make people work; it is perhaps Diego's nature to make trouble for
others. In other words, *niiky'* applies to individuals or things in
themselves. In people, it constitutes an intrinsic temperament that
acts rather than a human awareness that interacts.

In contrast to the corporeal presence of *iipin*, and the innate constitution of *niiky'*, "disposition," *naab'l* appears to enmesh individual singularity in an interpersonal "common sense"—common in
the sense of being both shared and normal—that abides in particular
places. Having *naab'l* remains at once individual and cognitive yet
shared and public, humanly distinctive yet rooted in particular human communities. Although it inheres in individuals, *naab'l* pertains to what goes on between them. Quite simply, it internalizes in
individuals a given "way of being" that makes them transparent and
intelligible to those who share the same sensibilities. Thus, when
Chimaltecos speak of the "arrival" of *naab'l* following sleep, infancy, or sickness, they refer not merely to regaining consciousness
in a cognitive sense but also to reestablishing a connectedness to
others that they construe as essential to their well-being. In other
words, the conventional associations of *naab'l* equate human awareness with belonging to a community, expressed through an individual recognition of—and ongoing commitments to—the others who
make up this community.

This inextricable link between personal "sense" and public "sensibility" likens *naab'l* to what Roy Wagner (1981: 94) sees as the
concept of "soul":

The definitive sense of "self" precipitated in tribal, peasant, and
ethnic "differentiating" traditions is that of an innate spark of
conventional discernment, of moral "rightness" or humanity,
called the "soul." It is experienced as a seemingly "internal,"
malleable, and highly vulnerable manifestation of the conventional order implicit in all things. . . . To put it simply, the soul
sums up the ways in which its possessor is similar to others,
over and above the ways in which he [or she] differs from
them. . . . The soul is precipitated in the course of recognizing
and responding to things, *and is experienced as that which rec-
ognizes and responds.* It knows itself. (Original emphasis)

Although not explicitly a soul, the soul-like quality of *naab'l* suggests its importance as part of Chimalteco moral affinity and local identity. More explicit concepts of soul bear this out.

Sensibility and "Soul"

Anthropologists have long noted in Maya communities throughout Mexico and Guatemala that the proper conduct of daily affairs depends heavily on the welfare of human souls. As Evon Vogt (1969: 371) observed of a community of Tzotzil Maya in the highlands of Chiapas, "The ethnographer in Zinacantan soon learns that the most important interaction going on in the universe is not between persons nor between persons and material objects, but rather between souls inside these persons and material objects." This preoccupation with souls differs from the otherworldly concerns of redemption and salvation in the Catholic cult of the eternal soul, which is also found in these communities (cf. Reina 1966: 168–172).

Chimaltecos recognize first an "inner soul" called *aanma*—probably derived from the Spanish word *alma*, or perhaps *ánima*, "soul" (cf. Maldonado et al. 1986: 16). It refers to a personal animating essence associated with the breath, *xeewb'aj*. Like the Christian soul, *aanma* survives death, and in the past *aanma* worked for *witz* inside their mountains. Sometimes today they wander the earth as ghosts, *taanma kyimni*, literally "soul[s] of the dead." For orthodox Christians, this is the soul that either goes to heaven or burns in hell. Chimaltecos also recognize the common Mesoamerican concept of *nagual*, a "spirit double" that shares the life and destiny of its human counterpart (cf. Foster 1944; Saler 1964; Vogt 1970; Gossen 1975). In Wagley's time, these spirits, called *kleel* in Mam, took the form of animals or natural phenomena (Wagley 1949: 65), but today the term usually refers to a guardian angel or saint. Of the two concepts, *aanma* plays the more prevalent role in everyday affairs.

Despite its obvious Christian associations and probable linguistic origins, *aanma* constitutes more than an artless reflection of Christian metaphysics because it can "go away" or be "lost" while the body lives. When Chimaltecos dream, they say that their souls wander abroad in the world. If they suffer *seky'pajleenin*, "fright," their souls can also "leave" the body: one man reasoned that fright "makes the soul think that the body has died," and so it departs. Mothers sweep the ground where a child has gotten hurt, softly urging the fallen soul to *we?ketza! we?ketza!*, "Get up! Get up!" I have also seen a man who slipped on a muddy path strike the spot with his machete so that his startled soul would not stay behind.

Perhaps most revealing of what Chimaltecos mean by soul is this soul-loss engendered by *seky'pajleenin*. They say that a fright can lead to loss of appetite, listlessness, insomnia, headaches, and "sadness." The cure involves a potion made mostly of *aguardiente* (sugarcane rum), mixed with black pepper, rue (*Ruta gaveolens*), and *agua espíritu*—literally, "spirit water," a patent medicine sold in city pharmacies composed largely of alcohol. A woman herbalist (see chapter 8) administers the medicine by spraying a mouthful on the patient's face and chest and then has her charge drink a good dose of it (cf. Gillin 1948; Rubel et al. 1984: 33); one Chimalteco laughingly remarked that curer and patient sometimes get drunk in the process. Indeed, the word *romey*, "remedy," from the Spanish *remedio*, often serves as a euphemism for *aguardiente*. Over a period of days or weeks, repeated dousings of the medicine serve to "heat" the patient's blood and so induce the soul to return. Recently, Chimaltecos have also begun resorting to injections, mostly of vitamins, which are said to be very "hot."[4]

Like *naab'l*, *aanma* relates closely to the blood, *chiky'*. Indeed, *aanma* refers as much to the corporeal "heart," and even to one's "sense of touch," as it does to the soul (cf. Maldonado et al. 1986: 16). According to Chimalteco conventions, then, heating the blood to cure *seky'pajleenin* literally restores *aanma*, putting the invalid back in touch with normal states of affairs. Unlike inhabitants of other Maya communities (cf. Vogt 1969: 442–444), Chimaltecos perform no other ritual cure for soul-loss, nor does Wagley (1949) mention one in the past. This suggests that just as sickness denotes absence of the physical, behavioral, and social normality of *naab'l*, the loss of *aanma* reflects an impaired, senseless state. Soul-loss in Chimbal does not necessarily connote the mystical imperilment that it does elsewhere (cf. Vogt 1969: 370). Instead, it involves a direct physiological impairment of one's body—in particular the blood. Soul-loss perhaps constitutes a culturally construed natural disorder rather than a mystical one.

By the same token, this would suggest that having a soul pertains to normal ongoing bodily states and individual capabilities as much as it signifies possession of some immaterial essence that confers well-being. In this sense, *aanma* may refer to a "stative" notion— that is, to a condition rather than a thing. This in turn closely approximates the normal sense and sensibility that having *naab'l* implies.[5] Indeed, Chimaltecos directly associate *aanma* and *naab'l* in this way. As one man observed, "*Qa kyuw tnaab'l, jaka tz'aajtz ti taanma tu'n xnaq'tzbil* [If (someone's) *naab'l* is 'hard' (i.e., a short-tempered, stubborn, impatient person), (the person's) *aanma* can come back through learning]," which implies that "incomplete" *naab'l* indicates a deficiency of *aanma* as well. Without the equanimity, sensibility—even sensitivity—of *naab'l*, how can one have much of a soul?[6]

Chimaltecos clearly distinguish *aanma* from *naab'l*, however, because *aanma* also refers to a personal animating essence that survives death, and in this sense it transcends the social normality of *naab'l*. On one hand, *naab'l* grounds the immediacies of Chimalteco habit and familiarity in a conventionalized—and therefore shared—awareness of their appropriateness. On the other hand, *aanma* associates this resulting sense and sensibility with the transcendent personal essence of soul—although Chimaltecos retain their everlasting souls only as long as they manage to make sense to other Chimaltecos by demonstrating that they have *naab'l*. This dialectic between the public and the personal, the emergent and the essential, at once enables *naab'l* to conventionalize the vagaries of individual practice into recognizable patterns of local identity, while also drawing on the transcendence of *aanma* to sanctify the action and identity of *naab'l* as self-evidently true. Each confirms the other, since proof of one's "immortal" soul depends on humanly acceptable—or at least intelligible—behavior, just as lacking the normal sensibilities of *naab'l* indicates some kind of "soul trouble." Far from arbitrary mystifications, *naab'l* and *aanma* pertain directly to the "rightness" of feeling, reasoning, acting, praying—in short, of living—in Chimalteco ways, whatever these might be at any given time or circumstance.

The Social Identity of Having "Soul"

Rather than any purely metaphysical notion, then, Chimalteco souls resemble "having soul" in North American black culture. In his book, *Urban Blues,* Charles Keil (1966) notes that "soul" encapsulates black identity as well as black solidarity by articulating a "common experience, [and the] shared modes of thinking about and expressing that common experience" (1966: 180). On one hand, soul alludes to an "unspeakable essence," "a mixture of ethnic essence, purity, sincerity, conviction, credibility, and just plain effort" (Keil 1966: 160, 164). It arises from having persevered in the face of life's adversities—as one blues musician put it, "[From] having been hurt by a woman, being 'brought up in that old time religion,' and knowing 'what that slavery shit is all about'" (Keil 1966: 152, 169–170). At the same time, black soul entails more than being or knowing: it requires the constant commitment of deeds as well—the improvisational style of speech, dress, walk, and repartee that demonstrates mutual recognition and affirmation, a kind of communion, not simply personal accomplishment (Keil 1966: 160–162, 180–181). Finally, for all its worldliness, black soul also presumes a sacred quality (Keil 1966: 176–177), a transcendent purity impossible to describe but instantly recognizable: whatever "it" is, those in the know realize immediately who has soul and who does not. Consequently, soul makes almost any social interaction a potential ritual of self-affirmation and collective affinity.

The analogy to black "soul" highlights several essential characteristics of Chimalteco concepts. First, "soul" in both cultures refers to a shared "way of being" rather than to an essential life force inside individual beings. Just as blacks often refer to soul in a singular sense, Chimaltecos speak of different degrees, not kinds, of *naab'l* that substantiate their own souls: a person's *naab'l* is "complete" or "incomplete" depending on how reasonably he or she behaves. Even "hard" or "bad" *naab'l* alludes more to infelicitous tendencies than to different natures. Like black soul, Chimalteco souls derive not from some innate essence but from relative participation in an inclusive nexus of social interaction. Chimaltecos continually work at having soul—they must demonstrate it, not simply claim it.

Second, as in black culture, having soul in Chimbal holds a canonically transcendent as well as pragmatically emergent meaning. The interrelated meaningfulness of *aanma* and *naab'l* remains at once culturally self-evident and behaviorally self-referential. On one hand, physical well-being within the familiar here and now that is Chimbal makes the normal sensibility of *naab'l*, and the *aanma* that this presumes, experientially real to Chimaltecos. As long as Chimaltecos accept *naab'l* and *aanma* as apt conceptualizations of everyday existence, the immaterial nature of these conventions leaves them unfalsifiable: no one can prove, or ever really bothers to question, whether souls exist or not. Such conventional self-evidence sanctifies—that is, asserts the motivated rather than arbitrary nature of—Chimalteco sociality by grounding individual behavior in the constancy of human souls (cf. Rappaport 1979b: 227–229).

On the other hand, this canonical sense of souls dictates no explicit standards for having a soul, only a consensus that souls do indeed exist. Thus, in sanctifying Chimalteco sociality, the self-evidence of Chimalteco souls makes the substantive meaning of having a soul largely self-referential: if everyone normally has a soul, soul must be as souls generally *do*. This does not mean that Chimaltecos can do whatever they please and call it "soulful," because, as in black culture, the propriety of having soul must be recognized and affirmed by others, not simply self-asserted. What Chimalteco souls do depends on the practical necessities of everyday life and, more importantly, on agreed upon—that is, morally constituted—precepts about how to meet those demands responsibly. Although canonically unspecified, having a soul acquires tacit definition through the exigencies of living in ways recognized by other Chimaltecos as proper.

Like black soul, Chimalteco souls precipitate a powerful language of moral affinity and local identity predicated on a people's common history, shared experiences, and knowing familiarity. Having a soul entails any individual action that expresses commitment to the spirit of that history, experience, and knowledge. The precise meaning of Chimalteco souls remains behaviorally emergent yet culturally transcendent, definitive of social boundaries yet undefinable in its own terms. Far from dictating explicit standards of social conformity, *naab'l* localizes—and through its association with *aanma*, internalizes—in individual Chimaltecos a diffuse consensus of what is right and proper. At the same time, the errant nature of *aanma* dramatizes the contingent inclusion of any given individual in this ongoing state of socially defined grace.

Even where the analogy breaks down, the contrast between soul concepts in the two cultures proves instructive. The ethnic community precipitated by having "soul" remains much more circumscribed in Chimbal than it does among American blacks, but this simply intensifies the power of souls and of soul-loss to define social boundaries. Similarly, Chimaltecos speak of souls in both a plural and a singular sense, internalizing in individuals the common social affinities that bind them together. Directly shared, yet deeply personalized, Chimalteco souls—more than black soul—make the most mundane interactions in Chimalteco life into tacit rituals of mutual identity, because to disregard these ways risks the loss of one's personal soul—that fundamental human connectedness to others that Chimaltecos live out from their earliest memories of life.

Acknowledging the indeterminacies inherent in any social situation between act and outcome, one's intent and other's inference, improper eccentricity and acceptable rationalization, the moral logic of Chimalteco souls demands an existential eloquence of continual engagement with other individuals, predicated on established cultural precedents.[7] Consequently, as Chimaltecos and Chimalteco life change, so do the pragmatic meanings of having a soul, although such latitude in creating a soul also engenders the existential terror of losing one. As will be seen, the power of souls to evoke local affinities stems largely from how Chimaltecos acquire soul; the morality of Chimalteco life arises from what they must do to keep it.

Acquiring a Soul

Acquiring _naab'l_, and thus having a particularly Chimalteco soul, demands more than simply being born in Chimbal: it requires behaving in appropriate Chimalteco fashion. For men, this means learning to grow corn with skill and perseverance, because in Chimbal _milpa_ constitutes the principal source of Chimalteco sustenance and its cultivation the clearest measure of Chimalteco manhood and maturity. Indeed, the Mam verb _aq'naal_, "work," denotes working in the fields, and those who cease to work regularly in their _milpas_ or coffee groves fall somewhat in the estimation of their neighbors.[8] For women, being Chimalteco means knowing how to weave, keep house, make tortillas, and raise children. These basic tasks remain essentially unchanged since Wagley's time; without them, and the interdependent sex roles they imply, life in Chimbal would be nearly impossible (cf. Wagley 1949: 32–34; Bossen 1984: 58–65). The few who eke out a living without farming are mostly Ladinos with other sources of income, mainly from teaching in the local school. Nearly all of these Ladinos come from outside Chimbal and keep their own company, an insulated society within the larger community.[9]

Language and dress constitute other obvious markers of Chimalteco identity. Like all Maya in Guatemala, Chimaltecos speak a distinctive dialect. While mutually intelligible to other speakers of Northern Mam (cf. England 1983: 4–6), Chimalteco speech differs in pronunciation, intonation, and lexicon. Maya ears are finely tuned to such distinctions, and men from neighboring communities will sometimes burlesque each others' accents with wicked accuracy. Differences in language indicate social distance, a fact brought home to me time and again when my greetings in Mam would transform wary trail encounters into smiles and nods, brief questions and courteous farewells. Chimaltecos stress that local Ladinos who speak only Spanish are not really Chimaltecos, even if they were born in Chimbal, whereas the few Ladinos who speak Mam are at least "good people."

Similarly, distinctive handwoven dress differentiates Chimbal from other Maya communities, although most Chimalteco men, like Maya men throughout the region, generally wear Western-style clothing. All Chimalteco women, however, still weave their own clothes. The quality of her dress proclaims a woman's skill as a weaver as well as her public propriety (cf. Annis 1987: 119–120). The long *corte*, "skirt" (*aamj* in Mam), consists of heavy navy blue cotton sewn into a tube; the woman steps into it, then folds it around her, securing it with a wide red and white striped belt, also hand-woven. The blouse, or *kaamixh* in Mam from the Spanish *camisa*, "shirt," is also worn folded and tucked into the wraparound belt. Distinctive not only for its bright red color and checked pattern of white and yellow lines, the blouse also has true sleeves and a short stand-up collar. In most other Maya towns, women's *huipiles*, "blouses," consist of two flat pieces of cloth sewn together at the top and sides, with slits for the head and arms. Chimalteco women wear their long hair gathered in back and wound in a long red woolen band (*si?pj* in Mam) tied elaborately on the top of the head. Unlike other Maya, they wear no necklaces or rings. Formerly, women went barefoot, but now most wear the black plastic shoes or sandals ubiquitous in rural Guatemala. One of the most striking images from my field-work remains the women and girls of this town dressed in the same style of vivid reds and deep blues, with their jet black hair tied up in identical fashion.

In contrast, most Chimalteco men no longer wear the white trousers (*weexj* in Mam), red sash (*k'alk'u?j*), handwoven striped shirt (*kaamixh*), black pullover woolen jacket (*kapixhay*), and red *k'alb'il*, "shoulder kerchief," of former times.[10] During the late 1960s, younger men began to adopt Ladino-style clothing, a transition nearly completed by the 1980s. A distinct age-grading appears at work here: men born before the 1930s still largely follow the traditional style, although they resort to store-bought shirts and white pants to wear with their red sashes and woolen jackets. Men born since the mid- 1930s opt for a more generic rural garb of cowboy hats and manufactured polyester shirts, trousers, and jackets. Old photographs reveal that many of these younger Chimaltecos dressed in traditional fashion until well into their twenties, suggesting that the shift represented some historically induced transition rather than a generationally induced one. On the whole, Chimalteco men appear to place no great import on their changing dress, attributing the switch to the practicalities of price and comfort.[11] Testament to the relativity of tradition, one older Chimalteco lamented this loss of local distinctiveness, even as he sported a newly acquired pair of black high-topped sneakers.

Between the pervasiveness of language and the vicissitudes of dress lie the myriad details of local life that evoke the rightness of having *naab'l*—from knowing how to handle a hoe and machete to knowing the proper consistency of corn dough for patting out tor-

Chimalteco woman weaving the sleeve of a *huipil* on a backstrap loom, July 1981.

The traditional woman's and man's dress in Santiago Chimaltenango, January 1988. The man's shirt and pants are commercially made of polyester, his jacket and the woman's hair bands are wool, and everything else is handwoven of commercial cotton thread. Note the grandson's Ladino-style clothing.

Two Chimalteco brothers, dressed in Ladino fashion, January 1988. Both wore the traditional man's dress until their early thirties, like many men of their age adopting the new style about 1970.

tillas. While these mundane activities remain largely unremarkable and by no means unique to Chimbal, their Chimalteco-ness lies in where they are practiced and how—and from whom—they are learned. In the first instance, Chimaltecos cultivate an intimate knowledge of their immediate world most readily apparent in the seemingly endless place names that order the local landscape (cf. Redfield 1962b: 178). Coming to know this landscape as only a Chimalteco would thus becomes an unequivocal expression of "being Chimalteco." Such familiarity, although tautological, remains not so much mystical as experiential. Practically, Chimaltecos come to know what best to grow where, or how much a given plot will produce. Socially, they learn who lives where and who owns, or used to own, which parcels of the ever-shifting patchwork of fields, fallows, and woods—no mean feat given the fragmented nature of holdings and the natural landmarks used to bound adjacent properties. Historically, they absorb the import of specific locales, from Txa'n Tzqiij Tnam, "at the edge of the dry pueblo," where their ancestors first found Santiago, to other locales where more recent events have occurred. In equating place and identity, Chimaltecos also come to identify what they do in this place as an inseparable part of it and, like the land itself, uniquely theirs.

Just as knowledge of place defines the Chimalteco-ness of local ways, so this sense of identity inheres in the individuals from whom Chimaltecos acquire this familiarity in the first place. Parents and grandparents, in particular, authenticate the generational continuity—if not absolute constancy—of practices that extend back to the ancestors who first settled the town, discovered Santiago, and built the church for him. Here again, local practices become Chimalteco by being personalized—that is, intrinsically associated with people living in Chimbal—regardless of whether the practices themselves are unique to the community.

In a more immediate experiential sense, the way Chimalteco children learn their culture imbues what they learn with an unanalyzable Chimalteco-ness. Learning for most Chimalteco children occurs informally as youngsters observe and imitate their elders (cf. Wagley 1949: 32–35; Nash 1967: 59–60). Infants spend much of their time in close contact with their mother, sleeping next to her at night and wrapped in a shawl on her back during much of the day. As they grow older, caretaking passes to older siblings who serve, along with parents, as the primary socializers. Children acquire the necessary skills and manners demanded in daily life by interacting with others, but few concessions are made to their more limited capacities. Chimaltecos engage in very little baby talk, and as children learn to speak, adults seldom explicitly correct their mistakes. Instead, adults will sometimes repeat the child's error and chuckle if the occasion warrants it (cf. Pye 1986). Behaviorally, parents rarely discipline their children beyond quietening them when play becomes too loud. If a squabble erupts, parents often ridicule the perpetrator by laughing rather than attempting to adjudicate. They seldom appeal to abstract standards of right or wrong but clearly convey their general displeasure at quarreling. Children soon learn that openly expressed anger is unacceptable, and play usually proceeds peacefully.

Boys fly kites during the windy months of November and December and spend hours rolling plastic hoops through the streets, propelling them with short sticks as they run alongside. They also play games with marbles and small disks of wax called *xkab'* in Mam (cf. LaFarge 1947: 6; Oakes 1951: 37). In recent years, a few bicycles have appeared on Chimbal's unpaved streets. Girls have fewer toys than their brothers, most commonly a doll carried in a shawl or rag, just as their mothers carry their younger siblings. In any event, the early years of play soon give way to increasing expectations and responsibilities for both boys and girls.

As children begin to master adult tasks, the tacit nature of socialization extends to specific aspects of Chimalteco learning. Little verbal instruction accompanies the acquisition of any skill, even in such complex tasks as weaving. Girls watch their mothers and older sisters weave long before they are allowed to try their hand. When they finally do, explicit guidance is rare, but a girl learns quickly about any mistake she has made. Long before they can actually perform the tasks, girls also mimic their mothers at washing clothes, grinding corn, and making tortillas, substituting rags and clumps of dirt for the real thing. For young boys, the mastery of expected skills similarly rests on observing and copying their fathers and older brothers when they accompany them to the fields.[12] No men's task is as intricate as weaving, but work in the fields with hoe, axe, and machete can prove more dangerous. In a place where a family's livelihood depends heavily on the well-being of its members to perform their allotted tasks, young boys must learn to work with prudence and perseverance because careless injury or thoughtless waste can never be easily, if ever, remedied or recouped. Knowing how to work hard demands not only the physical capacity to do a man's work, but self-mastery as well.

In addition to learning the practicalities of everyday life, Chimalteco children sporadically attend the local primary school. Girls usually attend more regularly than boys, who are often absent to help in the fields, but teachers remark that they soon forget what

A Chimalteco woman, two of her daughters, and a grandson, January 1988.

they have learned once they finish school, marry, and start a family (cf. Wagley 1949: 31–32).[13] Even within the school, instruction involves mostly rote memorization and copying exercises from text or blackboard. As with the acquisition of practical skills, school emphasizes mastery of form over understanding of content, and lessons encourage little originality or inquisitiveness (cf. Modiano 1973).

Education through observation conventionalizes Chimalteco maturity in two senses. Pragmatically, children shoulder the responsibilities of adults as their physical and mental capacities grow. Their mastery of requisite adult skills constitutes the surest sign of maturity, regardless of age, since children naturally learn according to their abilities. Adults sometimes excuse ineptitude by saying that a youngster is *k'waalx*, "still a child," occasionally implying that he or she is old enough to know better. Conventionally, this tacit process of learning also validates the reality of having *naab'l*. That is, the ability to perceive the mechanics of a task, the intuition that transforms such percepts into knowledge, and the capacity to remember and to replicate what has been learned all demonstrate faculties associated with having *naab'l*. Reaching adulthood becomes synonymous with demonstrating *naab'l* and thus having a soul.

On a deeper level, Chimalteco socialization and education imbue what is learned with a fundamental givenness that results in the formalism so typical of native Mesoamerican cultures. Anthropologists often encounter this formalism in the Mayas' lack of cultural exegesis, epitomized by the constant refrain *es costumbre*, "it is the custom," in response to questions concerning the reason behind local practices (cf. Vogt 1976: 1; Hunt 1977: 28, 248–249). I would argue, however, that such responses, rather than evidencing ignorance, disinterest, or obfuscation, reflect the manner in which most Maya learn their culture. Growing up in a one-room house, Chimalteco children continually encounter words, actions, and references that are obviously meaningful to their elders but whose precise meanings they lack the experience or capacity to understand (cf. Vogt 1969: 192–193). Even as familiarity and comprehension of the world grow, the tacit nature of instruction in Chimbal only partially rationalizes the reason for things. Children confront meaningful forms but are left to improvise meanings of their own within the bounds of public sensibility and personal experience. Meaning comes to rest more on usage than on referentiality; learning consists of improvisation rather than rationalization; and mastery of form ultimately takes precedence over understanding of content. In other words, Maya seldom explain their culture because, as often as not, it has never been "explained" to them.

How Chimaltecos learn their culture thus imbues it with a certain numinous immutability. Learning never rationalizes conventions as the best choice between possible alternatives—indeed, alternatives are seldom explicitly appraised. Instead, children must simply try to reproduce practices that they perceive in adult activities. Consequently, conventions acquire a transcendent sense of being the way things have always been—regardless of how recently they may have changed. With practical alternatives conventionally masked, learning comes to entail a choice between sense and nonsense—between mastery of given practices or denial of self-evident realities. It becomes the demonstration of common sensibilities rather than the cumulative acquisition of personal knowledge and understanding. The ability to learn acquires one a soul; what one learns takes on something of the canonical transcendence and compelling power of this soul through the very process by which it is learned.

Keeping a Soul

The notion of *naab'l* as the presumed sense and sensibility of normal Chimaltecos, and its association with concepts of soul, socialization, and learning, constitute the conventions of Chimalteco morality. What constitutes right and wrong, acceptable and unacceptable behavior, arises out of the personal equanimity and intuition associated with having *naab'l*. This involves relative compliance to outward form rather than absolute conformity of individual action and intent. Indeed, the largely tacit manner in which Chimaltecos learn their culture suggests that strong personal interpretations rationalize the meaning of shared conventions, and daily life in Chimbal, no less than elsewhere, constantly engenders differences of opinion, conflicting motivations, and idiosyncratic usages of convention. Chimaltecos remain acutely aware of individual variation, but *naab'l* leaves the moral justification—as well as resolution—of individual differences problematic because it only stipulates an unobtrusive intelligibility, not a strict adherence to explicit rules of conduct. Everyday morality thus involves the rationalization of personal motivations and behavior through constant appeal to the propriety presumed in having *naab'l*. Such manipulation, of course, threatens to falsify this sense of correctness by revealing its arbitrary nature, but the close association between *naab'l* and potentially errant Chimalteco souls preserves the sanctity of shared conventions by placing the onus of moral responsibility on the individual: individuals, not conventions, lose their souls.

While the formalism of Chimalteco morality precludes outright condemnation of all but the most extreme eccentricities or transgressions, disapproval of others often prompts Chimaltecos to emphasize their own skills or comportment: "My fields are well cared for and clean, not like other people's," or "I still speak pure Mam, and when those others were helping Padre Donaldo [to prepare a dictionary of Mam (see chapter 8)], they had to come to ask me the proper words for things." Given the diffuse propriety of having *naab'l*—and the obvious impropriety of criticizing or squabbling with others—disapprobation of others' behavior must take the more indirect form of appeal to one's own correctness. Ironically, masking one's opinions of others out of self-interested decorum implies that others are doing precisely the same thing. Such obliqueness leaves Chimaltecos uncertain of how others are evaluating their behavior, resulting in greater individual concern with an outward show of personal correctness.

Within the context of this relatively small but not exclusively face-to-face community, a Chimalteco's actions can rapidly become common knowledge, yet the reaction of the community remain conventionally indirect and diffuse. This produces a sensitivity to others' responses—real or imagined. The insecurity that accompanies this preoccupation often translates into suspicions of the jealousy or envy that others harbor toward oneself. For example, one enterprising Chimalteco complained that people gossiped about the presumptuousness of his many projects and ambitions, and he attributed this to envy of his successes. Another young Chimalteco gestured to some broken branches in his coffee grove and told me that people often damaged his trees as they passed by on the trail. When I asked why, he replied, "Maybe they're jealous because I have such good coffee trees here. I don't know." When he later fell ill with persistent pains in his neck and head, he mentioned that it might be due to the envy or jealousy of others. Any conspicuous self-distinction can prompt this uneasiness of what the neighbors must be thinking. Although these suspicions seldom crystallize into overt confrontations, it may be this diffuse fear of the jealousy or envy of others that creates the reserve found in Chimalteco interpersonal relations.

Retaining one's soul—that is, being morally correct—necessitates a precarious balance between individual ambitions and self-rationalizations and the tacit limits of public acceptability. Nowhere are the potential contradictions between these terms more crucial, nor Chimalteco souls more at risk, than in the pursuit of wealth. In Chimbal, wealth in itself is not inherently threatening to community stability, as some anthropologists have suggested for other Mesoamerican peasant communities (cf. Wolf 1957: 5; Foster 1965). Indeed, the pursuit of wealth through the acquisition of land has long pervaded Chimalteco economic motivations (cf. Wagley 1941: 76–81). The moral significance of wealth lies in how Chimaltecos acquire and use it, not simply in its possession. Wagley indicates that rich Chimaltecos were not always the object of gossip and envy simply because they were rich. If a man became rich through hard work and astute dealings, he was considered *muy honorable,* "very honorable," but not all wealthy men automatically gained such respect.

Diego Sacarias is now considered "very honorable," although people said that he has not always been so. He is said to have left the village as a "poor young man with less than twenty *cuerdas* [about 2.2 acres]." He worked for several years in Huehuetenango as a *mozo* for a rich ladino and returned with the money to buy more than a hundred *cuerdas*, a sugar cane mill, and one mule—a sum that might be estimated at about one hundred and fifty dollars. Diego claimed to have saved the money from his wages; some think he might have stolen the money. Diego has never been selected for high political office and I was told his request for a wife was refused by the fathers of several girls, in spite of his wealth. His status as "honorable" is still somewhat clouded by doubts about his past. (Wagley 1941: 78)

An honorable man is one whom no one doubts. He has taken his inheritance from his father and built on it wisely and industriously, open to the scrutiny of the entire community. In the past, a man often used his wealth to serve in public office (see chapter 5), but "working for his sons" also constituted an acceptable economic motivation (Wagley 1941: 80). This continues to be the case in Chimbal, as one middle-aged man suggests.

My father left me hardly any land, but through hard work and planning I now have nearly three hundred *cuerdas* [about 32 acres], and I have coffee trees in Rio Ocho. I have two houses but want to build a third so that each of my sons will have a house when I die. I think that in twenty years it will still be possible to make a living by farming in Chimbal. That's why I've decided to buy more land instead of sending my boys to school in Huehuetenango. It's better to buy land for my children, even though my father left me nothing. Who knows what my sons will be able to do for their sons? But it's impossible for anyone to solve everyone's problems forever.

Honorably gained and honorably used, wealth constitutes a legitimate pursuit in Chimbal. This, however, demands a transparency of personal motives and methods as well as acquiescence to proper form.

The antithesis of the honorable man is the *cholero*, or *choolil* in Mam, meaning "murderer." Formerly, a *choolil* killed his victims and sold their heads to *witz* for large sums of money (cf. Wagley 1949: 58–59). The contemporary Chimalteco concept of *choolil* no longer involves pacts with *witz*, but the term still refers to evil or unscrupulous individuals. Contemporary *choolil*, like their predecessors, acquire money from outside of the community, although not in so grisly a manner. For example, a Chimalteco merchant left for Guatemala City in the middle of planting season, leaving his son to sow the family plots of corn. One of the most active traders in the town, he often traveled to the capital to purchase luxury goods, such as clocks, wristwatches, radios, and tape recorders, which he then retailed in local markets. As his brother and I helped his son plant a field, the brother exclaimed, "My brother's gone to Guatemala again—he was there just last week! I don't know what he's up to. Maybe he's a *choolil*. He doesn't want to work anymore. He just chases after money." Despite demystification of the *choolil*'s source of wealth, the congruence between old and new usages of the term suggests that it is the lust for money and disregard for work in the normal sense of "working *milpa*" that morally damns the *choolil*.

Such disapprobation of wealth might be interpreted as another example of the resentment incurred by anyone who tries to succeed within the peasant "image of limited good"—a worldview in which life constitutes a zero-sum game where anyone's gain is everyone else's loss (cf. Foster 1965: 296, 297–298, 305–306). Such an economistic model, however, remains inappropriate in Chimbal for two reasons. First, although all *choolil* are rich, not all rich men are *choolil*. The convention simply condemns those who would gain their wealth in unconventional ways. Second, *choolil* do not prosper at the direct expense of fellow Chimaltecos. Even in the traditional sense, *choolil* seldom killed other Chimaltecos; in fact, strangers were preferable victims (Wagley 1949: 58–59; cf. Oakes 1951: 75–76). The true crime of the *choolil* thus involves neither disrupting the equilibrium of a zero-sum game nor robbing others of some finite communal good. His is the crime of cheating—of stepping outside the bounds of the community, then attempting to use his ill-gotten gains to buy his way back into society.

The moral issue here, I would argue, concerns not only general principles of fairness or integrity but also the larger cultural consequences of such deceit. By cheating, the *choolil* threatens to reveal the arbitrary nature of Chimalteco conventions. His success substantiates the possibility of alternatives that Chimalteco learning and the conformity of *naab'l* conventionally mask. While alternative and variation remain acceptable—even necessary—facts of life, *naab'l* also demands that proper form be observed. The *choolil* challenges the validity of these forms—forms that hold a significance far beyond their instrumental value. At stake is neither blind, inveterate conservatism nor the need to neutralize excessive individual initiative or power. The *choolil* sins not by becoming rich but by cheating, because in so doing he endangers the local conventions that—for historical reasons of military conquest, colonial exploitation, and abiding racism—define a social place where Chimaltecos need not be humble or servile but can be heard and even achieve an existential eloquence of their own. By challenging convention, the *choolil* threatens the humanity that Chimaltecos have struggled so long to preserve.[14]

Chimaltecos respect an individual's manner of working and making a living as much as they value success for its own sake, yet wealth is not automatically feared or disdained. Money is good, especially when it can be used to buy land, tools, fertilizer, coffee plants, or send one's children to school. But money has yet to acquire an intrinsic value of its own, and individuals lured from the daily tasks of being Chimalteco in pursuit of money for its own sake risk becoming modern *choolil*, assailants of the fragile bonds of moral sensibility that bind neighbors together.

The conventional reality of Chimalteco souls precipitates a local community morality that, within the limits of reasonableness, pertains less to what people do than how they do it. The normality presumed in *naab'l* imbues all behavior with intrinsic moral import through the ongoing encounters of daily life, not through strict adherence to explict norms or rules. Within the limits circumscribed by avaricious *witz* and murderous *choolil*, social propriety remains largely contingent on individual rationalizations of behavior and the eloquence to convince others of one's moral correctness. As with the community boundaries articulated in the opposition between saint and *witz*, *naab'l* grounds Chimalteco morality in the physical propinquity, interpersonal familiarity, and above all, conventional interpretability of life in Chimbal. It also associates this morality with the self-evident presence—or absence—of Chimalteco souls, which internalize in each individual a stative human normality that only finds validation through the recognition that it sparks in other Chimaltecos.

Ironically, this conventional transparency inspires neither personal intimacy nor any necessary love of traditional ways. Indeed, in fostering interpersonal intelligibility, it encourages a stoic equanimity, a reserved formality that safeguards the propriety of one's soul. A careful conformity, as well as traditionalism, results—in part from the common necessities and limited alternatives of local agrarian life, in part from the inescapable consequences of local reputation in an insular but not isolated community such as Chimbal, and in part from the conventional constraints of communicating with others in mutually intelligible ways. At the same time, despite this studied reserve, the precariousness of Chimalteco souls demands that their presence be constantly confirmed through meaningful interactions, even as the vicissitudes of such encounters exacerbate what Guiteras-Holmes (1961) knowingly called the "perils of the soul." Nothing guarantees against soul-loss, or worse, discovery of the *choolil* in one's soul, conjured there by self-doubt or the suspicions of others. The diffuse community sociality embodied by Santiago and circumscribed by the amoral intractability of *witz* remains forever problematic, dependent on the ongoing self-mastery of one's own—and everyone else's—soul.

5

✢ The Conventions of Responsibility ✢

In previous chapters, I examined cultural conventions that define Chimaltecos' sense of community as a physical place imbued with a social and moral "way of being." The spatial opposition between saint and *witz* situates the community within the routines and ongoing sociality of local life. Putative relations with these figures in turn conventionalize the relative, contingent nature of this sociality, while the ethnic transposition of Catholic saint into Chimalteco shibboleth, and Maya *witz* into Ladino earth lord, underscores the moral accountability that physical propinquity and social interdependence rightfully engender. Within the bounds of place and propinquity, conventional associations between the sense and sensibility of *naab'l* and the corporeal as well as immaterial essence of *aanma* personalize this moral accountability in individuals by obliging their participation in the local "way of being" that having a soul presupposes. For the most part, this ongoing engagement between neighbors involves making common cause of the necessities of everyday existence and survival. In addition to such diffuse pertinacity, however, Chimalteco men also continue to fulfill more explicit expectations of personal propriety through service in the local civil-religious hierarchy, or system of *cargos* (literally "burdens"). Through such formalized public responsibilities, the personal dictates of *naab'l* and the public import of the saints find further articulation as well as mutual confirmation.

Mesoamericanists have long viewed the cargo system as the core of contemporary Maya social structure (cf. Tax 1937: 442). Ideally, all men in the community participate in a system of rotating administrative and religious offices by holding a succession of ranked positions, or cargos, during lifelong public careers. Cargoholders usually serve for one year without pay. In addition to various administrative duties, they traditionally shouldered religious responsibilities that required considerable personal expense for ritual offerings and ceremonial meals. As a result, cargoholders "rested" between cargos while they repaid debts incurred during their previous service and accumulated money for the greater expenses of their next office. For those who succeeded in carrying cargos on all levels of the hierarchy, social prestige and no small amount of local influence, if not actual power, ideally awaited.

This chapter examines participation in the Chimalteco cargo system within the context established by local conventions of community and morality. It begins with Charles Wagley's description of the Chimalteco cargo system in 1937 to underscore continuities during the last fifty years. Despite various structural changes in the cargo system, these consistencies clearly reveal the enduring social significance of the institution. The broader economic and political functions of the cargo system, as well as the actual dynamics of change within it, will be analyzed in chapter 7.

The Cargo System in Chimbal

Structurally, the Chimalteco cargo system has changed little since 1937. Except for expansion in the overall number of cargos, it still consists of four levels of offices, three civil and one religious. In 1937, there were a total of forty-nine cargos; in 1988, there were seventy-seven (cf. Wagley 1949: 80–84) (see fig. 6). Considering that the population has more than doubled over the last half century, however, this increase has hardly kept pace. In Wagley's time, the major civil offices consisted of a mayor, called *likaal* in Mam (from the Spanish *alcalde,* "mayor"), twelve *xtool* (*regidores,* or "town councilmen"), and twelve *miyool* (*mayores,* "clerks," or municipal assistants). Heading the religious side of the hierarchy, five *sacristanes,* "sacristans," held office for life and thus were not technically part of the cargo system at all. They supervised four *martoon* (*mayordomos,* "stewards") who served the saints in one-year cargos.

While these civil and religious officials saw to the daily administration of the town, real political power lay with the four *principales* (*tojlaamaq'* in Mam)—town elders who had already passed cargos at all levels of the hierarchy—and with the *chmaan tnam,* the most powerful shaman-diviner in the community. These men had proven their integrity and wisdom through long and distinguished public careers, and once appointed, they held office for life. When one *principal* died, the remaining three selected his successor, just as they did upon the death of the *chmaan tnam.* Aided by the divinations and prayers of the *chmaan tnam,* they selected the new cargo officials each year, performed important *costumbre* for the

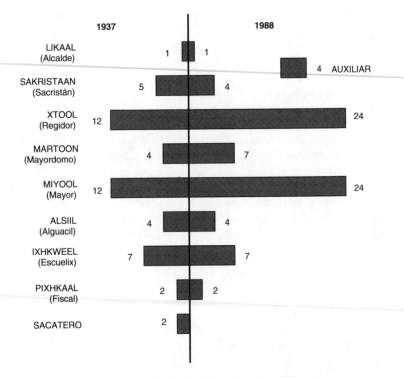

Figure 6. The Chimalteco cargo system, 1937–1988.

public welfare, and "[decided] on any issue of importance to the village as a whole" (Wagley 1949: 85–86).

Today, this basic structure still exists, but with two major exceptions. First, the *principales* no longer exert the influence that they once did on local politics, and second, a clear distinction now exists between officials chosen by national election and cargoholders who serve in the traditional manner (see chapter 7). Technically, in Wagley's time, the entire Chimalteco cargo system lacked legal recognition because in 1935 Chimbal had been reduced to the administrative status of an *aldea*, "hamlet," of the neighboring town of San Pedro Necta. Chimbal was thus legally entitled only to an *alcalde auxiliar* beholden to the Ladino officials in San Pedro. The community nonetheless managed to retain its cargo system and a semblance of local autonomy through the efforts of a delegation of Chimaltecos sent to Guatemala City by the *principales* (Wagley 1949: 8–10). When Chimbal regained municipal status in 1948, it fell under the guidelines for local government that resulted from the Revolution of 1944 (Gall 1980: 686; cf. Whetten 1961: 312, 316–319).

The offices of the Chimalteco cargo system chartered by the national government constitute what is known as the "municipal corporation." Until the political upheavals of the early 1980s, this body included the *alcalde*, five ranked *consejales*, "councilmen," (also called *xtool* in Mam), three alternate *consejales* (*suplentes*), and one *síndico*, "syndic," or magistrate, who represented the *alcalde* in legal matters, usually having to do with property or boundary disputes. All officials serve for four-year terms and are selected by popular vote during national elections.[1] The municipal government also employs a secretary and a treasurer, but Chimaltecos do not consider these positions cargos. They stressed, however, that if an *alcalde* proves ineffectual or irresponsible, the municipal secretary, who in the past was nearly always a Ladino, would often usurp administrative power in the pueblo through his literacy, fluent Spanish, and familiarity with national law (cf. Wagley 1957: xxiii). When I visited Chimbal in 1988, a young Chimalteco man filled the post of municipal secretary.

In addition to the municipal corporation, Chimbal retains all the traditional cargos described by Wagley, although they lack formal recognition from the national government. *Xtool* still assist the *alcalde*. Their number has grown from a total of twenty, including the five *consejales*, in 1979 to twenty-four in 1988, with the *consejales* being reduced to two. Serving under them are twenty-four *miyool*, young men who run errands for town officials, fetch the mail from San Pedro every other day, and maintain order as the town constabulary, especially during major fiestas. Four *auxiliares de aldeas* represent the municipal government in Chimbal's outlying hamlets. Completing the civil side of the cargo system, seven boys serve as *ixhkweel* who must tend the garden in the town plaza. They are supervised by two *pixhkaal* (*fiscales* in Spanish), older men who have the demeaning task of cleaning the plaza and sweeping out the marketplace each week. Men who have carried few if any previous cargos are chosen for this post. All these cargoholders serve for one year without pay and are selected each year by the outgoing *xtool*.

The religious cargos also survive but lack official recognition from either church or government. Four *sacristanes*, rather than the five noted by Wagley, now maintain the church and the images of the saints residing in it. They accompany Santiago and Santa Ana on visits to nearby towns during the fiestas of their patron saints and similarly welcome other saints when they come to call on Santiago during Chimalteco celebrations. *Sacristanes* continue to serve the saints for life, and when one *sacristán* dies, the *xtool* appoint his successor. Seven *martoon,* "stewards," act as assistants to the *sacristanes.* They represent the local equivalent of the *cofradías,* "religious brotherhoods," found in more complex cargo systems (cf. Mendelson 1965: 51–54; Reina 1966: 99–109; Bunzel 1952: 164–171), although the term itself is not used in Chimbal (cf. Koizumi 1981: 15).

Martoon hold office for one year, four taking up their cargos during the fiesta of Santiago and the other three entering at Corpus Christi. Like the other traditional cargoholders, they are chosen each year by the *xtool. Martoon* do not individually serve separate saints but collectively sponsor all the major religious fiestas celebrated each year. These include the fiesta of Santiago at the end of July, the feast of All Saints on November 1, Christmas, Easter, and Corpus Christi in June. In Wagley's time, officials had to finance the celebrations out of their own pockets (Wagley 1949: 83), but they now collect a small tax from each household to purchase the ritual paraphernalia needed for the procession of the saints without which any fiesta is incomplete.

The remaining religious cargos consist of four *alsiil* (*alguaciles* in Spanish), adolescent boys who assist the *martoon,* especially during the change-of-office ceremonies at the end of December.[2]

Carrying Cargos

Although the specific ritual duties and economic obligations involved in cargoholding have changed dramatically since 1937, the basic sequence of service remains very much the same. Chimaltecos still carry cargos, and with a few notable exceptions, they take them in the same order and at about the same age as their grandfathers (see figure 7). As in the past, men, not women, serve these offices.

Ixhkweel and Alsiil

Ideally, the first cargo that a young Chimalteco holds is that of *ixhkweel.* These ten- or eleven-year-old boys assist the two *pixhkaal* by caring for the small garden in the town plaza. On the Wednesday before Holy Week, the fathers of the *ixhkweel* must decorate the altar of the church with palm branches and fleshy red flowers called *ttxaʔn chmekyʾ,* "turkey wattles" (*pata gallo* in Spanish). Few boys actually begin their cargo careers as *ixhkweel,* however, both because of the relative unimportance of the cargo and because of the

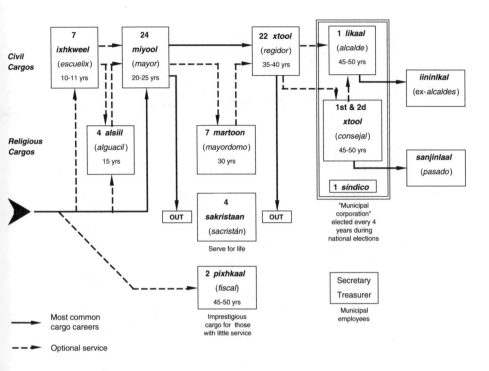

Figure 7. Pathways of cargo service.

limited number of cargos available. The same may be said of the *al-siil*, the lowest religious cargo, whose principal duties will be described below. The relative marginality of these cargos may explain why the number of *ixhkweel* and *alsiil* have not increased since 1937 (fig. 6). Then, as now, there were seven *ixhkweel* and four *al-siil*. Clearly, only a small proportion of eligible boys ever serve in either of these cargos, and once boys pass the appropriate age, they need not carry them.

Miyool

The first cargo that most young men actually serve is that of *miyool*, when they are between eighteen and twenty-five years old. Although many of these men still live in their fathers' house, by this age they have married and are considered adults. *Miyool* have relatively few duties—running errands, serving as night watchmen, collecting fees from the vendors in the weekly market, and ringing the hours of the day on the church bell. Each of the twenty-four *miyool* must spend one day every two weeks at the town hall to assist in daily municipal business. Most dealings, however, occur on Friday mornings when the weekly market keeps most Chimaltecos in town, so *miyool* usually have little to do other than toll the passing hours on the church bell or, more rarely, to fetch an absent *alcalde* or municipal secretary when a visiting official unexpectedly arrives. In addition to these biweekly duties, all *miyool* must be at the town hall each day from about 5:00 P.M. until dark, because municipal business often quickens when Chimaltecos return from their fields. Every afternoon, the *miyool*, along with the other civil officials, can be seen seated on the benches that run along the porch fronting the town hall—in the words of one former *xtool*, "doing very little."

Despite the relaxed duties of the *miyool*, their year in office constitutes a clear initiation into public life (cf. Moore 1979). For the first time, these young men hold a position of responsibility outside their families. *Miyool* have already proven their physical maturity by working in the fields alongside their fathers and by becoming husbands and fathers in their own right; most, however, have yet to play any publicly acknowledged role in the community at large. The minimal duties of *miyool* constitute a semblance of such responsibility. At the same time, the *miyool* gain recognition in the community by undertaking the "burden" of office. Even if the principal demand is only for their time, the cargo entails an incipient—but real—transition into public life.

Equally important, *miyool* develop their social skills while learning the rudiments of civic etiquette and authority. Socially, they experience belonging to a formally constituted group with an esprit de corps of its own. Many of Wagley's informants recalled their year as *miyool* as a carefree time when they learned to drink and carouse (Wagley 1949: 94, 96). Young Chimaltecos still enjoy their time in office, and one friend spoke of the *tb'aʔnil yool*, "good words"—the stories, jokes, and local lore—exchanged during the late afternoon sessions on the porch of the town hall. At the same time, although their formal duties subordinate them to the authority of higher cargo officials, *miyool* have power of their own, especially over the disorderly drunks they arrest or the citizens they call to the town hall on official business. Through the camaraderie, the duties, and the authority of their office, *miyool* acquire a more immediate sense of Chimbal as both social community and sovereign authority. For these young men, their year of service furthers the tacit socialization begun in infancy, while publicly demonstrating their growing maturity.

More than any other cargo, the office of *miyool* has survived with few changes during the last fifty years. One might argue that this constancy simply reflects the relative simplicity and unimportance of the office, but the number of *miyool* has doubled from twelve in 1937 to twenty-four in 1988. This suggests that, unlike the similarly marginal cargos of *ixhkweel* and *alsiil*, the office continues to fulfill some kind of meaningful function. Indeed, *miyool* is the only cargo that many Chimaltecos will ever serve, as in the past when Chimaltecos who lacked the ambition or resources to pursue a cargo career nonetheless served at least as *miyool* (Wagley 1949: 94–97). Because the duties of *miyool* have never expressly prepared cargoholders for the responsibilities of higher office (cf. Wagley 1949: 81, 91), serving this cargo has perhaps always been an end in itself. I suspect that the office serves primarily to establish a man's standing in the community, over and above its formal function as entry into the age-graded hierarchy of the cargo system. The responsibilities of the office reinforce this suspicion.

At the beginning of their year in office, *miyool* receive public affirmation of their status during the change-of-office ceremony, and while on duty they have the right to carry the stubby, tasseled batons that serve as their badge of office. *Miyool* also must perform the ritual dance with Judas that opens and closes the celebration of Holy Week, further demonstrating their growing social competence and maturity. While a more detailed examination of these cargo rituals will be presented below, suffice it to say for the moment that, like the cargo of *miyool* as a whole, these rituals of recognition and responsibility clearly represent conventional expressions of community membership. They emphasize the importance of personal participation over the mastery of complex performances, stipulating an acquiescence to conventional form that at once validates both self and conventions (cf. Rappaport 1979a: 191–194). Through their participation, the young *miyool* demonstrate the recognition of local social forms that having *naab'l* entails, while their acceptance of conventional constraints—both the literal and metaphorical "burden" of cargo service—substantiates firsthand the power of these conventions to order their lives. In other words, the cargo of *miyool* establishes the readiness of these young men to assume fuller responsibilities of community membership.

Martoon

After a year as *miyool*, a Chimalteco ideally next serves as *martoon*, "steward" (derived from the Spanish *mayordomo*), assisting the *sacristanes* with upkeep of the church and care of the saints. *Martoon* are generally in their thirties, although they can be older. The *xtool* choose the seven *martoon* each year, three at Corpus Christi and four at the fiesta of Santiago. On the night before Corpus Christi and again on the first night of the fiesta of Santiago, each outgoing and incoming *martoon* invites the former *alcaldes* and all cargoholders to their houses for coffee and shots of *aguardiente*. On these nights, one can hear a marimba being played in distant houses, then the *chirimía* and drum marking the passage of the company from one house to another. As mentioned before, *martoon* have no day-to-day obligations to individual saints but organize the major fiestas celebrated in Chimbal each year. This involves collecting money from each household and buying the skyrockets, candles, and incense that accord the proper honor to Santiago and Santa Ana during their processions around the plaza and church.

Martoon also accompany Santiago and Santa Ana when the *sacristanes* take them to visit the patron saints of neighboring communities. Santiago travels to San Juan Atitán for the fiesta of San Juan at the end of June, and on the fiesta of Santa Cruz at the beginning of May he visits Ixconlaj, an *aldea* of the neighboring community of Colotenango. The image of San Juan and a pair of angels from Ixconlaj pay return visits to Santiago at Christmas, Corpus Christi, and the fiesta of Santiago.[3] Until 1978, Chimbal also exchanged saints with San Pedro Necta, but that year when Santiago arrived for the titular fiesta, the Sampedranos failed to bring out their saints and barely accorded Santiago any of the other proper courtesies. The following year, Santiago refused the invitation to attend the fiesta in San Pedro. As one disgruntled Chimalteco told me, "If the people do not remember why we perform these acts, it's best to forget them once and for all." Evidently, the *alcalde* in San Pedro—a Ladino and staunch evangelical convert—cared little if Santiago received his proper due or not. A similar quarrel put an end to Santiago's visits to Colotenango in the 1930s (Wagley 1949: 82–83).

The cargo of *martoon* entails more substantial duties than that of *miyool*, as befits the greater age of the men who fill it. It demands organizational skills as well as the social assurance that enables *martoon* to represent Chimbal at the fiestas of neighboring communities. In the past, the financial burden of sponsoring fiestas also required the economic security that a Chimalteco man in his thirties would have ideally begun to attain. Nonetheless, today the cargo appears structurally marginal to the rest of the cargo system in three ways. First, unless a man later becomes a *sacristán*, *martoon* is the only religious cargo that he will ever hold. Like their civil counterparts, however, *martoon* deal largely with administrative matters rather than with esoteric religion, which perhaps reduces the distinctiveness of the cargo. Second, *martoon* do not participate in the change-of-office ceremonies with other cargoholders but enter office at staggered times of the year, publicly separating this cargo from the others. Third, and perhaps of most practical significance, the limited number of positions at this level automatically restricts the number of Chimaltecos who can take *martoon* as their next cargo after their year as *miyool*. Thus, most cargoholders now move directly from *miyool* to *xtool* without incurring disapprobation. The increase from four to seven *martoon*, in contrast to the *miyool*, may have more to do with the logistics of organizing fiestas in a growing town than with a desire for more cargos at this level.[4]

Xtool

After serving as *martoon*, a Chimalteco ideally becomes a *xtool*, or "town councilman" (*regidor* in Spanish). By the time of his selection for this office, a man is usually in his early forties and has attained a stable social and economic standing in the community, although the cargo requires little of the expense and none of the ritual duties that it did fifty years ago. Indeed, day-to-day commitments of *xtool* now differ little from those of *miyool*. *Xtool* spend one day every two weeks on duty at the town hall and must be present there each afternoon. As suits their higher rank, however, *xtool* have the authority to represent the *alcalde* in local litigation: commissions to investigate civil grievances—usually concerning boundary disputes or property damage—include at least two *xtool* as well as the municipal *síndico*. Structurally, *xtool* also preside over the traditional offices of the cargo system administratively and through the yearly selection of cargoholders. Toward the end of their term, each *xtool* appoints his own successor and one *miyool*, and then together they choose the remaining cargoholders. The *alcalde* and *consejales* intervene only to persuade a reluctant candidate to accept a cargo.

Beyond this, *xtool* have few specific duties. Perhaps more than with lower-ranking cargos in the hierarchy, the privileges of *xtool* have suffered from the ascendancy of the nationally constituted municipal corporation. Since they hold only local recognition, *xtool* cannot legally represent the community in official matters, as can the *alcalde* and *consejales*. The increasing presence of the national government in local affairs makes this restriction ever more apparent, reducing *xtool* to low-level municipal functionaries much like *miyool*. Clearly, this cargo no longer expresses the individual accomplishment or ambition that it once did. At the same time, however, the cargo has also lost the heavy ritual expense and personal inconvenience that merited its former prestige and greater standing. Consequently, service as *xtool* has become largely a matter of form, because *es costumbre*, "it is the custom."

Alcalde, Consejal, and Síndico

Service as *xtool* completes the cargo career of most men. Those with higher ambitions must ally themselves with one of the nationally recognized political parties and stand for *alcalde, consejal,* or *síndico*, during national elections. As the highest municipal official, the *alcalde* holds responsibility for public works as well as for maintaining civil order. He judges local disputes and ideally initiates projects to improve community welfare. In the past, his greatest power lay in allocating the town's communal lands, but the individualization of property and the penetration of national authority to the local level have abrogated this prerogative, leaving him the administrative matters of a minor civil servant. The first *consejal* (*tneejil xtool* in Mam) acts for the *alcalde* when he is absent or incapacitated, but generally the *consejales* simply assist and advise the *alcalde*. Except for the *alcalde*, none of these officials receives a salary, although the *síndico* draws a small commission from the fees that he collects, and *consejales* may pick up incidental assessments for commissions on which they serve. In 1979, the *alcalde* in Chimbal earned about Q40.00 a month.

The discontinuity between the legally recognized public offices of the municipal corporation and the informal traditional cargos has transformed the rationale of the cargo system. In the past, service as *xtool* could lead directly to the cargo of *tneejil xtool* (first *regidor*) or *alcalde*, positions of great responsibility and administrative power within the community. Today, however, access to higher office "depends on politics," meaning at the very least joining a national political party and publicly campaigning for office, rather than simply appealing to previous cargo service. Participation in the lower cargos no longer automatically qualifies individuals for high local office, vitiating the structural role of these cargos as the legitimate avenue to political power in the community. Nonetheless, Chimaltecos continue to carry the lower cargos, and the social value of cargoholding evidently still persists despite its enfeebled political significance. This persistent social meaning of cargoholding becomes clearer through an examination of the cargo rituals that have survived the last fifty years.

Rituals of Recognition: The Change-of-Office Ceremony

Perhaps the most colorful of all Chimalteco cargo rituals is the change-of-office ceremony. A public ritual occurs the day before Christmas to name the incoming *auxiliares de aldeas, miyool, alsiil, pixhkaal,* and *ixhkweel,* and a second ceremony on New Year's Day formally inaugurates the new *xtool.* Because Chimaltecos mark the beginning of the day from sunset (Watanabe 1983; cf. Wagley 1949: 115), preliminaries for the first ceremony begin on the evening of December 23, when the first *regidor* hires a marimba to play in front of his house to initiate the celebration. All the outgoing *xtool* gather there with the four *auxiliares de aldeas,* where they drink and dance to the marimba. On this night, the *auxiliares* provide the *aguardiente* for the other officials. Meanwhile, the *miyool,* who will complete their cargos the next day, meander through the streets beating a large drum.

Two *alsiil (alguaciles),* adolescent boys about sixteen years old, don costumes in preparation for their single most important duty. One dresses as a man in red trousers topped by a black woolen jacket with gold piping. Around his head he wears a red cloth called a *tzute,* and over his left shoulder he carries a wooden baton hung from a leather thong and a red handwoven *paa,* "shoulder bag" (*morral* in Spanish). In his right hand he carries a large gourd rattle to warn others of his coming. The other *alsiil* dresses in the navy blue skirt worn by all Chimalteco women and a white, sleeveless handwoven *huipil* with colored designs around the collar. This *huipil,* which bears no resemblance to the red blouses normally worn by Chimalteco women, recalls the *huipil* worn by women of the neighboring community of San Juan Atitán. Juan de Dios Rosales, who saw this ceremony in 1944, claims that the *huipil* comes from Quezaltenango (Wagley 1949: 135), but I was unable to verify this. The female figure muffles his face with a shawl wrapped around his head, and he carries a small stuffed animal called *we?ch* in Mam.[5]

Beginning about 11:00 P.M., the two *alsiil,* also called *k'ooj,* "masks," in Mam, run through the streets accompanied by younger children. At midnight, they climb the bell tower of the church and ring the bell to call the *xnaq'tzoon,* "cantors," to celebrate a sacred mass. The four *xnaq'tzoon* arrive with the marimba from the house of the first *regidor,* and the musicians place it at the back of the church just inside the door. The *xtool* and a group of men and boys enter the church and sit on the benches nearest the door with their backs to the altar. Instead of the normal trio of musicians, a single man plays a dirge on the marimba—a piece played only one other time each year, during the Thursday night procession of Holy Week. The *xnaq'tzoon* chant in accompaniment. Although several Chimaltecos told me that this ritual of reversal supposedly parodies the mass, the men and boys nonetheless maintain a respectful silence. One stated that this mass serves in part to bid farewell to the old year and to welcome the new.

After three or four responses lasting about three-quarters of an hour, the musicians move the marimba to the porch of the town hall, where they strike up more lively tunes. The two *alsiil* dance in front of the marimba, face to face and at arm's length, their hands on each other's shoulders. Skyrockets and bombs are set off. About half an hour later, the *alsiil* set off through the streets, knocking on doors to ask for small gifts of tamales, the holiday corn cakes prepared in every Chimalteco home. During the night, the *alsiil* are supposed to visit the oldest inhabitants of the town to celebrate their passing another year. At about 5:00 A.M., the young men retire for a few hours' rest before the change-of-office ceremony begins.

On the morning of the twenty-fourth, a holiday market slowly comes to life, and the *xtool* gather once more at the house of the first *regidor* to share *jícaras* (gourds) of *xtxuun,* a ceremonial drink made from corn and cinnamon. At about 8:00 A.M., the outgoing civil officials arrive in the plaza to begin the ceremony. The municipal salon becomes the reception hall for the new cargoholders, pacaya leaves (*Chamaedorea elatior*) (cf. Recinos 1954: 137–138) adorn the door, and *miyool* erect an arch of palm branches in front of the church steps. Wives of the retiring officials arrive with pots of coffee to serve the participants. Musicians set up their marimba on the porch of the town hall and begin to play, while the two *alsiil,* costumed as they were the night before, dance in front of the marimba for a few moments.

As the ceremony begins, the *xtool,* who have entered the hall, hand the names of the new cargoholders to the *alsiil.* Each sets off at a run to "capture" the new officials, accompanied by several *miyool* and trailed by excited children. Although the names of the cargoholders chosen at the end of each November are supposed to remain secret, word invariably leaks out, so the new cargoholders wait at home, dressed in their best clothes. The *alsiil* arrives, names the new official, then delegates two *miyool* to escort him to the reception hall. The *miyool* grasp their prisoner by the upper arms, one on either side, and walk him to the plaza, where they pass under the arch of palm leaves in front of the church, circle the fountain in the center of the plaza, and then cross into the municipal hall.[6]

The *alsiil* first capture the four *sacristanes* and the four *xnaq'-tzoon*. Even though these men hold their positions for life, they participate in the ceremony each year to renew their office (cf. Wagley 1949: 92). Next the *alsiil* seek out the twenty-four *miyool*, followed by the four new *alsiil*, the seven *ixhkweel*, the four *auxiliares de aldeas*, and finally the two *pixhkaal*. Because this last, imprestigious cargo is for older men who have neglected their public obligation to carry cargos, the new *pixhkaal* often arrive in the plaza blind drunk and occasionally belligerent.

Capturing the new officials takes most of the morning. During this time the marimba plays almost nonstop, the holiday market crowd looks on, and the outgoing *xtool* and *miyool* drink and dance to celebrate the end of their year in office. The officials gradually get drunker, and the *alsiil* run slower, sweat pouring down their faces as they trot off again, until finally all the new cargoholders have gathered in the municipal hall. Each new official then takes a pacaya leaf, and they file out of the hall with the most senior cargoholders last. Led by a *miyool* beating a drum and the male *alsiil* walking backwards and shaking his rattle, the procession circles the fountain, passes under the arch of palm branches, and enters the church, where each official deposits his leaf as he files past the altar. The new cargoholders then go to the house of the *alcalde* to share large *jícaras* of *xtxuun*. The new *miyool* take up their duties immediately, strolling self-consciously around the plaza, dressed in their best clothes and proudly carrying the tasseled batons that signify their office. A week later on the morning of New Year's Day, a much more staid ceremony in the town hall with speeches by the *alcalde* and other local luminaries formally inaugurates the incoming *xtool* and the four *auxiliares de aldeas*.

The installation of civil officials described by Wagley (1949: 89–90; cf. pp. 135–136) reveals that very few changes have taken place in the actual ceremony during the last fifty years. The most striking difference lies in the absence of *costumbre* performed before and after the ceremony, especially the divinations once conducted during the selection of officials and the *costumbres* required of the new cargoholders once they had entered office (Wagley 1949: 87–94). Close reading of Wagley's monograph, however, yields two relevant points. First, the heaviest ritual obligations during the selection and installation of new officials fell to the highest-ranking cargoholders, and second, even in the past, the lower cargos—those other than *alcalde*, first *regidor*, first *miyool*, and the four *martoon*—required little ritual validation (cf. Wagley 1949: 88–89).

The disappearance of *costumbre* associated with the change-of-

office ceremony perhaps reflects the fact that the highest civil officials now change every four years in June after the national elections
rather than annually each December. That is, cargoholders whose
ritual obligations figured most prominently in the transfer of authority to new officials no longer participate directly in the ceremony. This suggests that the loss of these rituals resulted as much
from changes in the mode of selecting high officials as from broader
economic or religious concerns. It also suggests that the underlying
purpose of the ritual capture of new officials was—and remains—
primarily social rather than political. The ceremony publicly expresses the social legitimacy accorded incoming cargoholders by their
selection. Where such selection once entailed the supernatural approval of God, Santiago, and the *witz*, today it means commanding
the social estimation of one's fellow Chimaltecos. To see the proud
smile on a young Chimalteco's face as two *miyool* escort him
through the crowded plaza on a clear December morning, resplen-
dent in gleaming white trousers, red sash, and new navy blue shirt,
is to understand the enduring power of this estimation.

Rituals of Initiation: Holy Week

During most local fiestas, *miyool* serve primarily as constables,
keeping the peace when drunks become unruly or belligerent. The
four-day celebration of Holy Week, however, involves more specific
duties for the *miyool*. First, in the days before the fiesta, they fabricate a life-size straw effigy of Judas and clothe it in tatters—a dingy
white shirt, a weather-beaten hat, an anthropologist's worn cor-
duroy trousers. An old wooden mask with round staring eyes, a long
twisted nose, and a slash of a grimace for a mouth serves as a face,
and battered boots and a red necktie complete the costume. Late in
the evening on Wednesday of Holy Week—Thursday "morning" by
Chimalteco reckoning—the *miyool* sally forth into the streets to
dance with their creation, accompanied by a marimba. Three *miyool* masquerade as *juuris*, "monsters," (probably from the Spanish
judíos, "Jews," characterized by colonial Catholic priests as the killers of Christ). They wear ragged clothes, and small wooden masks sit
low on their hooded faces, giving them the appearance of being
hunchbacked. The *juuris* take turns carrying Judas on their shoulders as they dance the shuffling two-step typical of Chimbal. The
other *miyool* carry the marimba from house to house, followed by a
large crowd of men and boys. Occasionally, the owner of a house
offers coffee and sweet bread to the dancers and musicians and, more
rarely, to the spectators. The revelry lasts late into the night, and

when the dancers finally retire, they string up their Judas on a tall post in front of the church, where the effigy hangs until the end of the fiesta. The infectious magic of the marimba, the hunched figures of the *juuris* capering in the moonlight with the towering specter of Judas astride their shoulders all inspire a vivid and eerie opening to Holy Week in Chimbal.

On the following night, the beginning of Good Friday by Chimalteco reckoning, the *miyool* once more engage in ritual, this time as intermediaries between the revelry of young boys disguised as bulls and the solemnity of the *alabanza de Cristo*, "praise of Christ," a procession conducted by the religious officials and former *alcaldes*. This procession is the longest, and perhaps the most beautiful, of the public rituals celebrated in Chimbal. An hour or so before it commences, boys and youths arrive in the plaza to dance as *waakx*, "bulls." They don disguises of mule saddles adorned with horns in front and leather tails behind. On top, many place cardboard boxes with designs cut in the sides and covered with colored cellophane, lit from within by a candle much like Halloween jack-o'-lanterns in the United States. A marimba begins to play on the steps of the town hall, and the bulls dance in crazy circles while the boys blow small horns. One man reported that the bulls used to try to gore each other, resulting in fights. "But now boys aren't so bad." Above the din, the church bell tolls incessantly, punctuating the lively music, the trumpeting of the bulls, and the laughter of the crowd. After about an hour, the *miyool* move the marimba down the main street toward the eastern *ttxaʔnja* shrine, preceded by the cavorting *waakx.* As the evening progresses and the *aguardiente* begins to flow, young men in women's dress or clad as nondescript animals join in what becomes increasingly drunken revelry.

In the meantime, a second procession emerges from the church led by four *miyool* carrying a marimba (cf. Wagley 1949: 115–116). A single musician plays the repetitious, mournful notes of the *alabanza de Cristo*, while two men playing the drum and *chirimía* follow behind. One *sacristán* rings a small bell; the others swing *xaawak'* (*pichachas* in Spanish), clay censers filled with pungent copal incense. Behind the musicians, eight former *alcaldes* carry an image of Mary and the smaller statue of Christ, which has a cross tied to his back; both statues are wrapped in palm leaves, signifying that Christ is "hidden" in "the other world" and that his mother mourns for him. The four *xnaq'tzoon*, "cantors," who chant prayers in Spanish, and the *martoon* who portion out cigarettes and shots of *aguardiente* to the other participants, complete the company.

Accompanied by about fifty people, many carrying candles, the

procession stops at fourteen stations as it circles the pueblo. According to Chimaltecos, each station, marked by a small cross and a scattering of pine needles, represents a place where Christ fell while
carrying the cross to Calvary. At each stop, the four *xnaq'tzoon* recite prayers in Spanish, one pair echoing the stanzas chanted by the
first, as the marimba plays. After ten or fifteen minutes, the procession moves on to the next station, to the slow cadence of drum
and *chirimía*. Candlelight illumines a face here and there, the
pungent odor of burning copal fills the air, and above all the waning
moon hangs shrouded in a cloudy sky.

Upon leaving the church, the procession moves clockwise around
the town, making one stop before reaching the eastern *ttxa'nja*
shrine. It then descends to the lower main street, where it passes
through the raucous bull dancers and continues on to the cemetery
at the western edge of town. The procession ends at the *ttxa'nja*
near the cemetery well after midnight. Formerly, the two saints remained in the small chapel there in the care of the *martoon*, but orthodox Catholic catechists stopped that practice, objecting to the
drunkenness that invariably accompanied the vigil (see chapter 8).
Now the two saints return quickly to the church, and the officiants
hurry home to bed or join the festivities in the plaza, where the
other marimba and dancers have also returned.

At dusk on the Monday following Easter Sunday, the *miyool* again
take to the streets with Judas to close the fiesta of Holy Week. The
three *juuris* dance with Judas to the music of a marimba, retracing
the clockwise route of the procession on Thursday night from the
plaza to the eastern and western *ttxa'nja* and then back to the plaza.
There the *miyool* strip Judas of his mask and boots (to be saved for
the following year), pour gasoline over him, and burn him, ending
the celebration of Holy Week in Chimbal.[7]

Two elements mark these rituals as rites of passage for *miyool*.
First, Holy Week celebrations represent the first responsibility that
young Chimalteco *miyool* have for preparing and staging a public
ritual. By successfully performing their duties, they prove their competence to fulfill more substantial community obligations. Second,
the symbolic associations of *miyool* with Judas and the revelries of
the bull dance underscore the social initiation inherent in this cargo.
Alexander Moore (1979: 60–62, 69–71) observes that in the pseud-
onymous community of Atchalán, the equivalent of *miyool* serve as
a mock *cofradía* for Judas during Holy Week, in much the same way
that Chimalteco *miyool* do. In his study of Santiago Atitlán (1965;
cf. Tarn and Prechtel 1990), E. Michael Mendelson further identifies
Judas as an aspect of *Maximón*, a figure that mediates the opposition

between the sexually potent but socially uncontrolled state of youth and the sexually sterile but socially powerful condition of old age. By fetching fruit from the lowlands to feed *Maximón* during Holy Week, young civil officials in Santiago Atitlán demonstrate the social "ripeness" that transforms their sexuality into the fertility of true maturity.

While Judas lacks such explicit associations in Chimbal, the ritual duties of *miyool* during Holy Week constitute a similar threshold between boyhood and manhood, as well as portray their status as novices in public life. On one hand, during the procession on Thursday night, *miyool* carry the marimba that plays for the *waakx* but no longer dance themselves. On the other, they carry the marimba for the *alabanza de Cristo* but similarly neither recite the prayers nor directly attend the images of Christ and Mary. Literally as well as figuratively, the *miyool* stand between the young boys dancing as bulls, who precede them in the procession, and the aging former *alcaldes* bearing the saints who follow behind. While the *miyool* still fancy the excitement and abandon of the young "bulls," their responsibility for Judas and their tentative mastery over the *waakx* constitute a conventional expression of their present self-control and a model for their future maturity.

Rituals of Community: Corpus Christi

Processions honoring Santiago formerly took place during all major fiestas, including the Ceremonies for Rain, in Mam *qaanb'il jb'aal* (literally, "asking for rain"), performed at the beginning of the rainy season each May (cf. Wagley 1949: 108–109, 115–116, 118–119, 121). This procession, along with the cargo rituals associated with it, has disappeared completely. In addition to Holy Week, however, processions still occur at Corpus Christi, the fiesta of Santiago, and on Christmas Day, the most elaborate being the one during Corpus Christi in June. On the day before the fiesta, men from each *cantón*, "ward," build four small chapels of saplings and pine boughs in the plaza, representing the four original subdivisions of the pueblo (cf. Wagley 1949: 10). A minor saint from the church is placed in each chapel. These images no longer represent the patron saints of each *cantón* but are chosen at random (*solo por gusto*), and their placement varies from year to year.

Each year, four men from each *cantón* take responsibility for building their chapel and collecting money from the *cantón* to buy candles for their saint and refreshments for those who watch over the image throughout the night. As one young Chimalteco noted, "This isn't like taking a cargo where you have to work for a whole year. This is just for one night, so what does it matter?" At nightfall, the *martoon* set off skyrockets, and men from each *cantón* arrive to take part in the vigil for the saint in their chapel. A marimba plays on the steps of the town hall, providing illusory comfort from the chilling rain that often falls at this time of year. The men in charge of each chapel burn candles for their saint and portion out cigarettes, hard candy, sweet bread, and coffee to others who have come to keep them company. These men keep their vigil throughout the night, but others are free to come and go.

On the actual day of Corpus Christi, a procession including Santiago, Santa Ana, and the visiting saints from San Juan Atitán and Ixconlaj emerges from the church to make a counterclockwise circuit of the plaza and marketplace, pausing at each chapel. Two men playing drum and *chirimía* lead the procession, followed by the pair of angels from Ixconlaj, the "wife" of San Juan, San Juan himself, Santa Ana, and finally Santiago. The image of Santiago stops in front of each chapel while the first cantor lights two candles and recites a brief prayer in Spanish. The ubiquitous marimba plays in front of the town hall, and *martoon* shoot off skyrockets. In less than half an hour the procession is over, and Santiago and the visiting saints reenter the church. Shortly thereafter, the chapels are dismantled and the other saints returned to the church without ceremony. Each year, one man also volunteers to serve *xtxuun*, the ceremonial corn drink, to all who come to his house after the procession. Although not a formal cargo, this is no mean obligation, since each person receives nearly a liter of the drink, and a marimba must be hired to play for much of the afternoon.

One elderly Chimalteco catechist explained to me that the fiesta of Corpus Christi commemorates the appearance of Christ before the apostles sixty days after his resurrection, and the chapels represent the four corners of the world where he sent them to preach. Most Chimaltecos, however, pay little heed to such universal interpretations and enjoy the fiesta in a more immediate sense. Indeed, Santiago, not Christ, makes the round of the chapels to link the different quarters of the community to the town center, bringing the inhabitants together in common—albeit brief—ceremony. Beyond this, the fiesta serves as an opportunity to stay up late and have a good time, as fiestas probably always have.

Such pragmatism, of course, has also dispossessed the minor saints in the church of whatever magical individuality that they may once have had, relegating them to namelessness. Santiago too has suffered a certain disenchantment. While still accorded much honor and respect, interaction with him has come to conventionalize the diffuse spirit of local sociality rather than the actual personage that Chimaltecos once took him to be. Despite this transformation from saintly interlocutor to local emblem, Santiago continues to draw Chimaltecos together as the protective presence that watches over Chimbal from heaven (see chapter 8). The church remains the house of Santiago, the physical and spiritual center of the community, and the wooden image of Santiago still affirms the singular identity of Chimbal through its uniqueness: no other place has a Santiago on horseback just such as this, and no other pueblo performs precisely these rituals for their saint. Therein perhaps lies the most enduring importance of these celebrations for Santiago.

Cargoholding in Chimbal no longer constitutes the demonstration of wealth, the exercise of power, or even the acquisition of prestige that it once did. Despite obvious changes in the extrinsic economic and political rationale of cargo service, however, Chimaltecos continue to carry cargos and have expanded the number of available positions to accommodate growth of the town's population. This persistent participation in the cargo system clearly attests to the intrinsic social value of cargo service as a formal expression of inclusion in the local community. Thus, when Chimaltecos say that they still serve their cargos because *es costumbre,* "it is the custom," they invoke not the blind habit of tradition but the imperative to participate in the ongoing life of their community. More enduring than the rituals that once legitimated it—or even the administrative autonomy that once empowered it—the simple social fact of fulfilling a cargo remains unequivocal proof of inclusion in the community, a standard by which to gauge the commitment of others to one's neighbors and to demonstrate publicly one's own Chimalteco-ness.

Saints, Souls, and Service: The Conventional Reality of Chimbal

In the preceding chapters, I have tried to delimit the community of Santiago Chimaltenango in terms of the local conventions that Chimaltecos use to shape their lives and make them meaningful. To a great extent, these conventions rest on the quotidian experiences of daily routine and seasonal round, on attachment to place and past, and on proper comportment and shared public responsibilities in an ongoing here and now. A symbolic opposition between nearby saint and distant *witz* sanctifies community boundaries by conventionalizing physical propinquity as the consequence—rather than the cause—of enduring local sociality. Chimalteco notions of soul and *naab'l* in turn define this sociality as an individual internalization of mutual recognition that stems from acknowledgment of conventional forms and mastery of familiar acts. Such recognition, however, involves an emergent social engagement rather than strict behavioral conformity. Public responsibilities of cargoholding formally substantiate for Chimalteco men the personal capacities and commitments incumbent on having a soul through explicit—if now largely formulaic—obligations to the community at large. Despite crucial economic, political, and ritual changes in these obligations, the abiding importance of cargo service to both community and individual identity remains evident in the rituals of social recognition, public initiation, and local sovereignty that survive.

At the same time, however, Guatemalan history, touched on so briefly in chapter 2, clearly belies any presumption that these community affinities reflect the persistence of some pristine Maya identity—much less, the inherent equilibrium of some isolated community. Conquest, colonialism, and racism, and the iniquities that they spawn, have created a society in contemporary Guatemala that denies Chimaltecos any meaningful place outside their own community. Thus, in a very real sense, Chimalteco conventions of community directly attest to this negative, encompassing presence. On one hand, the moral imperative of Chimalteco souls finds ready confirmation in the common humanity that convention preserves within Chimbal but which is found so lacking immediately beyond its bounds. On the other hand, the intrusiveness of the larger world, dramatically personified by *witz*, continually demands a pragmatic opportunism rooted not immutably in place or practices but in the emergent, highly personalized social familiarity that local life precipitates. The community of Santiago Chimaltenango exists precariously between the felt propriety of enduring moral affinities and the equally great need to accommodate the vagaries of changing historical circumstances: if conventions prove too exacting, community boundaries will shatter; if too malleable, abiding commonalities succumb to the empty formalism of habit.

In the end, Chimaltecos remain wary of the new and the strange because to entertain unfamiliar alternatives always runs the risk of revealing the ultimate arbitrariness of the conventionality—the "way of being"—that has long fostered Chimalteco life and livelihood. The fear that assails Chimaltecos is one of meaninglessness, not one of change. It is the dread of subverting the commonality with one's neighbors that has sometimes been the only defense against a world full of oppression, lies, and prejudice.

✠ Part Three ✠

A Changing World

6

✛ *From Livelihood to Labor* ✛

Thus far in this inquiry into the meaning of community in Santiago Chimaltenango, I have focused on how Chimaltecos identify and engage each other socially through certain cultural propositions that they share—notions about saints and *witz*, souls and soul-loss, public recognition and community service. I have also suggested why they should foster such affinities in the first place, emphasizing the immediacies of place and daily experience as well as the iniquitous legacy of conquest and colonialism.

Despite their very real historical roots and social consequences, however, the cultural conventions of Chimalteco identity remain essentially ineffable—meaningful but irreducible to fixed meanings: saint and *witz* personify contingent social distinctions, not absolute ethnic essences; errant souls presume an emergent normality, not explicit standards of social conformity; cargoholding incorporates men into public life through acts of participation, not mastery of specific skills. Rather than reducing such indeterminacies to singular cultural axioms, or worse, reifying them into sterile analytical truisms, I have tried to convey the meaningfulness that these conventions hold for Chimaltecos. Consequently, the previous chapters have only circumscribed a formal language of community—how, and perhaps partly, why, Chimaltecos interact as they do—without conveying much sense of what Chimaltecos are actually doing as they use this language.

My task in the next three chapters, then, is to relate this language of community to concerns that confront Chimaltecos as they live their lives. I do so by examining how Chimbal has changed during the twentieth century. Far from a complete recounting of Chimalteco history, I draw on Charles Wagley's study of Chimbal in 1937 (1941; 1949) and on my own research there since 1978 to highlight general patterns of change that have substantiated as well as transformed the sense and sensibility that Chimaltecos have of themselves and their community. Specifically, this chapter deals with the problems of livelihood in the face of growing overpopulation and inextricable dependence on a market economy; chapter 7 focuses on the encroachment of the Guatemalan state and the subsequent loss of local sovereignty and political self-legitimation; and chapter 8 examines the decline of folk Catholicism in Chimbal.

This conjunction of cultural conventions and social change neither presumes nor confirms the persistence of some timeless Chimalteco culture. Neither will it decry the demise of once-pristine traditions before the inexorable march of global modernity. Such mechanistic formulations would belie the findings of earlier chapters on the diffuse, emergently meaningful cultural conventions that inform Chimalteco life. Indeed, the formalism of such conventions tends less to homogenize the community into a definitive conformity than to orient Chimaltecos toward common, if not necessarily always constant, consistent, or even compatible, interests and concerns. As Dan Sperber (1975: 137) has rightly noted, "Cultural symbolism focusses the attention of the members of a single society in the same directions. . . . [It] creates a commonality of interest but not of opinions." The following chapters treat salient Chimalteco interests and concerns as part of an ongoing nexus of cultural meanings and historical conditions, neither of which ultimately determines what Chimaltecos actually do. Instead, Chimaltecos constantly alter both conventions and conditions, if only inadvertently, as they try to make sense of an inconstant world and act to survive in it.

Maya communities in highland Guatemala have changed markedly since anthropologists first undertook intensive ethnographic study of them in the 1920s and 1930s. Nowhere is this change more apparent than in economic affairs—superficially in the ubiquitous presence of such things as wristwatches, radios, plastic shoes, and bottled beer, and, more fundamentally, in the structure of local livelihood itself. The significance of these changes goes well beyond how people manage to feed themselves. Established anthropological wisdom—most notably Eric Wolf's model of the "closed corporate peasant community" (1955; 1957; 1986)—has long equated the cultural vitality of Maya communities with local economies predicated on subsistence corn farming on locally controlled lands, an egalitarian ethic of "shared poverty," and abiding resistance to incorporation into a wider market-dominated society. Recent times, however, attest to increasing differences in wealth both within and between Maya communities; to the advent of private property, with the concomitant buying and selling of land even across municipal boundaries; and to ever-greater dependence on local cash-cropping, migratory wage labor, and petty trade and manufacturing.

This chapter examines the nature of these changes in Chimbal since Charles Wagley's visit in 1937. I begin by comparing present economic pursuits with Wagley's (1941) findings on land tenure and maize production and then discuss the impact of economic diversification and stratification on Chimalteco identity: if Chimbal is no longer socially closed or institutionally corporate, in what sense—if at all—does it remain a community (cf. Watanabe 1981a)?

Corn: Land and Livelihood

Corn still constitutes the mainstay of Chimalteco life. With few exceptions, living in Chimbal means provisioning a household with enough corn to last from one harvest to the next. As in Wagley's time, Chimaltecos recognize two principal types of maize, white *saq* and yellow *q'an*, each divided into "winter" and "summer" varieties (cf. Wagley 1941: 27). Summer maize, called *a?k'l* in Mam, derives its name from the dry season when Chimaltecos plant it. Sown in March, well before the rains begin, fields of summer corn grow in *che?w tx'otx'*, "cold land," high on the mountainsides above the pueblo. The cooler conditions there dictate a longer growing season as well as lower yields, although some Chimaltecos contend that *a?k'l* is more nourishing because its slower growth gives it more *iipin*, "strength." In general, however, the harvest of *a?k'l* in November merely tides people over until the main harvest of winter corn in late January.

Winter corn, called *a?qwaa*—literally, "our food"—in Mam, makes up most of the corn crop. Grown on the lower, sheltered slopes below the town, fields of winter corn are sown at the beginning of the rainy-season winter in May and ripen in September, well before the rains end. While the corn is still tender, Chimaltecos pick a few ripe ears, called *i?xh* in Mam, for roasting, for making into a corn gruel called *sqaa*, or for sweet, cornbreadlike tamales (*suub'in i?xh*). Most of the ears, however, dry on the stalk into *jal* (in Spanish *mazorcas*, "Indian corn") until harvest time under the clear, dry January skies. Chimaltecos say that the yellow corn keeps best, so they store white corn where it can be used first.

Being rugged, cold, and remote, Chimalteco lands never suffered direct expropriation by Ladino *haciendas* or plantations (cf. Wagley 1941: 56). Consequently, Chimaltecos have until recently practiced extensive bush-fallow hoe cultivation, ideally using a plot for two years and then letting it lie fallow for at least four. Despite a rapid drop in yields after the first year that always forced a shifting of fields, Chimbal was known as a relatively land-rich *municipio* (Wagley 1941: 31, 56; cf. Stadelman 1940). Unlike Maya in other towns of the region, however, Chimaltecos in 1937 had no other specialization to supplement their income through trade. They remained entirely dependent on maize for subsistence, and any surplus was sold or bartered for needed commodities and a few luxuries (Wagley 1941; 21–24). Wagley concluded that

> to support adequately a family of five from agriculture, without working for wages, a man must plant at least sixty *cuerdas* [about 6.5 acres] of milpa each year. To plant sixty *cuerdas* each year, he must control at least one hundred and twenty *cuerdas* [13 acres], since much land must lie fallow each year. The sixty planted *cuerdas* should yield fifty to sixty *quintales* [1 *quintal* = 100 pounds] of shelled maize, leaving him a surplus beyond the family's consumption of ten to twenty *quintales*. From the sale and exchange of this surplus, he must obtain all other necessities of life. This represents a rock bottom minimum since the income from the sale of only ten *quintales* of maize would hardly purchase all the family needs; any Chimalteco would supplement this basic income by work for his richer neighbors or at the coffee harvest on a plantation. (Wagley 1941: 55)

Despite these calculations, the actual size of fields planted in 1937 averaged only 38.5 *cuerdas*. Although some households worked 150–200 *cuerdas* of *milpa*, 30 (12 percent) planted less than 15 *cuerdas*, and only 58 (23 percent) cultivated more than 60 *cuerdas* (Wagley 1941: 73).[1]

A man's success depended directly on the amount of land that he had. Ideally, he built on the inheritance from his father by borrowing or renting land from richer relatives and neighbors on which to grow surplus corn for cash. By combining any proceeds with savings from plantation labor or work for other Chimaltecos, he could buy more land of his own. Once a man controlled enough land to produce a consistent surplus, he could hire poorer Chimaltecos to work his *milpas* while he engaged in more lucrative enterprises such as trade and transport. Those with capital often bought mules to haul coffee to Huehuetenango for two plantations that had recently been established west of Chimbal (Wagley 1941: 30, 45–47, 76–77).[2] Profits from muleteering could then be invested in more land or used to buy trade goods, making the successful man even wealthier.

In reality, few Chimaltecos ever realized this dream of success. As early as 1937, more than three-fourths of the town owned less than the minimum amount of land that Wagley deemed necessary to free them from outside wage labor (1941: 72–73). Although most households had access to sufficient land through family or rental, overuse of the same plots year after year gradually eroded *milpa* production and exacerbated the need to buy corn. Even those with enough land to feed themselves still needed cash for tools, food staples, clothing, thread for weaving, and other necessities. With only a limited amount of work available locally, many Chimaltecos resorted to migratory wage labor on the coffee plantations of Guatemala's Pacific coast, eight days' walk away, where they earned between 10 and 20 centavos a day (Wagley 1941: 30, 73–74). Nonetheless, few families had no land at all, and "most Chimaltecos work[ed] for wages only to supplement, slightly or greatly, their incomes from cultivating their own fields" (Wagley 1941: 75).

In concluding his study, Wagley attributed Chimalteco wage-labor dependency not to an absolute shortage of local land but to its unequal distribution. This had originated in the alienation of property made possible after Guatemala abolished communal land tenure in the late nineteenth century (Wagley 1941: 60–61, 82; see chapter 7). Wagley predicted that ever-greater disparities in land ownership would eventually divide the town into a majority class of land-poor wage earners captive to plantation labor and a much smaller class of large landowners who would gradually accumulate their neighbors' land as fragmentation through equal inheritance made these holdings too paltry to provide a livelihood (Wagley 1941: 82–83).

By the time of the national agricultural census of 1964, Wagley's predictions appeared prophetic. The population of Chimbal had nearly doubled from his estimate of 1,500 in 1937 to 2,647 for the *municipio* as a whole (Wagley 1941: 9; Gall 1980: 687). The mean size of landholdings in the town had halved from 101.5 *cuerdas* to 52.25 *cuerdas,* and land productivity had fallen from 75–100 pounds of corn per *cuerda* to less than 60 pounds (Wagley 1941: 31, 72; DGE 1968; 1971). Over 90 percent of Chimalteco households lacked the 120 *cuerdas* that Wagley felt necessary for self-sufficiency, and fully half the town lacked the 30–40 *cuerdas* then needed to grow enough corn for a single year, let alone fallow any land for the next (see fig. 8, table 1). Townspeople relied increasingly on migration to the coastal coffee plantations for money to buy corn. One Chimalteco reported that demand for corn drove prices as high as Q25.00 per *quintal* (100 pounds).[3] Consonant with Wagley's predictions, those who could subsist on their lands now comprised less than 4 percent of

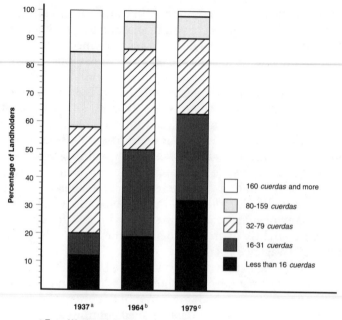

ᵃ From Wagley 1941:73.
ᵇ From DGE 1968.
ᶜ From DGE 1982.

Figure 8. Distribution of land by size of landholding, 1937–1979.

Chimalteco households, but they controlled a quarter of local lands; by contrast, in 1937, the top 4 percent of landowners in Chimbal controlled less than 20 percent of the land (cf. Wagley 1941: 72).

During the late 1960s and early 1970s, this situation slowly began to change. Agricultural programs sponsored by the Maryknoll Fathers in San Pedro Necta introduced chemical fertilizer to Chimbal, prompting a dramatic improvement in land productivity and shifts in patterns of land use. Chimalteco *milpa* production jumped from 60 pounds per *cuerda* in 1964 to 150–200 pounds per *cuerda* by 1979. Even agricultural census figures, always notoriously underreported, set maize production in Chimbal at 108 pounds per *cuerda* in 1978–1979 (DGE 1983). Chemical fertilizer also allowed Chimaltecos to use the same *milpas* for several years running, reducing the need for extensive land in fallow. Accordingly, by the late 1970s, Chimaltecos had to plant only about 15–20 *cuerdas* of *milpa* to feed their families, half to a third less than they had needed ten years before.[4] The smallest amount that I knew of personally was 8 *cuerdas*

Table 1. *Distribution of Land by Number of Producers, 1937–1979*

Size of Holding	1937[a]	1964[b]	1979[c]
0–15 cuerdas	29	100	215
16–31 cuerdas	19	165	211
32–79 cuerdas	97	188	180
80–159 cuerdas	69	55	53
160 cuerdas and above	39	20	13
Totals	253	528	672

[a] These figures are first approximations derived by linear interpolation from figure 3 in Wagley 1941: 73.
[b] From DGE 1968; includes corn and coffee holdings.
[c] From DGE 1982; includes corn and coffee holdings.

planted by a thirty-year-old man to support his wife and four young children; the largest was 40 *cuerdas*, worked by an older man and his two grown sons for their combined families. Direct observations during the harvests of 1979 and 1980 corroborated Chimalteco estimates of 150 pounds of shelled maize from a well-fertilized *cuerda* of winter corn, as well as the much reduced acreage cultivated by individual families.[5]

Only such intensified land use explains how Chimaltecos, rich and poor alike, could assure me that everyone had enough *milpa* to feed themselves, despite a growing municipal population then close to 3,500 (cf. DGE 1977; 1984). According to the agricultural census of 1979 (DGE 1982), such growth had reduced mean land-holdings in Chimbal to less than 40 (38.81) *cuerdas*, and two-thirds of the town lacked even this much land (fig. 8). Clearly, old patterns of land use would never have allowed Chimaltecos to claim such self-sufficiency. At the same time, the "green revolution" left the town no more self-sufficient than it had been before. Nearly a third (31.3 percent) of Chimalteco households reported holding less than 15 *cuerdas* of land, a benchmark minimum even with fertilizer, and another four households (0.6 percent) had no land at all (DGE 1982). Furthermore, in order to make what land they had sufficiently productive, Chimaltecos needed enough cash to buy 5–7 *quintales* of chemical fertilizer each year—about Q60.00–80.00 in 1979 when wages on the plantations brought Q2.50 a day (see table 2). Chimaltecos had altered, but not escaped, their deepening dependency on wage labor.

Table 2. Local Wages and Prices, 1937–1988

	1937[a]	1965[b]	1979	1980	1988
Wages					
Local	10¢	40¢	Q1.50–2.00	Q2.00	Q2.50–3.00
Plantation	10–20¢	70–80¢	Q2.50–3.00	Q3.00–4.00	Q5.00–6.00
Corn					
(per *quintal*)	50¢–Q2.00	Q5.00	Q8.00	Q10.00	Q20.00
Coffee					
(per *quintal*)	Q4.00–6.00	Q25.00	Q60.00–65.00	Q90.00	Q175.00–200.00[c]
Chemical fertilizer					
(per *quintal*)	—	Q6.00	Q12.00	Q16.00	Q25.00
Land					
(per *cuerda*)	Q1.00	Q5.00	Q100.00–500.00[d]		Q1,000.00[d]

[a] From Wagley 1941: 23–24, 65, 75.
[b] From Appelbaum 1967: 28–29, 33, 39, 55; and Chimaltecos' statements to me.
[c] These prices reflect devaluation of the quetzal between 1980 and 1988 from par to Q2.50 on the dollar, not a rise in international coffee prices.
[d] These figures reflect the rising demand for suitable coffee land.

Nonetheless, the reduction in *milpa* size brought about by chemical fertilizer definitely eased access to land for poorer Chimaltecos, if only because they had to rent less of it from richer neighbors. The agricultural census of 1979 (DGE 1982) shows that about 100 households (15 percent) in Chimbal rented some or all of their land, although apparently none more than about 16 *cuerdas*. Similarly, even those with excess land seldom planted more than the 15–20 *cuerdas* needed to feed themselves. Instead, if they had suitable land, larger landholders cash-cropped in coffee, and many rented small parcels to neighbors, often in return for labor. On the rest of their land, they grew firewood or occasional crops of summer corn.[6]

Thus, between 1937 and 1980, the population of Chimbal more than doubled, and average landholdings shrank by nearly two-thirds, but the amount of *milpa* needed to feed an average family dropped by about half, due to the introduction of chemical fertilizer. While I am confident of the relative accuracy of these comparisons, the census figures to which I have referred should not be taken at face value. Because Chimaltecos fear government taxation and suspect the envy of their neighbors, they never readily reveal the extent of their holdings even to friends, much less to a census-taker who is either a

Winter corn and coffee planted on a steep valley slope below the town, December 1987. The lighter areas are corn surrounding the rows of coffee trees interspersed with shade trees at center. Both houses (*center, far left*) have small cement patios for drying the hulled coffee beans.

Ladino outsider to be mistrusted or a neighbor to be discreetly parried. I have no illusions that townspeople were any more frank with me. Chimaltecos also know that, given the long fallowing of plots scattered over some thirty-five square kilometers of mountainous township lands, their statements about total landholdings remain practically impossible to verify.

To relativize matters further, townspeople do not necessarily quantify their land in abstract terms of area. Chimaltecos know and carefully respect the *mojones*, "boundary markers," that divide their fields, but land titles seldom specify plot size. Instead, they name the owners of adjacent parcels who testify to the mutually acknowledged boundaries (see chapter 7). A Chimalteco normally gauges land according to the quality of the plot rather than by set acreage. Experience, not size, dictates what combination of often widely scattered fields will produce the corn that a family needs each year. Chimaltecos clearly know the extent of their own holdings, but only inquisitive census-takers—or anthropologists—prompt them to quantify their land, more often than not with offhand estimates and calculated understatement. It should be noted, however, that unreported property consists largely of the marginal upper reaches that make up so much of the town's rugged land.[7]

Coffee: Cash-Cropping and Wage Labor

To keep their shrinking plots of land viable, Chimaltecos must find a way to buy the fertilizer that they need. This cash comes almost exclusively from coffee that they grow on their own land or pick for wages on Ladino-owned plantations outside Chimbal. On one hand, these contrasting involvements with coffee confirm the differentiation that Wagley predicted long ago between land-rich and land-poor Chimaltecos. On the other, like the use of fertilizer, cash-cropping and wage labor in coffee have enabled marginal landholders to survive, thus postponing, at least for the moment, irrevocable splits along class lines.

With most of its land at well over 6,500 feet (2,000 m), Chimbal lies on the extreme upper margins of coffee production. The high altitude and cool climate slows ripening and reduces yields, yet Chimaltecos have converted nearly all suitable land from corn to coffee. In 1937, only one Chimalteco spoke of growing coffee, and another grew some sugarcane (Wagley 1941: 47, 79). By the 1950s, more Chimaltecos had begun to plant coffee, first in the lower reaches of the Rio Ocho valley north of town and then on the south-facing valley slopes below the town. By 1964, as many as 74 Chimaltecos owned 240 *cuerdas* of coffee, with another 432 *cuerdas* planted but not yet producing; total production amounted to 413 *quintales* of dried coffee beans (DGE 1971). In other words, about one in seven households (14 percent) grew coffee in groves covering 2.4 percent of all land reported in the census (DGE 1968; 1971) (see table 3).

The boom in coffee prices during the mid-1970s further expanded production. By the end of the decade, the number of local growers had tripled to 241 (35.7 percent of producers), and the amount of land in coffee had risen nearly three and a half times to 2,299 *cuerdas*, almost 9 percent of total landholdings (DGE 1983) (table 3). In 1979, Chimaltecos sold close to 1,540 *quintales* of dried coffee, grossing about Q93,000.00. Despite guerrilla warfare and a deteriorating national economy, coffee production continued to rise during the 1980s. Between 1979 and early 1988, the local coffee cooperative tripled in size to 380 members, representing perhaps half the households in the town, and Chimaltecos reported that in 1987

Table 3. Coffee Producers and Coffee Land, 1937–1979

Year	Number of Producers		Land (in cuerdas)	
	With Coffee	All Producers	Planted in Coffee	Total Land[a]
1937[b]	0[c]	253	0	25,688
1964[d]	74	528	672	27,600
1979[e]	241	672	2,299	26,085

[a]For a discussion of the discrepancy in these figures, see text, note 7.
[b]From Wagley 1941: 72.
[c]Wagley (1941: 79) mentions one Chimalteco who had "recently bought a small plot of land deep in a *barranca* near San Pedro Necta, where he can raise some [sugar] cane and coffee," but he makes no other reference to actual coffee production in Chimbal.
[d]From DGE 1971.
[e]From DGE 1983.

the cooperative sold about 4,500 *quintales* of coffee worth over Q900,000.00.[8]

As impressive as these figures appear, most Chimaltecos remain small producers who sell less than 10 *quintales* of coffee each year (see fig. 9). In 1979, average production hovered around six and a half (6.39) *quintales* (DGE 1983), but more than half the town's growers produced less than this (see table 4). Nine growers reported no harvest at all, because their groves had not yet matured. In contrast, eight growers (3.3 percent) harvested more than 20 *quintales* of coffee; the largest produced 50 *quintales*. Since 1979, average coffee production in Chimbal has almost tripled, but I do not know to what extent this reflects new groves as opposed to maturation of established ones. By 1988, Chimaltecos who ten years before had harvested only 5–10 *quintales* of coffee from young groves told me that they were producing 50, 60, or even 80 *quintales* a year; a very few growers enjoyed harvests in excess of 100 *quintales*. Well over half the growers in Chimbal, however, own less than 10 *cuerdas* of coffee (fig. 9), meaning that they can never hope to produce more than 5–10 *quintales* of dried coffee a year. The dearth of additional land and the prohibitive capital investment that planting coffee demands suggest that production in Chimbal has peaked.

Indeed, except those who already own coffee groves, few can now realistically afford to become growers. When coffee prices soared during the mid-1970s, so did local land prices (table 2). By 1979, vir-

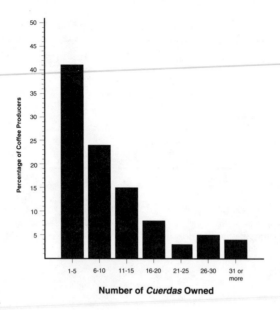

Number of *Cuerdas* Owned

Source: Based on a sample of 393 census forms that the director of the 1979 agricultural census in Chimbal allowed me to examine as they were being collected. These forms included 189 coffee producers reporting coffee holdings from 1 to 59 *cuerdas*. They comprise more than three-fourths (78.4 percent) of the 241 producers and 2,034 of the 2,299 *cuerdas* (88.5 percent) of the coffee land included in published census figures (DGE 1983). The missing coffee growers tend toward the lower end of the scale, which would further skew the distribution presented here.

Figure 9. Distribution of coffee producers by size of coffee holding.

tually no coffee land could be had in Chimbal, and what little was available cost as much as Q500.00 a *cuerda*, up from Q5.00 a *cuerda* in the mid-1960s. During the 1960s, a number of Chimaltecos began buying property in the neighboring *municipio* of La Democracia, where the warmer climate and sparser population made coffee land more readily available. Even there, however, prices rose to Q100.00 a *cuerda* by the mid-1970s and to as much as Q1,000.00 a *cuerda* by 1988.

Even if a prospective grower manages to obtain suitable land, coffee seedlings must be purchased or grown from seed for a year in a nursery, then carefully transplanted to the grove. At about 100 trees per *cuerda*, seedlings cost from Q20.00 to Q30.00 a *cuerda* in 1980. After planting, the trees take three to six years to begin producing, and all the while they must be weeded, fertilized, and carefully tended. A bad frost, pests, or blights can destroy years of work, and even after the grove matures, the income from the initial harvests often goes to pay off debts or to make additional investments in

Table 4. *Coffee Production, 1978[a]*

Production (in quintales)	Number of Producers
0	9[b]
1–5	84
6–10	44
11–20	25
21–30	5
31 or more	3

Source: Based on a sample of 374 census forms that the director of the 1979 agricultural census in Chimbal allowed me to examine as they were being collected.

[a]This table includes 170 coffee producers, representing just less than 71 percent of all growers in Chimbal at that time (cf. DGE 1983). Figures refer to the 1978 harvest. For reasons I now find inexplicable, I failed to correlate figures on production with size of coffee holdings; nor do published census figures allow any detailed calculations in this regard.

[b]These growers reported land planted in coffee that had yet to begin producing.

needed machinery to hull the ripe coffee berries or cement patios to dry the beans.

One of Chimbal's largest producers described this long process to me. He owned about 45 *cuerdas* of coffee in Chimbal and another 125 *cuerdas* in La Democracia. In 1979, about half his groves were producing, yielding a combined harvest of 60–70 *quintales,* and he hoped eventually to sell about 200 *quintales* a year. Although most of his coffee land lies in La Democracia, he lives in Chimbal for much of the year and takes an active role in community affairs.

My father and I planted our coffee in La Democracia sixteen years ago [1963], but it was six years before we earned anything. For the first three years, we didn't have any harvest at all, and for the next three there wasn't much. With the money from the first harvest we built a [cement] drying patio; with the second we built a proper house to live in when we went down [to La Democracia] to work; with the third harvest, we bought a sugarcane press because we had planted sugarcane to sell until the coffee matured. But it's been ten years now that I've been able to enjoy the rewards of all my work.

Becoming a coffee grower in Chimbal clearly demands capital in land and money, self-sacrifice, perseverance, and no small amount of luck.

Once the coffee trees have matured, there are still upkeep costs to meet. During most of the year, small producers and their families can maintain their groves themselves, weeding, fertilizing, trimming, and replanting trees. Fertilizer constitutes a major ongoing expense since 1.5 to 2 *quintales* per *cuerda* each year are required. Expenses rise dramatically at harvest time, when all but the smallest growers must hire workers to help pick their coffee. Large producers may employ twenty or more workers during the peak harvest season between February and April. In addition to paying daily wages, which rose locally from Q1.50 in 1979 to Q3.00 in 1988 (table 2), employers feed and sometimes house their workers, especially if their groves lie several hours' walk north of town in the Rio Ocho valley.

Because most workers are also neighbors, local hiring has yet to become a completely commoditized exchange of labor for wages. Owners still toil alongside their workers and speak of the need to treat them well, if for no other reason than to forestall resentment and envy. Equally important, however, employers know that workers can leave for the coastal plantations, where they might earn nearly twice what they do in Chimbal—but only far from home and under much worse working conditions. Rather than attempting to match commercial plantation wages, Chimalteco growers try to capitalize on the familiarity of working in Chimbal. This ultimately means setting flexible work quotas, usually based on days worked rather than amounts picked, and buying substantial amounts of corn to feed workers during the harvest season. In the end, this undercuts what growers save by paying lower wages, yet it fosters a sense of neighborliness with their workers that higher wages alone could never engender.[9]

After the ripe coffee berries are picked, they are hauled to town and hulled by hand-cranked machines to extract the ivory-colored bean from its fruity pith. A thorough washing and soaking follow; then the beans are spread on cement patios to dry for at least three days—brought out each morning, periodically turned with rakes, then gathered back into large sacks each evening. Processing the coffee constitutes a tedious, monotonous task, especially since about 450 pounds of coffee berries must be picked, hulled, and dried for every 100 pounds of dried beans produced. Except for the actual picking, however, the grower's family usually does most of this processing without hired help.

Once they dry and bag the beans, Chimaltecos face the problem of selling their coffee. Like growers the world over, they remain at the mercy of the highly volatile international market. As local coffee production grew during the 1960s, prices stood at Q20.00–30.00 a *quintal*, but they skyrocketed in the mid-1970s to Q200.00 and more because of crop failures in Brazil. By the end of the decade, however, prices had fallen back to Q60.00–90.00 a *quintal*, as inflation further eroded profits through the rising costs of fertilizer for production and gasoline for transport (table 2). Devaluation of the Guatemalan quetzal during the 1980s raised the local price of coffee once again to over Q200.00 a *quintal.*

Whatever the price, Chimaltecos must always cope with the immediate problem of getting their crop to market. Until the early 1980s, the town's relative inaccessibility meant that growers had to ship their coffee in one-and-a-half-ton pickup trucks, since these were the only vehicles that could negotiate the precipitous road into the town. Most small growers usually succumbed to Ladino middlemen, aptly dubbed "coyotes," who came through town and bought up small lots of coffee at below-market prices and made their profit by shipping the coffee to Huehuetenango in greater bulk than any small producer could do alone. Chimaltecos had founded a coffee cooperative during the mid-1970s when local growers had withdrawn from the Ladino-dominated cooperative in San Pedro Necta, ostensibly over the municipal taxes they had to pay to sell their coffee there. Collective efforts, however, had yielded prices little better than coyotes offered because of the same constraints of transport. A better road, built in 1982 in conjunction with the army's counterinsurgency campaign against Guatemala's leftist guerrillas (see chapter 7), enabled the Chimalteco cooperative to begin using ten-ton trucks to ship its coffee to Huehuetenango. This reduced transport overhead and bypassed at least a few middlemen in Guatemala's labyrinthine coffee market. The ability to offer better prices increased membership sharply, and by the late 1980s, the cooperative was able to build a combined warehouse and meeting hall.

Obviously, fluctuations in coffee prices and production costs, especially for fertilizer and transport, dramatically affect how much Chimaltecos earn from their coffee and consequently how much coffee a household needs to produce to free itself from wage labor. About 10 *cuerdas* of coffee probably represents the break point between relatively consistent self-sufficiency and varying degrees of wage-labor dependency. Only with this much land in coffee can a Chimalteco grower ensure sufficient income to hire workers, buy fertilizer for corn fields and coffee groves, purchase staple goods and tools, and meet incidental household expenses.[10] As mentioned previously, over half the growers in Chimbal own less than 10 *cuerdas* of coffee land, but even the income from a few *quintales* helps to diminish time spent in wage labor.

For nearly two-thirds of the town, however, the point remains moot, since these families own no coffee land at all and must rely on working for other Chimaltecos or the coffee plantations on the Pacific coast for the cash that they need. I do not know to what extent recent increases in coffee production in Chimbal have absorbed local needs for wage labor, but in 1988, many townspeople—"perhaps half," some said—still went to the coastal plantations every year. In 1978, roughly two-thirds of Chimalteco households sent at least one member to the coast every year, but most went for two months or less; fewer than one in ten families migrated for more than three months, the maximum being five months (see table 5).

Migration to the plantations severely disrupts Chimaltecos' lives, not only because of the unfamiliar, often abhorrent conditions and the hotter, unhealthy climate but also because of prolonged estrangement from Chimbal. One Chimalteco, now a fairly prosperous coffee grower, recounted a trek to the coast that he took as a boy with his grandparents.

In the old days, there used to be a lot of exploitation. Many people went to the *fincas* [plantations], yet they earned very little. Most Ladinos called us *inditos* [little Indians] and treated us like dogs. They wouldn't even let us ride in their trucks, so my poor grandfather and grandmother and I had to walk for seven days just to get to the *finca* to begin working. On our way back to Chimbal, my old grandparents got tired, so we asked some Ladinos for a ride. They laughed at us and called us names, but they finally let us climb into the back of their truck. I still remember how happy my grandparents were when they got to ride all the way to Huehuetenango!

Even then, the three faced a day's walk over steep mountain trails to reach Chimbal from Huehuetenango. In the past, the dislocation resulting from migration was palpable and absolute.

In recent years, however, better roads and faster transport have eased these disruptions somewhat. The trek that formerly took a week Chimaltecos now make in a day or less on buses or, more often, on the large trucks that plantations use to transport their workers. Although neither accommodating nor comfortable—and often dangerous to boot—the improved transportation has prompted many Chimalteco migrants to intersperse stints on the plantations with periodic visits home to tend their fields and see family and

Table 5. *Migratory Wage Labor, 1978*

Days Worked on Plantation	Number of Households [a]
0	133
30	18
60	139
90	57
More than 90 [b]	24

Source: These figures come from a sample of 371 census forms that the director of the 1979 agricultural census in Chimbal allowed me to examine as they were being collected.

[a] These represent 55 percent of all households in Chimbal at that time (cf. DGE 1983). When I recorded these numbers, I was only interested in rates of migration and thus did not make correlations directly with other factors. The proportion of nonmigrants to migrants, however, parallels the proportion of Chimaltecos with sufficient corn and coffee lands to those without (see text).

[b] The maximum time spent on the plantations was five months.

friends. Those who remain in Chimbal sometimes counter the long absences by going down to visit relatives working on a plantation, remaining a few days and then returning home. Workers also carry letters back and forth between highland communities and the plantations—terse notes in stilted Spanish that reassure loved ones that all is well and that untended *milpas* have not suffered, or that admonish a father alone at home not to drink too much. For a small fee, radio stations broadcast personal messages to and from workers on the road or far from home concerning expected arrivals, unexpected delays, changes in plans, or family emergencies.

Improved transportation and communication has also bettered Chimalteco knowledge of the labor market. Prospective migrants no longer remain completely at the mercy of local *habilitadores*, "labor recruiters." In Wagley's time, labor recruiters often contracted workers by offering cash advances or liquor on credit, indebting them before they even left for the plantations (cf. Wagley 1941: 74–75). When I lived in Chimbal at the end of the 1970s, labor recruiters still worked local fiestas, but many plantations also began in July to advertise on the radio for harvest work, specifying daily wages and rations and where their trucks would pick up workers. Chimaltecos could compare various offers—often much the same—but more importantly, they also talked with returning workers about wages, work quotas, and living conditions on different plantations. By the late 1970s, many Chimaltecos apparently left for the plantations without contracts, signing on for a *quincena*, or two weeks, once they arrived, then renewing their contract or not, when it expired. Workers tended to remain at or return to places where they found conditions most tolerable. Hard as it is to gauge the effect that even such limited choice had on plantation conditions, wages that Chimaltecos earned on the coast rose steadily during 1979 from Q2.00 or Q2.50 a day to more than Q3.00 by the end of the year—well above the then-official minimum wage of Q1.12 a day.[11] All this perhaps reflects what Carol Smith (1984b: 217–219) has interpreted as an increasing labor shortage in Guatemala's plantation economy during the late 1970s.

In addition to the changing avenues of seeking employment, perceived motivations for Chimaltecos to migrate have also changed. In the past, Chimaltecos migrated to the plantations for lack of land, but the use of chemical fertilizer today means that most families have access to enough land to feed themselves as long as they can buy the fertilizer to make it sufficiently productive. In other words, Chimaltecos now migrate for lack of money, not land. As one man put it, "I have corn, I have beans, I have firewood, I have coffee—but I don't have *pisto* [cash]!" Given the high cultural value placed on sustaining a family from one's own land, migrating workers now leave behind a more meaningful economic base in the community than they did before the introduction of fertilizer. Consequently, most migrants can plausibly view plantation labor as an extension of their own economic concerns rather than as alienation from their lands and way of life. The complementarity of the corn and coffee cycles in Guatemala reinforces this perception: for Chimaltecos, most *milpa* work falls between April and August, while the coffee harvest on the coast runs mainly from August to December. Workers can thus migrate to the plantations without unduly neglecting their own fields. One Chimalteco went so far as to refer to plantations that pay an "honest" wage and provide sufficient rations as a "great help" to the poor. False consciousness aside, Chimaltecos know full well that migratory wage labor allows them a place in their community that they might not otherwise be able to maintain.

In no way, however, do Chimaltecos accept plantation labor as wholly beneficial or even benign. They decry the very real human costs that migration entails: workers are crowded into small, dirty rooms or barrackslike *galeras* where smoke from cookfires chokes the air, and dust constantly sifts down between the planks as people walk across the floor above. They weary of work in the stifling heat where *caporales*, "overseers," constantly urge everyone to hurry, yet impose fines for careless work or for the slightest damage to a coffee tree. They encounter more drunks than at any fiesta when rare days off turn people to the only available diversion of drink. And they suffer the malaria, mosquitoes, infections, and dysentery—and not occasionally the death—that infest the coast (cf. Appelbaum 1967; Pansini 1980; Menchú 1984).

Chimaltecos also deplore the alienation and anonymity of plantation labor. Work in Chimbal may be hard and inexorable, but as one man observed, "Here there's no *patrón* [boss] or *obligación* [contract]. If you get tired, you can always rest for a little while *sin pena* [without worry]." A young Chimalteco who has already spent a good part of his life on the coast spoke of the hard work and constant orders and, in particular, of how no one cares about anyone else: strangers too easily get killed down there. In contrast, people he knows in Chimbal invite him in for a cup of coffee or a bite to eat out of neighborliness. "*Minla?y qokyim tzaluu?* [literally, "No one can die here (in Chimbal)"] he concluded over and over again— meaning that no Chimalteco would just let another die. For those who can retain even a toehold in the community, the plantations offer needed income but little else. Migration can clearly radicalize some Guatemalan Maya (cf. Menchú 1984), but because Chimaltecos often migrate in family groups and speak a language different from Ladinos and other Maya, their exposure to new ideas and experiences remains limited. Indeed, Chimaltecos learn few skills on coffee plantations that they have not already mastered at home, nor does rural plantation life lure them with "the bright lights of the city."

Whether grown in local groves or on Ladino plantations, coffee has thus absorbed whatever labor that Chimaltecos save in cultivating fewer *cuerdas* of *milpa* than they did fifty years ago. Indeed, agricultural techniques have changed little over the years, if only because the land is so rugged that, short of massive terracing, more intensive irrigation or plow agriculture remains impossible. Chimaltecos still need much the same time for clearing, planting, weeding, and harvesting—roughly two to three days per *cuerda* each year (cf. Wagley 1941: 29; Stadelman 1940: 182–183). Only the careful fertilizing of fields has replaced the third and sometimes fourth weedings noted by Wagley. Although greater land productivity, and thus smaller fields, means 30–40 days fewer a year working *milpa*, poorer Chimaltecos now spend at least this much time on coastal coffee plantations, just as local coffee growers use this time to tend their own groves and process the resulting harvest. In typical peasant fashion, Chimalteco innovations in corn production and cash-cropping have intensified use of the scarcest resource of local land at the cost of greater exploitation of their own labor.

Class Stratification and Community

The changes of recent years have bound Chimbal inextricably to Guatemala's market economy, yet at the same time, they have allowed local *milpa* agriculture to persist, if only in greatly modified form. It might be argued that from the point of view of local subsistence, only those things have changed that had to change for everything else to stay the same—a kind of Chimalteco Romer's rule (cf. Rappaport 1979b: 229–230). It is important to note, however, that this conservatism does not abide in immutable patterns of Chimalteco culture but in the effects of ongoing natural, conventional, and political conditions—both local and regional—that have shaped Chimalteco responses to changing historical circumstances. It remains, then, to situate the changes that I have discussed within the context of these encompassing parameters.

Local population growth has clearly undermined Chimalteco household resources, especially land, yet the advent of chemical fertilizer and cash-cropping in coffee has changed how Chimaltecos measure the wealth implied by these resources. In Wagley's time, families' fortunes rested directly on the amount of land that they controlled: more land meant a greater corn surplus, which enabled them to hire labor and diversify into more profitable pursuits such as muleteering and trade. Today, Chimalteco corn and coffee production presumes a more intensive use of selected plots of land that largely abrogates any direct relation between size of landholdings and wealth. Instead, the quality of land—especially its suitability for coffee—has become more important than quantity. Small parcels of good coffee land far outweigh more extensive tracts of *che'w tx'otx'*, "cold land," good only for *milpa*, that once would have qualified a family as rich. Similarly, chemical fertilizer allows Chimaltecos to rotate their fields less often with correspondingly less concern for the lands they hold in fallow.

Changes in use have thus relativized the perceived value of land: it no longer represents the absolute good that it once was in Chimalteco eyes. I would argue that this relativization of land underlies the now-open sale of property between *municipios*—something "frowned on" in Wagley's time (Wagley 1941: 65). Not only do Chimaltecos buy coffee land in La Democracia, as already mentioned, but they also sell plots of "cold" *milpa* land to neighboring Maya from San Juan Atitán and Colotenango. Rather then demonstrating the disintegration of local values—or worse, the last desperate acts of a proletarianizing peasantry—such sales suggest changing ideas about the perceived value of particular kinds of land. At least for the moment, Chimaltecos have less need for the land that they sell than for the capital to buy coffee land wherever they can find it. At the same time, however, this by no means repudiates abiding Chimalteco attachments to local land. Even those who now live permanently near their coffee groves in La Democracia rarely sell all their *milpa* in Chimbal, and many return home to visit at least during fiestas.

Changes in the perceived value of land also presuppose greater competition for the limited amount of local land temperate enough to grow coffee. This in turn might suggest increasingly rigid stratification within the community, simply because local coffee land can no longer be readily had. In 1937, Wagley (1941: 76) noted that most Chimalteco men acquired the bulk of their wealth during their lifetimes because equal or split inheritance fragmented all but the largest estates. A generation later, the image of the self-made Chimalteco perhaps still held true. At least a few of the now-prosperous local coffee growers began their careers by migrating to the plantations during the 1950s and 1960s and investing their savings in local land that they later planted in coffee.

They could do this because land at that time remained relatively cheap in Chimbal, especially overworked parcels that no longer "gave good *milpa*." Several Chimaltecos said that they bought "ruined" fields for bargain prices that they later rejuvenated into valuable *milpa* land when chemical fertilizer became available. Indeed, one Chimalteco contended that the earliest coffee growers in Chimbal only began planting coffee on plots that had become useless for corn. Once Chimaltecos found local coffee production not only possible but, with the mid-1970s boom in prices, highly profitable as well, mounting land prices made it nearly impossible to acquire new coffee land. Only those who already owned suitable land could convert it from corn to coffee. A number of Chimalteco families who had been land-rich became relatively poor, because they failed to make the transition to coffee production.

Given this situation, it appears that few young Chimalteco men today will duplicate the rags-to-riches success that the introduction of coffee permitted in their fathers' time. Land prices have outstripped wages by so much that few can hope to acquire coffee land of their own. Nonetheless, while the difference between rich and poor in Chimbal has grown sharper, I am not at all sure that the gap will soon ossify into polarized classes of coffee growers over against wage laborers. Although half the coffee land in Chimbal belongs to only 20 percent of the growers, the other half remains in the hands of producers owning fifteen *cuerdas* or less (see figs. 9, 10). As in the past, inheritance may tend to split larger coffee holdings, making it difficult for families to reproduce their wealth in the next generation. In a few cases that I know personally, it appears that some growers may be trying to minimize the fragmentation of family holdings by investing in the education of "noninheriting" sons. So far, most young men who have gone on to school outside Chimbal have sought jobs as school teachers in rural *municipios,* but it remains to be seen how successfully they will transcend their dependence on family lands.

At the same time, the relative value of even small plots of coffee land in supplementing household income makes it unlikely that smallholders will sell their marginal groves to larger growers. As long as the price of coffee remains high enough to offset the costs of production, even small groves can generate a useful cash surplus. To complicate matters further, smallholders, like the Chimaltecos without coffee holdings whom they hire at harvest time, often work for other local growers, futher blurring incipient class distinctions. Thus, a growing population with circumscribed resources, the downsizing pressures of split inheritance, and the relative worth of even small plots of coffee suggest increasingly entrenched, but by no means inexorable, economic stratification in Chimbal.

Equally important, within the wider realm of social possibilities and cultural values, even the richest Chimaltecos express no desire to leave Chimbal for a more comfortable Ladino-style life in the cities. Although wealthy by local standards, few have the wherewithal or the job skills to live any better in the cities than they do in Chimbal. Consequently, wealthier men may speak better Spanish, travel more often to Ladino market towns, and buy more consumer goods, but women and children in these households often have less direct experience of life beyond the town. Chimalteco women and children most commonly travel outside Chimbal to work as seasonal laborers on Guatemala's commercial plantations, but wealthier families seldom migrate, leaving these women and children even more embedded in the immediacies of local life. In other words, increased prosperity does not necessarily lead to accelerated ladinization. Although

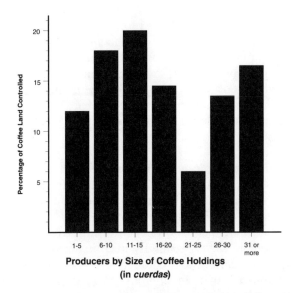

Source: Based on a sample of 393 census forms that the director of the 1979 agricultural census in Chimbal allowed me to examine as they were being collected. These forms included 189 coffee producers reporting coffee holdings from 1 to 59 *cuerdas.* They comprise more than three-fourths (78.4 percent) of the 241 producers and 2,034 of the 2,299 *cuerdas* (88.5 percent) of the coffee land reported in published census figures (DGE 1983). The 11.5 percent of coffee land unaccounted for is mostly owned by growers with 10 *cuerdas* or less, which would raise the percentage of land that they control accordingly.

Figure 10. Distribution of coffee land by size of producer.

readily apparent, the material changes in these households come piecemeal, introduced by the men from outside the community and accepted by their families and neighbors as local innovations rather than as transformative new ideas and practices.

Richer Chimaltecos do occupy larger, multiroom houses; they often have electric lights instead of candles or lanterns; and they may sleep on spring mattress beds instead of planks drawn over sawhorses. They eat more meat and bread than their neighbors; they are more likely to have tooth fillings than pulled teeth; and they wear newer clothes and leather rather than plastic shoes. Even the wealthiest women and girls still wear the town's traditional dress, although they may cook on raised adobe stoves rather than over open cookfires on the floor. Beyond these creature comforts, however, consumption by the wealthy in Chimbal largely conforms to local circumstances and standards.

As in the past, excess wealth that richer men cannot convert into land is invested in transport and trade. In 1988, four Chimaltecos owned Toyota Landcruisers—the four-wheel-drive vehicle of choice in rural Guatemala—and two more had small buses that, when not broken down, made regular trips to Huehuetenango. Until the Pan American Highway was built during the mid-1950s, a round trip to Huehuetenango took three days on foot or by mule (Wagley 1941: 45), but Chimaltecos now travel there and back in less than a day in trucks and buses that leave early in the morning and return by mid-afternoon. In good weather, the ride to Huehuetenango takes only about two hours.

Given that a truck can haul much more than the mules of times past, improved transport has drawn more Chimaltecos into petty trade. Aspiring merchants buy staple goods and household necessities from Ladinos in Huehuetanango to retail in Chimbal for a few cents' profit. The high cost of transport, limited capital, and circumscribed market, however, generally keep inventories to less than a few hundred quetzales. Most Chimaltecos sell mainly in the Friday market, established in 1943, and only incidentally from housefront stores that dot the town.[12] One notable exception is a man who has turned a room of his house into a true *tienda*, "shop," with glass-fronted display cases and wooden shelves lining two walls from floor to ceiling. He travels to Guatemala City twenty or thirty times a year to replenish his stock and has had the experience of being robbed by one of the many youth gangs that prowl the city. He is the only Chimalteco who sells luxury items like tape recorders and radios, as well as high-quality leather shoes and boots, in addition to the usual sundries. His corner on the luxuries market allows him a greater markup than most merchants, but the inherently high price of such goods and their intermittent sale tend to offset any immediate profit he might make. Costlier items and customers with little ready cash also push him to sell on credit, but since he does not charge interest, profit margins must cover any defaults. Extending credit only to individuals he knows and interacts with regularly helps to insure eventual, if not necessarily prompt, payment.

All the capital for his goods comes from coffee profits. In a very real sense, he can afford the risk of fewer but larger transactions and delayed or defaulted payments largely because his income from coffee allows him literally to leave his money on the shelf longer, tied up in slower moving merchandise. Indeed, the growth of his inventory in recent years to perhaps Q10,000.00 reflects the continual infusion of coffee money rather than any burgeoning demand for consumer goods in Chimbal.

The weekly market in Chimbal, January 1988. The corrugated metal roof was constructed in 1980.

Despite the town's more active commercial life, no Chimalteco merchant lives primarily on commerce. Local demand for most goods remains too small and inelastic to keep profit margins very high. The proliferation of small stores in Chimbal, with their great redundancy of goods, further undercuts the prices that any single merchant can set. Local truck and bus owners best illustrate the strain of reconciling the exigencies of a wider market economy with the frugality of a local subsistence-oriented clientele. When higher gasoline prices during the late 1970s prompted truckers to raise fares, many Chimaltecos chose to walk two hours down to the Pan American Highway and three hours back with their cargo to save Q1.00 in bus fare to Huehuetenango. Two of the three truckers in Chimbal in late 1978, both Mayas, lost or sold their vehicles within six months of my arrival. Said one, who planned eventually to buy another truck secondhand, "I'm not going to provide regular [transport] service for other people when I get my next truck. A truck owner actually does people a favor when he makes trips to Huehuetenango because he never earns a thing. Why should I spend Q20.00 [for gas and a driver] and wear out my truck when I can ride to Huehuetenango on somebody else's truck for Q1.50?"

Since 1982, when the new road was built, two buses have taken over the bulk of public transport, and pickup truck owners today mostly tend to their own affairs, hauling cargo for others only on commission or when it suits them. Bus owners, however, still face the same problem of high costs and low returns, buffered only by the greater number of paying customers that they can carry each trip. As in marketing local coffee, Chimbal's relative inaccessibility on western Guatemala's "peasant periphery" limits both the possibilities and profitability of local trade and transport (cf. Smith 1978).

Regardless of these inherent constraints, however, no Chimalteco entrepreneur ever really aims to become a full-time merchant in the first place. Almost all capital still comes from coffee, and coffee remains the primary concern. Nowhere is this more apparent than in the fact that local commerce follows the yearly rhythms of agricultural production in Chimbal. Inventories are largest and most varied just after the coffee harvest in April and May, when growers have cash to buy merchandise and workers have earnings to spend from the coast or work in Chimbal. Business noticeably slackens after the fiesta of Santiago in late July, as migrants depart for the coast, and entrepreneurs turn their earnings to the more immediate demands of labor and fertilizer for their own coffee groves and *milpas*. Between September and December, the weekly market shrinks and merchants let inventories fall. By the end of the year, however, workers returning for the corn and coffee harvests in Chimbal once again stimulate local trade. This pattern suggests that commerce serves mostly as a way for Chimaltecos to capitalize surplus cash until they reinvest it in yearly agricultural production. This may hold true especially for those with insufficient capital to buy more land. Commercial activities in Chimbal thus represent diversification, not differentiation, of the town's basic agrarian economy. Even as merchant entrepreneurs, Chimaltecos remain firmly rooted in the immediacies of their land and town.

Behind this abiding localism rests a recognition by all Chimaltecos of their vulnerability to circumstances beyond their control. Whether of natural or human agency, the vicissitudes of their world make retrenchment an ever-present contingency in Chimalteco life, even in the best of times. As the ultimate hedge against unforeseen disaster, all Chimaltecos, from poorest migrant to richest coffee grower, aim first and foremost to plant enough *milpa* to feed their families each year. "What would I do if I lost my coffee crop and didn't have my *milpa?*" asks one of Chimbal's largest growers. Another grower, faced in 1981 with inflation, falling coffee prices, and increasing political violence, told me that Chimaltecos would survive the coming crisis because they were used to getting by with less than Ladinos. "We don't need to buy radios or wristwatches or other luxuries. About the only things that we can't do without are salt and sugar. Beyond that, a cup of coffee and a few tortillas will do." In production as well as consumption, Chimaltecos decline to enter fully into the marketplace.

As long as Chimaltecos hope to eke out a livelihood in Chimbal—and little in Guatemalan society presently tempts them to do otherwise—such retrenchment also demands the minimal goodwill of their neighbors when misfortune hits. Today's hired worker may become tomorrow's companion in adversity, and neither rich nor poor can afford the alienation of open rifts. One man's recent rise to prominence as a truck owner and merchant has transformed a profit-minded opportunist into a civic-minded leader, twice town *regidor* during the mid-1980s and an active member of the town betterment committee. His public service, however, rests on more than a newly awakened altruism. One evening, after a long string of visitors to his store, I joked with him about the hard work of tending shop. We laughed, but then more thoughtfully he said that, yes, sometimes it was bothersome. It took a great deal of patience, he added, to have people constantly stopping by, but then with patience—meaning by this, I think, a general neighborliness—people would keep coming back, and when they came, they always brought their money with them. And he smiled. Another coffee grower, who chose to invest in land and houses for his sons rather than risking the marketplace, ended one of our conversations with a reference to the prophet Isaiah's denunciations of rich men who ignored the word of God. Although no longer the active catechist that he once was, he said that rereading the Book of Isaiah had made him take more care to treat his workers fairly and to admonish his sons not to act *bravo* or *macho* because they were better off than others.

Both of these Chimaltecos, each in his own way, express the realization that, despite their wealth, the success of their endeavors depends in no small part on the goodwill of their neighbors. Without them, there would be no one to help work their coffee and corn fields or to frequent the store of one and the informal medical and dental clinic of the other. Because Chimbal is where they choose to live—and strive to belong—both remain beholden to neighbors, friends, and family, as perhaps these others depend on them. Thus, in the interstices of change and self-interested ambition, a moral economy of community persists (cf. Scott 1976)—but far from saintly altruism or enforced egalitarianism, it derives from the felt certainty that, given the world as it is, life is still better in Chimbal than anywhere else, and it behooves them to mind how best to stay there.

7

✤ The Struggle for Sovereignty ✤

In tracing patterns of economic change in Chimbal during the last fifty years, the previous chapter focused primarily on the immediacies of land and livelihood and how Chimaltecos have responded to chronic deficiencies in both. An ever-growing population, finite local resources, and limited access to wider markets and opportunities most directly shape Chimalteco ambitions and efforts, while embeddedness in their community tempers the outcome of such endeavors. Nonetheless, beyond the tacit sovereignty of Chimbal's immediate possibilities and Chimaltecos' abiding commitments to each other, the eminent domain of Guatemalan state and society motivates a more explicit sense of political sovereignty. Increasing wage-labor dependency, for example, reflects Chimalteco land shortages as well as the wider exigencies of Guatemala's plantation economy, just as enduring Chimalteco affinities affirm not only the positive bonds of local familiarity and mutuality but also the alienation and discrimination that Chimaltecos often suffer beyond the bounds of their community. Thus, the way that Chimaltecos respond to the changing dictates of life and livelihood in Chimbal remains inextricably linked to how they contend with the interests, intentions, and actions of others within a larger realm of human and historical possibilities.

In this chapter, I turn to Chimalteco concerns with political autonomy, specifically their changing relations with the Guatemalan state since the late nineteenth century. Not surprisingly, in an agrarian society such as Guatemala, land as the source of Chimalteco livelihood and the touchstone of Chimalteco sovereignty has been the focus of confrontations with the state. This nexus of land and sovereignty relates directly to two changes in the Chimalteco cargo system noted in chapter 5: first, almost all the ritual obligations formerly required of cargoholders have disappeared; and second, participation in national political parties has superseded, without entirely replacing, advancement through the hierarchy of cargos as the primary avenue to high political office in the community. This chapter examines in greater detail the role of cargo rituals in substantiating the community's sovereignty while also legitimizing individual cargoholders as worthy officials—and thus as rightful members—of the community. This "politics of consensus" based on ritual legitimation, however, eventually dissolved in the face of jurisdictional disputes over land within Chimbal, between Chimbal and neighboring towns, and with the national government, paving the way for the nominal presence of national party politics in the town.

While recent institutional changes in Chimalteco politics have all been decreed from outside the community, these events demonstrate that changing local conditions—not governmental fiat—provided much of the impetus for Chimaltecos to neglect established political conventions and then, less completely, to entertain imposed alternatives. In assessing the impact of local and national influences on political change in Chimbal, I distinguish Chimaltecos' disregard for the old and their acceptance of the new as two distinct moments in the process of change. The contingent relationship between these moments clarifies the apparent contradiction in Chimalteco political history of, on one hand, opportunistic recourse to state authority and, on the other, a continued resistance to Ladino authorities.

Cargo Rituals and Political Legitimation

Inquiry into traditional Chimalteco cargo rituals suggests that they once played a central role in legitimizing the exercise of political power within the community. Contrary to culturalist or historicist explanations of Mesoamerican cargo systems, Chimalteco cargo rituals served neither immediate administrative purposes nor wider socioeconomic ends.[1] Administratively, cargoholders participated in numerous rituals and processions, but these involved neither lengthy prayers to memorize nor complex ritual formulas to master. The daily administration of the community required little religious expertise, and most officials probably left office with no deeper religious knowledge than they had had before (cf. Wagley 1949: 98–104). Socioeconomically, cargo service entailed little leveling or redistribution of wealth within the community. Indeed, Wagley found that "the richest men of the village seldom bother with public office. . . . They have enough prestige from wealth alone" (Wagley 1949: 97–98). Although cargo rituals did exact increasingly heavy obligations from higher officeholders, Chimaltecos seldom went into debt to meet such expenses, because a man could refuse a cargo if he lacked the wherewithal to finance it, especially if he had already served lower cargos (cf. Wagley 1949: 97). Nor did cargo expenditures necessarily indebt Chimaltecos to Ladino merchants outside the community, since most ritual necessities—copal incense, sacrificial chickens and turkeys, food for ceremonial meals, and even musicians—originated locally or came from neighboring Maya towns (cf. Wagley 1941: 23).[2] Thus, although important, the socioeconomic implications of cargo rituals in Chimbal appear to have remained too specifically individual or too sociologically diffuse to account for the rituals, expenditures, and structure of the cargo system itself.

The actual rituals, however, suggest that the rationale behind them lay most immediately in the annual transfer of cargos and in the legitimation of new officeholders. According to Wagley (1949: 87–94), the heaviest ritual obligations fell at the beginning and end of officials' terms, with the *alcalde* and first *regidor* bearing the brunt of the burden. Responsibilities included expenses for ritual paraphernalia and ceremonial meals, pilgrimages to shrines in and around the pueblo, and sexual continence before performing these rituals. Upon taking office on January 1, new officials participated in four rituals during the first twenty-day Maya calendrical cycle of their term. Beginning on the first day, and every five days thereafter, the *chmaan tnam*, the most powerful shaman-diviner in the community, performed *costumbre* at the house of the first *regidor* and then led the new cargoholders on a prayer round of the church and nearby mountain shrines, where he prayed for the welfare and trustworthiness of the incoming administration. On the twenty-fifth day after taking office, the *chmaan tnam* dispatched each new cargoholder to a mountain shrine specified by his divinations. There, the new official prayed to God, Santiago, and the *witz* "for the health and welfare of the village during his year in office. . . . By early afternoon of that day, almost every important shrine of the entire *municipio* [had] been visited by the *principales*, the *Chimán* or one of the higher officials of the new village administration" (Wagley 1949: 91). Ritual meals provided by the *alcalde*, the first *mayor*, and the first *alguacil* completed the ceremony. Cargoholders made three more pilgrimages to the mountain shrines, one every five days, until the second twenty-day cycle of their term had ended. Completion of these rituals without mishap or misfortune indicated supernatural approval of the new administration, and the cargoholders were then considered officially installed (Wagley 1949: 92).

During their year in office, cargoholders, especially the *alcalde* and first *regidor*, participated in—but did not necessarily sponsor—

periodic celebrations for the saints (see chapter 5). At the end of their
term, ritual responsibilities turned again to selection of new officials. Together with the *principales*, "town elders," the *alcalde* and
first *regidor* submitted names of possible *alcaldes* to the *chmaan
tnam*, who performed divinations and eliminated nominees if their
prospects for the coming year proved unfavorable.[3] Once a candidate
was selected and approved, the *chmaan tnam* performed *costumbre*
for him and then set out on a prayer round with the other officials
to ensure "the health and success of the new *Alcalde*" (Wagley
1949: 88). The selection process ended with a ceremonial meal provided by the outgoing *alcalde* and first *regidor*. On the next two
days, the new first *regidor* and first *mayor* were selected in the same
fashion. The *principales* and outgoing *alcalde* and first *regidor* then
chose the other *regidores, mayores,* and minor officials by common
consent without ritual approval from the *chmaan tnam* (Wagley
1949: 87–89).

Traditional cargo rituals clearly focused on the selection and confirmation of Chimalteco cargoholders. Divinations, prayer rounds,
and ceremonial meals substantiated the installation of new officials:
the higher the office, the more elaborate and costly the rituals associated with it. Cargo rituals also served as "models of" as well as
"models for" the proper conduct of officials (cf. Geertz 1973: 93–94).
In their representational aspect, the collective and individual pilgrimages of new officials to all of the important shrines in the *municipio* symbolized Chimalteco bonds to the surrounding *witz* as
both the literal and figurative mountains on which local life depended. In turn, the direct association of ritualist and shrine imbued
the cargos of individual officeholders with the enduring legitimacy
embodied by the lands of the community itself. Similarly, annual
cargo rituals performed for the saints at crucial stages of the agricultural cycle and on their feast days enacted ongoing concerns as well
as local interdependencies (cf. Watanabe 1990). Through these iconic
representations—or dramatizations—cargo officials reaffirmed community boundaries and affiliations.

In their performative aspect, cargo rituals demonstrated the fit-
ness of particular individuals to hold office. They did so formally,
conventionally, and practically. In formal terms, the performance of
cargo rituals publicly confirmed individual acquiescence to conventional form, regardless of personal belief in the practices themselves
(cf. Rappaport 1979a). Significantly, successful completion of cargo
rituals depended less on the minutiae of correct performance or sincerity of purpose than on strict sexual continence the night before
performing *costumbre*—an unequivocal subordination of individual

will to conventional constraint (cf. Wagley 1949: 92). In conventional terms, omniscient saint and *witz* tacitly corroborated the intentions and actions of individual cargoholders: if an official failed in his responsibilities, the gods would eventually strike him down or send misfortune to the community (Wagley 1949: 92). Conversely, if he passed his cargo without mishap, the cargoholder had proven worthy. In other words, the capricious nature of Chimalteco deities left the propriety of incumbent officials forever problematic, contingent only on the absence of any major calamities. Perhaps this uncertainty encouraged officials to behave appropriately—or to worry more about their conduct. Finally, in practical terms, regardless of the formal and conventional sureties conveyed through successfully completed cargo rituals, the very real economic and personal sacrifices demanded of higher officials served as collateral against possible improprieties. On one hand, the ability to finance an important cargo suggested managerial skills on which the community might rely (cf. Farriss 1984: 250); on the other, the greater the influence wielded by an official, the heavier his ritual responsibilities. While self-sacrifice never guaranteed that a cargoholder would respect the privileges of office, it did increase the cost to any individual who might abuse them.

The timing and performance of traditional cargo rituals thus reveal their intrinsic political rationale, whatever their extrinsic social or economic consequences. Through these rituals, local officials—especially the *alcalde* and first *regidor*—demonstrated their worthiness to serve in public office by reaffirming the local sovereignty and conventions of the community that they administered. The need for ritual sanctification of both officeholder and office within the community as a whole, however, does not explain what motivated individual Chimaltecos to serve cargos in the first place. Given the high expense and personal inconvenience of office, why did Chimaltecos bother to carry cargos at all? Appeal to some collective Chimalteco consciousness, to human desires for power and prestige, or to the dictates of colonial or capitalist modes of production provide little insight into why such global realities should have taken shape in precisely this way in this particular place. Analysis demands further inquiry into the nature of the political power and the practical privileges that cargo rituals legitimized.

The Need to Serve and the Objective of Power

One of the principal tasks of traditional cargoholders in Chimbal appears to have been administration of the town's communal lands. As

noted in chapter 2, shortly after the Conquest, the Spanish resettled
the Maya into new Christian communities, each granted one square
league (about 6.5 mi²) of *ejido*, or common land, to be administered
by local officials for the use of the settlement's inhabitants. In addition to the *ejidos*, Wagley notes, "Many inaccessible villages also
had under their jurisdiction certain areas called *baldíos* or
'uncleared' land, which were often cleared and used without legal
title by many men of the village and were thus frequently incorpo-
rated according to ancient native procedure into the common lands
of the village, increasing considerably the size of the communal
holdings" (1941: 59). Through payment of a yearly rent called the
censo enfitéutico, members of the community received usufruct
rights to specific plots of land that could be passed on to their heirs.
Land remained inalienable, however, and reverted to the community
if it stood idle for too long or if rent went unpaid. One of Wagley's
informants assured him that until the late nineteenth century, "men
applied to the *Alcalde* for the right to use common land for milpa
and were assigned as much as they could plant. Year after year these
men planted the same plots paying *censo* to the *Alcalde*. Sons divided the plots of their fathers and continued to cultivate them, applying to the *Alcalde* for the right to clear more land if necessary"
(Wagley 1941: 61).

As the highest-ranking official, the *alcalde* regulated access to
community lands, ensuring that no man held more than he and his
sons could work, although wealthier Chimaltecos could evidently
claim more land by paying larger rents (cf. Wagley 1941: 72).[4] Because the Guatemalan government assessed the *censo enfitéutico*
on the basis of community landholdings as a whole without regard
to the actual distribution of land within the community, the *alcalde*
could exercise final authority in any dispute that arose over plots
left too long in fallow.

Far from empty prestige, then, the office of *alcalde* involved administrative control over town lands. This responsibility, and the
real or perceived dangers of misusing it, in turn suggest that the hierarchical, rotating structure of the cargo system served as a simple,
reliable mechanism for delegating and circumscribing the *alcalde*'s
authority. To begin with, the need to pass lower-ranking cargos established a public record by which to gauge the suitability of prospective *alcaldes*. Second, the age-grading inherent in both the requi-
sites of previous service and the escalating economic and personal
costs of higher cargos meant that only older men, hopefully more
experienced and responsible, would ever qualify for consideration in
the first place. Finally, the yearly rotation of cargos kept any single

individual from wielding power for too long, while it also produced a surfeit of former *alcaldes,* including the *principales,* whose proven integrity could—and often did—serve to safeguard the public interest (cf. Wagley 1949: 96).

Thus, administrative power over the community's common land could certainly have motivated ambitious Chimaltecos to undertake a cargo career, at the same time that the structure of the cargo system effectively regulated the pursuit, as well as exercise, of that power. Not all men, however, possessed the requisite skills or ambition to become *alcalde,* yet nearly all carried at least one cargo during their lifetimes. Indeed, Wagley (1949: 97) found that "informants could remember only two [men] without at least a year of service, one an imbecile, and Diego Sánchez, who was born blind." Any man who neglected cargo service ran the risk of being chosen as *pixhkaal* in his old age, his duty of sweeping the plaza every few days an ignominious public reminder of a lifelong lack of civic spirit. The tacit presumption that every man carry cargos suggests a motivation besides the willful pursuit of political power or social prestige. As argued in chapter 5, the most obvious—and perhaps most enduring—social meaning of cargoholding appears to have been to define, recognize, and enact membership in the community. Even politically unambitious men thus would have reason to carry lower, less onerous cargos, as long as they felt the need to affirm their proper standing within the community.

In this regard, I would argue that just as the traditional cargo system defined access to administrative power, so it also defined access to community resources—particularly the common land that the *alcalde* administered. By unequivocally distinguishing those who served from those who did not, cargoholding could restrict the right to use town lands to those who had fulfilled their public obligations. Given the overwhelming importance of land in Chimalteco life, willing service to the saints in the church or civil service at the town hall not only demonstrated a man's personal acumen and public ambition but also legitimized his claim to livelihood within the community. This suggests that rather than epitomizing some singular ethnic solidarity or cohesive social conformity, the need to serve in the traditional Chimalteco cargo system comprised a multiplicity of individual interests and motivations: for some, cargo service initiated lifelong public careers; for others, it constituted the minimal obligatory dues of social participation. Despite such diversity, however, participation in the cargo system still precipitated an abiding sense of common concern regarding a resource crucial to all Chimaltecos—namely, the town's communal land.

In organizationally elegant fashion, the traditional cargo system in Chimbal appears to have bounded as well as ordered the community by regulating access to both public resources and political power. Not incidentally, it also provided older, well-established—and wealthier—men with control over the public life of the community. The personal repute derived from carrying cargos thus served neither solely as an end in itself nor as empty compensation for Chimalteco marginality in Guatemalan society and economy. Instead, it substantiated individual claims to livelihood within the community, while also legitimizing the authority of certain individuals to administer community lands and affairs.

If the Chimalteco cargo system and the diverse commitments of Chimaltecos to serve in it hinged on the fundamental importance of communal land in Chimbal, then the traditional logic behind cargo-holding and ritual expenditures undoubtedly began to unravel as local patterns of landholding changed from communal to individual tenure beginning early in the twentieth century. To assess the impact of this on Chimalteco sovereignty, the individualization of land ownership must be examined in more detail.

The Demise of Communal Land Tenure, 1879–1950

Thus far, I have dealt with the traditional Chimalteco cargo system in terms of its internal logic of ritual legitimation and administrative allocation of power and property within the community, especially regarding the appropriateness of local men to serve cargos. Beyond these immediate concerns of land and legitimacy, however, an intrusive state presence also fundamentally shaped the Chimalteco cargo system. For all his ritual legitimation within the community, the *alcalde* remained a functionary of the Guatemalan state, obliged to carry out any decree handed down by Ladino officials for taxes, public works, forced labor, and the like (Wagley 1949: 101–102). This, of course, constantly relativized the prerogatives of power brokers like the *principales* or *chmaan tnam* and reminded all Chimaltecos how easily the *alcalde* could betray the community to outsiders. Fear of co-optation by Ladino officials reinforced Chimalteco preferences for honorable men as *alcaldes* who would minimize outside involvements. Such was the *alcalde* in 1937: "a quiet conservative man; he speaks little Spanish and is not, therefore, very friendly with the *ladinos*. He does not have a reputation for chasing women; thus his *costumbres* are 'good.' He is not *bravo* (aggressive, mean, or tough)" (Wagley 1949: 96–97). At the same time, such stoic Chimalteco respectability made *alcaldes* ineffective in contesting

Ladino dictates or divining Ladino machinations. Thus, any Chimalteco rationale behind cargos and cargoholding necessarily entailed not only local concerns but also the dilemma of a community sovereignty bound to the very state authority that Chimaltecos sought to evade in the first place.[5] Not surprisingly, this ongoing tension between state and community also turned on questions of jurisdiction over local lands.

As I have described it, the traditional Chimalteco cargo system rested on two crucial factors. First, it presumed the integrity of community lands and the autonomy of local officials to administer them. Second, the distribution of communal land, based on the needs and capacities of individual households to work it, necessitated a ready surplus of land. For much of Chimalteco history—or at least from the mid-1600s to the late 1800s—these two conditions held relatively true (see chapter 2). Only in the latter half of the nineteenth century did communal landholding towns like Chimbal begin to erode in the face of internal and external pressures. Increasing population and growing economic differentiation within Maya communities weakened their former self-sufficiency, and the expansion of commercial agriculture following the triumph of the Liberals under Justo Rufino Barrios in 1871 further eroded Maya autonomy with new demands for land and labor (Smith 1984b; 1990b; LaFarge 1940).

In perhaps the most significant development of the Liberal program, the Barrios government revoked the *censo enfitéutico* in 1877, requiring that rents or taxes on land be paid on an individual basis: "All lands were henceforth to be held by individual title only; arrangements were set up by which people who had held land by rent could acquire private title. Efforts were made to distribute the common lands among the dwellers of the municipalities" (Wagley 1941: 60). Although communal land tenure was not abolished outright (McCreery 1988: 239–240; 1990), protracted legal struggles often jeopardized the "uncleared" *baldío* lands that many Maya communities had traditionally held through usufruct, especially if Ladinos wanted this land for commercial coffee production.

While various forms of communal land tenure survived in many parts of western Guatemala well into the twentieth century (cf. Stadelman 1940: 102), Chimaltecos became aware quite early of the need to acquire legal title to their land, even though its negligible commercial value left them little to fear from Ladino encroachments.[6] On May 19, 1879, a delegation of Chimaltecos led by Diego Carrillo, the municipal *síndico*, petitioned officials in Huehuetenango for formal title to their municipal lands.

I, Diego Carrillo, *síndico* of the *municipio* of Santiago Chimaltenango . . . , declare that since our pueblo lacks the lands necessary for our fields, and not having title for even the *ejido* lands
that by law belong to us, I come now in representation of my
pueblo to claim formally the public lands that since time immemorial we have possessed in good faith. . . .

For the *síndico* who does not know how to sign his name, it is
done by the secretary of the same pueblo, Juan Carillo (AGCA:
ST, *paquete* 12,#2; my translation).[7]

Under oath, four other Chimaltecos—Juan Hernández, Pedro Lopez,
Sebastián Lopez, and Diego Aguilar—all aged sixty-five or seventy,
delineated the boundaries of Chimbal's *ejido*, adding that "the land
is only good for cultivation of maize."

Disputes with neighboring *municipios* over the boundaries claimed
by Chimbal rapidly ensued. On June 20, 1879, San Juan Atitán pro-
tested that lands included in the Chimalteco declaration actually
belonged to them and had been claimed as part of their *ejido* in October 1873. In November 1879, San Pedro Necta claimed the *aldea*
of Niyá as theirs, saying that they had a title to it. Similarly, the village of San Martín, now an *aldea* of Todos Santos (cf. Gall 1983: 98),
disputed Chimalteco possession of the *aldea* of Tujumuc on the
grounds that they had had it "for two hundred and nine years." In
December 1879, Chimbal denied these counterclaims and asked
that a surveyor establish the proper boundaries, since a search of the
archives in Guatemala City on December 15, 1879, had revealed
that neither "the pueblo of Santiago Chimaltenango nor that of San
Pedro Necta have the lands that they possess measured or titled."
The only document pertaining to either *municipio* stated that "the
pueblo of Santiago Chimaltenango and that of Todos Santos Cuchumatán requested protection of their lands in 1670" (AGCA: ST, *paquete* 12,#2; cf. *paquete* 1,#1).

A surveyor was commissioned on April 27, 1880, and the survey
of Chimbal's *ejido* was completed in June of that same year by Juan
María Ordoñez. In his report, he wrote:

It is the case that the interested parties possess much more land
[than the one square league of *ejido* to which they were legally
entitled] that they would have never consented to have had only
partially measured, since they assured me that other neighboring
pueblos would then augment their possessions with less right [to
the land] than they; that the poor quality of the land on the one
hand and the farmers who are its only inhabitants on the other

make it absolutely necessary that the former be of sufficient and considerable extent so that there be enough for everyone. For these reasons, I thought it proper to make an inspection of all land that the Chimaltecos possess, measuring their extent and noting it in the survey. (AGCA: ST, *paquete* 12,#2; my translation)

This initial survey included 38 *caballerías*, 45 *manzanas* of *ejido* (17.3 km²) and 119 *caballerías*, 59 *manzanas* of *baldío* (53.6 km²). A civil engineer (*ingeniero revisor*) reviewed the survey on May 5, 1883, noting that it amounted to slightly more than the "one square league" of *ejido* legally allotted to the community. The municipal land title, however, was not formally granted until September 10, 1891. This title ceded to the jurisdiction of Chimbal 1,746.38 hectares of *ejido* (17.4 km²) and 2,925.56 hectares of *baldío* (29.2 km²). No mention of the 24.4 square kilometers of *baldío* lost to Chimbal appears in the final land title, but Wagley later noted that "Chimaltecos told me that (about 1900) San Pedro and San Juan took some of their terrain" (1941: 56n).[8]

Examination of this municipal title suggests two important facts. First, although Chimaltecos obviously recognized the importance of titling their land, their initial efforts centered on acquisition of a municipal title, despite national pressures against communal land tenure. While inconclusive, this suggests that Chimaltecos were attempting to preserve an extant system of communal lands, a possibility reinforced by the fact that in 1893 no Ladinos lived in Chimbal, and even by 1921 there were still only twenty (DGE 1923). In 1937, Wagley's older informants recalled that in their fathers' time before the turn of the century, "there was much more *monte* (brushland) and one could always get permission from the *Alcalde* to clear it" (Wagley 1941: 61), again suggesting that a system of usufruct rights to communally administered lands apparently still held sway.

The title also reveals that competition for land with neighboring Maya communities was nearly as intense as contention between Maya claims and Ladino commercial interest elsewhere in the Cuchumatán Highlands (cf. LaFarge 1947: 3–5; Davis 1970; McCreery 1988). As early as the eighteenth century, Maya communities in this region had resorted to litigation to defend their lands from each other (cf. Lovell 1983a: 223–226), but as land became increasingly scarce toward the end of the nineteenth century, such struggles intensified. In this region of little commercial value, population growth appears to have most directly motivated this escalating competition for land. Compared to preconquest levels, population densities in western Guatemala remained relatively low throughout the colonial period (Lovell and Swezey 1982). After reaching a nadir in the mid–seventeenth century, Maya in the Cuchumatán Highlands began to make a slow but sporadic recovery from the devastation wrought by Old World infectious diseases introduced at the Spanish conquest. Even late in the eighteenth century, however, the smallpox epidemic of 1780–1781 carried off nearly 15 percent of the region's Maya population, while typhus similarly ravaged the Cuchumatanes repeatedly between 1796 and 1810 (Lovell 1988). Despite such setbacks, the population of Chimbal nearly tripled during the nineteenth century, from 502 in 1797 to 1,345 in 1893. By 1937, Wagley estimated the number of Chimaltecos at about 1,500 (1941: 9; but cf. Wagley 1949: 11 for a slightly lower estimate).[9]

A growing population placed mounting pressure on the surplus lands essential to traditional Chimalteco practices of communal land distribution. A transformation in local patterns of landholding did indeed result, such that by 1937, Wagley found that almost all Chimaltecos held their lands privately, although most men still lacked formal titles to their plots (1941: 63–64). This transition from communal to individual ownership, however, did not happen overnight. Under the *censo enfitéutico*, Chimaltecos had exercised individual and heritable usufruct rights to land that only denied them the power of alienation. As Wagley (1941: 62) observed, "The plots which had been used by families for several generations were what later became their private property through titles." As increasing numbers of Chimaltecos brought nearly all the arable land in the *municipio* under individual usufruct rights, the old system of allocation, use, and redistribution slowly crystallized, leaving younger generations dependent on fields inherited from their parents and on buying and selling already existing properties. Larger landholders sometimes sold or gave land to poorer Chimaltecos or to Sanjuaneros in exchange for serving their turns in the forced labor drafts that prevailed until the mid-1930s (cf. Wagley 1949: 102; Jones 1940: 151–158). Older Chimaltecos told me that these laborers could occasionally use their token wages from forced labor to purchase more land upon completing their work contracts. Long after the transition to private ownership had begun, however, Chimaltecos still considered the municipal land title more important than titles for individual plots, and they frowned upon the sale of local lands to outsiders (Wagley 1941: 62, 65).[10]

Finding that in 1937 many Chimalteco men claimed to have bought most of the plots that they then possessed, Wagley concluded that alienation of land probably began during the first decade of this century (1941: 65), and examination of municipal land records confirms this supposition. The oldest municipal records in Chimbal date only to 1948, the year that Chimbal became a *municipio* again after thirteen years as an *aldea* of San Pedro Necta.[11] During their administrative subservice to San Pedro, most Chimaltecos refused to go there to register land or land transactions (cf. Wagley 1941: 64), but once Chimbal regained municipal status, townspeople readily registered their holdings at their own town hall. Nearly all the ninety documents in the *Actas de la Municipalidad* for 1948 deal with the sale, inheritance, or titling of land. At least thirteen documents represent retroactive claims involving transactions dating from four to forty-seven years previously. Several bear specific mention.

Acta 38 involved a dispute over terrain that the owner claimed to have bought from a Sanjuanero in 1908. In *Acta* 42, an elderly Chimalteco bequeathed land to his children that he had "possessed in a public and peaceful manner these last thirty years," including a plot that for forty-seven years he had "possessed peacefully without interruption." *Acta* 69 constituted a retroactive land claim in which a witness, aged eighty-five, verified that the owner, aged fifty-six, had bought land near the cemetery in 1915 and had "planted it each year in *milpa* without interruption."

The seventy-eight documents of the *Actas de la Municipalidad* for 1949 continue in much the same manner. The vast majority are petitions for "certified copies" of property transactions and land claims, although they seldom specify the precise extent of the plots involved. Instead, acknowledgement by the owners of adjacent fields sufficed to establish property boundaries, implying that, much as it had in Wagley's time, "public recognition, not documents" still constituted final proof of ownership (1941: 64). In one such document, a woman's neighbors testified that "she is the legitimate owner of a plot of land that was inherited from her deceased father . . . who died more than ten years ago without leaving her title; but her surrounding neighbors affirm their recognition of her claim and beseech that the title be given." Only one document, *Acta* 47 of 1949, mentions any previous title: a man bequeathed to his child a "lot with a small house, bought from one Carlos Diaz, now deceased, according to a document at hand that was granted to him in this office on October 23, 1923." In 1950, the number of *actas* fell to fifty-five, again the majority recording land transactions "that guarantee the holder as legitimate owner." In 1980, the municipal secretary assured me that most of the *actas* he drew up still dealt with land.

An examination of changes in Chimalteco patterns of landholding since the late nineteenth century suggests that, despite legislative attacks on communal land tenure beginning in 1877, the exercise of individual rights of alienation in Chimbal coincided more closely with local circumstances than with national law. The transition appears to have fallen into three phases. First, a community-wide response to encroachments by neighboring *municipios* resulted in a petition for a municipal title in 1879, which was finally granted in 1891. During this time, titling disputes—if not conflicts over land— occurred mainly between communities rather than within them, and according to Wagley's older informants, unoccupied communal land was still available. The second phase, perhaps under way by 1900 but certainly by 1910, involved increasing alienation of land within the community as the population grew. Gradual incorporation and cultivation of most arable municipal lands froze a system of usufruct rights into a fixed pattern of individual landholdings, with acquisition by purchase replacing grants of uncleared land from the *alcalde*. The third phase was observed by Wagley in 1937, in which competition for land within the *municipio* transformed conventions of possession from usufruct rights established by consensus to litigation based on legal titles (cf. Davis 1970: 86). This phase culminated in the late 1940s and early 1950s, when essentially all Chimaltecos registered their land. By that time, the population of Chimbal had reached 1,818 (DGE 1953), due largely to decreasing mortality rates beginning in the 1940s (cf. Early 1982: 172–174). Such accelerated growth, rapidly outstripping the capacities of local lands and agricultural techniques, could have only further encouraged Chimaltecos to assure claim to their shrinking plots through acquisition of legal titles.[12]

At the same time, this gradual Chimalteco recourse to municipal and individual titles demonstrated the increasing penetration of the Guatemalan state into local life. True, the protracted transition to legal titles during some seventy years suggests that national legislative decrees provided the means by which to adopt new patterns of landholding, while local conditions established the motivations. Nonetheless, these means, enacted by national legislation and conditioned by economic demands for land and labor from commercial coffee plantations, channeled local claims to land in institutionally specific ways and steadily usurped the authority of Chimalteco cargo officials to control the emerging patterns of ownership and work. In seeking legal titles—whether municipal or individual—to safeguard their lands, Chimaltecos in effect abdicated sovereignty over that land by appealing to state authority to validate their claims. Town sovereignty fell increasingly to the mercy of Ladino bureaucrats and their lackeys, as evidenced by the loss of nearly half the town's *baldíos* in the 1891 land title.

In defending what they saw as their indisputable rights to land and livelihood, Chimaltecos abrogated the dictates of communal land tenure that had once motivated—and justified—participation in the cargo system. Assailed from without and within, the sovereignty of the Chimalteco cargo system became not simply a matter of retrenchment, but a question of whether it would survive at all. I now turn to just how this sovereignty broke down and what remnants of it have survived.

The Vicissitudes of Legitimacy, 1937–1960

By the end of the nineteenth century, the two conditions on which the traditional Chimalteco cargo system depended no longer applied. An encroaching state presence had undermined local administrative autonomy, demonstrated by Chimbal's ability to title barely two-thirds of the land that it had originally claimed. Similarly, population growth had depleted reserves of uncleared communal lands and left Chimaltecos dependent on private land transactions rather than on public allocations from the *alcalde.* Although national land legislation had not immediately transformed local patterns of landholding and authority, it established the legal grounds whereby individual claims eventually came to supersede the traditional jurisdiction of the *alcalde.* Successive regimes of the Guatemalan government further eroded Chimalteco sovereignty.

During the 1930s, dictator Jorge Ubico centralized the national government by replacing local *alcaldes* with a system of rotating municipal *intendentes* and departmental *jefes políticos*—Ladino officals answerable to the president rather than to local constituencies. Although for a time Chimbal had its own resident *intendente,* the effect of his presence on the community probably remained minimal. On one hand, lacking a local Ladino elite—or more precisely, any Ladino population at all until well into this century—Chimbal took little part in regional political interest groups, let alone national ones (cf. Smith 1984b: 208–209). On the other hand, as a Ladino as well as outsider, the *intendente* probably administered the town indirectly. "In practice, the *intendente* as often as not found it easier to work through . . . already existent organizations [such as cargo systems or *cofradías* headed by local community leaders]. This was especially true where the Indians were predominantly monolingual, and there were few Ladinos in the community. As a result, the structure of the Indian towns was not so immediately affected as was that of the Ladino communities" (Adams 1970: 179).

A more dramatic instance of local subservience to the Guatemalan state came when Chimbal lost its status as a *municipio* on December 11, 1935 (cf. Gall 1980: 686). Forty-odd years before, the state had deprived the town of a substantial amount of land, but this second, seemingly arbitrary decree of the national government in effect dispossessed Chimaltecos of their lands entirely by reducing Chimbal to an *aldea* of nearby San Pedro Necta. Prompted by fear for town lands as well as by local pride, the *principales* delegated five Chimaltecos to go to Guatemala City to petition for the return of Chimbal's independence. To lead the group, they chose a young man named Diego Martín because, despite his youth, he spoke Spanish fluently and "was not afraid of *ladinos*" (Wagley 1949: 9).

After an eight-day trek to the capital, the delegation met with the minister of the interior, who, impressed with their sincerity, "issued an order that their title, their government flag, and their picture of the president be restored to their own native officials, whom they might continue to select as before" (Wagley 1949: 9). Although a moral victory for Chimbal, the episode underscored the waning ability of the *principales* to defend the community against outside interference. The town remained administratively beholden to Ladino officials in San Pedro, and—perhaps even more telling—young Diego Martín returned a hero, having accomplished what his elders could not. As younger, more worldly Chimaltecos proved better at dealing with Ladino officials, the traditional relationship between age and authority implicit in the hierarchical ranking of cargos became increasingly problematic (cf. Brintnall 1979: 142–143).

Despite these encroachments, however, the actual structure of the Chimalteco cargo system remained fairly stable until after the Revolution of 1944. With the nearest *intendente* a two-hour walk away in San Pedro Necta, Chimalteco cargo officials retained a semblance of day-to-day autonomy long after losing their legal authority to direct community affairs. The *alcalde* continued to adjudicate local land disputes and civil cases, legitimizing his authority in the traditional manner through performance of cargo rituals (cf. Wagley 1949).

Nonetheless, abiding concerns for land within the community eroded even the semblance of administrative autonomy as Chimaltecos came to realize the power of legal land titles. By the late 1930s, the inevitable conflict between traditional concepts of possession through consensus and legal ownership through title finally erupted:

All informants agreed that until a few years ago, all land disputes were brought before the Indian *Alcalde* and settled by him;
such cases rarely came to the attention of the ladino officials.
Lately, however, with the realization that the government is
more powerful than the local authorities, added to the growing
native interest in private titles, recourse is sometimes taken
to the government officials in San Pedro Necta or Huehuetenango. . . . At San Pedro weight is put on titles and bills of sale;
people with titles for land go there knowing full well that they
will win the case. (Wagley 1941: 65)

Although documents still carried little weight with the *alcalde* in
Chimbal, those without titles were at an obvious disadvantage if the
dispute went before Ladino officials. Wagley cites an extreme case:
"At the death of their father, one brother (who is *muy listo pero muy
bravo*—very ready or smart but very aggressive) rushed off to Huehuetenango and succeeded in registering and obtaining documents
for almost all of his father's lands, thus robbing his brothers of their
share of the inheritance. There was nothing the local Indian *Alcalde*
could do about it. At any dispute, the man with the title hurries to
San Pedro and secures a decision over the *Alcalde*'s head because he
carries documentary proof" (Wagley 1941: 66). Such opportunism, of
course, compelled others to do likewise to protect their land.

Ironically, because control and accumulation of land remained so
central to Chimalteco life, defiance of traditional conventions of
ownership and challenges to the authority of the *alcalde* made a certain degree of sense both conventionally and pragmatically, especially if these actions succeeded in securing land rights. As with the
varying motives to serve cargos, a multiplicity of interests—both
competing and complementary, public and private—bound Chimaltecos in a common, if at times contentious, social nexus, but not
into a unitary conformity. Abiding concerns for land, and not necessarily growing anomie or an upsurge of greedy individualism, perhaps best explained the growing subversion of the local status quo.

By the Revolution of 1944, the scope and exercise of political authority in Chimbal had come to favor younger men more familiar
with Ladino ways. Juan de Dios Rosales, who visited Chimbal for
research on Maya diet for the Carnegie Institution, found that many
Chimaltecos took out certificates of citizenship and voted in the
elections of 1944. A few younger men even campaigned for their
candidate, Juan José Arévalo (Wagley 1949: 133–134). Significantly,
Rosales noted that "several Indians from Chimaltenango went to
the reception for Dr. Arévalo, candidate for the Presidency of the Re-

public. One of them succeeded in speaking to the Doctor, asking him to restore the *aldea* (Chimaltenango) to the status of a *municipio.* . . . Dr. Arévalo said that he would make Chimaltenango a *municipio* again if he became President. The Indian was very satisfied and returned to tell all his companions" (Wagley 1949: 124). Arévalo won the election, and on February 2, 1948, Chimbal became a *municipio* again (Gall 1980: 686). A commission collected a tax of Q1.50 from each household to pay the necessary fees and went to Guatemala City to secure the decree. One elderly Chimalteco recalled that the governor of Huehuetenango came to Chimbal for the celebration, and everyone got drunk. "It was a happy day when Chimbal became a *municipio* again!" he assured me.

The men who now dominated the political life of the community no longer aspired to become *principales* through lifelong service in the cargo system. Indeed, three of them ceased to carry cargos at all, instead investing in mules to haul coffee to market for the plantations near San Pedro Necta (cf. Wagley 1941: 46, 79; 1949: 9, 97–98, 129, 131, 134). An element of class conflict undoubtedly entered this confrontation between the old regime of the *principales*, predicated on communal land tenure and ritual legitimation, and the new order, focused on private land, hired labor, and capital investment in mules, trade, and transport (see chapter 6; cf. Arias 1990). The interests of both groups, however, remained neither absolutely nor diametrically opposed, because the new Chimalteco *políticos* could not simply rely on self-interested profits or making common cause with Ladino merchants and bureaucrats for their power. Their influence still lay in brokering relations between Chimbal and these outsiders through their relative familiarity with Ladino language and customs. Like the *principales* before them, the new *políticos* remained rooted in the community. Rather than appeal to ritual sanctification from God, saints, and *witz*, however, they depended on pragmatic political skills and their neighbors' growing realization that the community's fate depended more on an ability to appease distant bureaucrats in Guatemala City than on placation of capricious or unseen deities.

The upheavals of land reform and peasant politicization following the Revolution of 1944 (cf. Adams 1972; Handy 1990) undoubtedly furthered the triumph of the new political order in Chimbal. Greater contact with government officials and encouragement to participate in national affairs attracted a number of younger men into local politics. Nonetheless, without any sizable Ladino or Chimalteco landholdings to denounce or defend, townspeople apparently acquired little enthusiasm for radical agrarian politics. Instead, the advent of electoral party politics in Chimbal during the early 1950s hastened the demise of old modes of political legitimation. By 1956, when Wagley made a brief visit to Chimbal, he found that the "recently elected" *alcalde* and first *regidor* had begun to neglect their ritual duties, prompting older Chimaltecos to complain that "the young men had blundered by having elected" officials who spent too much time in private pursuits and not enough attending to the public welfare (Wagley 1957: xxiii–xxiv).

The electoral process had abrogated cargo rituals by publicly endowing local officials with bureaucratic rather than ritual legitimation. At the same time, this meant that the *alcalde* no longer acted as absolute giver of Chimalteco law—an official whose power had to be carefully circumscribed by ritual sanctions and whose integrity rested on the conventional confirmation of ritual performances. Instead, he had become the civil servant of Ladino laws. By the end of the 1950s, only those cargo rituals with social import remained (see chapter 5). For example, an elderly Chimalteco proudly told me of the Q200.00 that he had spent as first *regidor* in 1952, but when his son served as *regidor* eight years later, he only had to sponsor a ritual meal at the beginning and end of his term.

Undermined by local and national circumstances, as well as demographic growth and institutional alternatives, the sovereignty of the old Chimalteco cargo system disintegrated. Encroachments by the state vitiated the political rationale of cargo rituals, but equally important, service in the cargo system had ceased to guarantee access to land within the community. The individualization of town lands lessened the need to define community boundaries through cargoholding, while also nullifying the pragmatic motivation for paying the costs of cargo service. As the cost of cargoholding came to exceed the practical returns in land or power that service had formerly offered, reduction of ritual expenditures—if not elimination of the cargos themselves—became inevitable. Significantly, the loss of cargo rituals in Chimbal coincided closely with the advent of routine titling of local lands.

In contrast to the development of private land ownership, however, the conditions leading to the disappearance of old forms of political legitimation assured neither immediate acceptance nor a clear understanding of national party politics. This fundamental inconsistency in Chimalteco political life persists today, manifested in a continuing ambivalence toward the Guatemalan state and its Ladino functionaries.

The Politics of Marginality, 1960–1980

By the 1960s, Chimalteco politics had outwardly come to conform to national practices. When I lived in Chimbal during the late 1970s, each of the four major Guatemalan political parties had a Chimalteco representative to recruit party candidates and organize campaigns for municipal office. On election day, voters cast ballots for parties rather than individual candidates. The winning party filled the offices of *alcalde*, first and fifth *consejal*, and *síndico*, while the losers divided the remaining posts of second, third, and fourth *consejal*. All officials served four-year terms in accordance with national law. Despite outward appearances, however, national politics inspired little interest in Chimbal, and few if any ideological differences separated local candidates. Voters were more swayed by a candidate's personal qualities and local affiliations than by party line. During campaigns, the incumbent party simply defended its record against the opposition parties' usually justified accusations of bureaucratic sloth. In 1955, for instance, the municipal government identified its most pressing problems as lack of vehicular access to the town and construction of school buildings (Gall 1980: 687). Twenty-five years later, major campaign issues still centered on completing a bus road into Chimbal and the need for more classrooms in the school.

Such political indolence reflects more than a venerable tradition of empty campaign promises. First, despite the new mode of selection, the actual duties of the *alcalde* have changed very little since Wagley's time. Although affiliation with a political party is essential for nomination, such ties seldom matter once an *alcalde* takes office. As in the past, the *alcalde*'s principal responsibilities involve civil administration and keeping the peace. He authorizes licenses to vendors in the weekly market and signs land titles; he jails offenders for minor infractions—usually drunkenness—and even in fairly serious criminal cases his judgment prevails as long as litigants agree not to appeal to a higher court. Because Chimbal still lacks a substation of the National Police, the *alcalde* remains the town's only legal authority and thus retains a certain degree of independence in his rulings. Chimaltecos' abiding mistrust of outside authority reinforces this fragile autonomy; if an *alcalde* refers too many disputes to Huehuetenango, litigants try to resolve their differences privately.[13] Thus, the *alcalde*'s actual political involvements rarely, if ever, extend much beyond the formalities of getting elected to office.

A second reason for the dormant state of Chimalteco politics lies in the military apparatus that has dominated Guatemala since the CIA-sponsored Counterrevolution of 1954 (cf. Immerman 1982). Not only do party affiliations make little difference in Chimalteco elections, but nationally the Guatemalan military continues to exercise final say regardless of which party wins at the polls (cf. Black et al. 1984). Through no fault of their own, Chimalteco party coordinators can neither effectively nor consistently elicit favor from a government intended essentially to command, not serve. The frustrations of an intractable Ladino bureaucracy in turn reaffirm the skepticism of other Chimaltecos for party politics and national affairs. In a real sense, then, control over the formal electoral process fails to give Chimalteco *políticos* an authority equivalent to that of the old *principales*. Caught between self-absorbed Ladino bureaucrats and politicians, a wary Chimalteco constituency, and their own limited means and local aspirations, Chimalteco politicians have become marginalized rather than indispensable to their community. As one Chimalteco commented, "Those *políticos* earn a salary during the elections, and that's reason enough [for their involvement in politics]." An intrusive yet unresponsive national government thus effectively undermines the credibility of local politicians and leaves their constituents politically impassive.

A third reason for political disinterest in Chimbal stems from the nature of public service itself, which discourages most Chimaltecos from seeking high office. For one thing, actively soliciting the approval of others runs counter to common experience, and few readily submit to the public scrutiny of campaigning. For those who do, service still begins with the lower cargos, even though these no longer prepare politically ambitious Chimaltecos for the necessities of campaigning or the realities of office. Ironically, those most familiar with bureaucratic procedures, usually learned in the local agricultural cooperative or in various church organizations (see chapter 8), often decline the burdens of public office for more rewarding private pursuits. Also, the time commitment of being *alcalde* is more than most Chimaltecos can afford. During his four-year term, an *alcalde* has to hire others to work his fields and must let most personal endeavors languish because of his duties at the town hall each day.

As the ranking public official in the *municipio*, the *alcalde* holds legal responsibility for the welfare of the community and, unlike party coordinators, is often criticized for the shortcomings of his programs. Although Chimaltecos generally mistrust the government and suspect that *alcaldes* might betray the community to outsiders, they can also be quick to criticize *alcaldes* for failing to use their position and power to benefit the community. In other words,

the more clearly the *alcalde* becomes a creature of the national government in the eyes of the community, the more vulnerable he becomes to charges of incompetence. Unfortunately, election to office
seldom transforms *alcaldes* into savvy bureaucrats or masterful
politicians. They still suffer the same barriers of language, culture,
and ethnic discrimination that leave any Chimalteco bewildered
and frustrated by the complex, impersonal structure and indifferent
policies of the national government. Many townspeople consider
the job of *alcalde* a thankless task, one that destroys the man who
holds it. Alcoholism appears to be an occupational hazard: the mo-
notony of being at the town hall every day and the frequent lack of
pressing tasks evidently makes the proffered bottle of a favor-seeker
or passing acquaintance often too welcome to ignore.

Despite the introduction of national political parties into the community, the realities of Guatemalan politics minimize local interest
and involvement in national affairs. Similarly, as the young *políticos*
of the 1940s and 1950s have aged, former associations between age
and authority have reasserted themselves. Consequently, throughout the 1960s and 1970s, Chimaltecos continued to elect middle-
aged or older men as *alcaldes,* preferring individuals of traditional
dress and outlook who largely maintained the status quo. This pattern finally changed in April 1980, when a Chimalteco in his early
thirties won the election for *alcalde.* During the campaign, an alliance between two of the major national parties, the Partido Revolucionario (PR) and the Partido Institucional Democrático (PID), did
little to help Chimalteco party coordinators find candidates willing
to run. Growing political violence in the country undoubtedly reinforced natural Chimalteco diffidence. As one older man reasoned,
"*At nkoojni, at nchooki; ti? tiil política?* [I have my land and my
hoe; what use is politics?]." The Democracia Cristiana (DC), which
had won the previous two elections in Chimbal, had to resort to a
non-Chimalteco—an evangelical convert from the Q'anjob'al town
of Santa Eulalia—as its candidate, while the PR-PID alliance nomi-
nated a young Chimalteco who had recently served as treasurer of
the agricultural cooperative. The obvious religious and ethnic handi-
caps of the DC candidate did not keep the election from being close:
PR-PID won 206 votes, DC 179, and other parties 74. Opponents of
the newly elected *alcalde* feared that he would be like the outgoing
alcalde because "he knew how to drink," while the DC candidate
was a teetotaler and "a good, humble man." Supporters of the victor
countered by citing the need for an energetic *alcalde.*

Much of the impetus for a younger *alcalde* came from within the
community itself, not from the dictates of party politics. As men-

tioned before, construction of a bus road connecting the pueblo to the Pan American Highway represented a major issue in the 1980 campaign. Local coffee growers, whose numbers had grown substantially during the boom of the 1970s (see chapter 6), pressed hard for the new road. With a better road, the coffee cooperative could ship its produce in greater bulk than could be handled by the two-ton pickups then in use, resulting in both lower transport costs and access to better markets. As a member of the coffee cooperative himself, the new *alcalde* stood to benefit directly from the road.

One of the founders of the cooperative noted that the outgoing *alcalde* had done little about the road: "This *alcalde* [in 1979] does nothing. When the engineer came to survey the route for the new road, the *miyool* closed the town hall just before he arrived because the *alcalde* was drunk. *Gracias a Dios*, we had a meeting of the cooperative that day and one of the *miyool* came to tell us about the engineer. I was the one who went with him to show him where we wanted the road." This man, one of the largest coffee growers in Chimbal, served on several commissions concerning the road and later became third *consejal* of the new administration.

The new *alcalde*, when entering office in June 1980, inadvertently underscored his own vested interest in the new road. In concluding his inaugural speech, he reminded everyone that despite his youth, he had handled over Q90,000 as treasurer of the cooperative without problem or complaint—a tangible sign of his administrative ability and personal integrity. With a better road, of course, these profits would have been even larger. Unfortunately, increasing political violence in Guatemala militated against the efforts of even a young and vigorous Chimalteco *alcalde*. By the early 1980s, guerrilla warfare and counterinsurgency state terrorism had descended on Chimbal, wrenching local concerns from the possibilities of progress to mere survival.

Revolution and Repression, 1980–1988

After the end of my fieldwork in September 1980, I returned to Chimbal for a brief visit during the summer of 1981 just as leftist guerrillas intensified their struggle against the Guatemalan army for control of the western highlands. Chimaltecos remarked on the freedom that gringos had, voicing their own fears of going even to Huehuetenango. Everyone asked me if the United States had similar problems with guerrillas. They told me that shortly after I had left Chimbal ten months before, a small detachment of guerrillas belonging to the Organization of the People in Arms (ORPA) had passed through the town at night, scattering leaflets and painting slogans on walls.[14] In February 1981, ORPA executed three Ladino plantation owners in San Pedro Necta who had been warned about substandard wages and poor working conditions. Their actions provoked a four-day army occupation of San Pedro and an upsurge in death squad disappearances of suspected subversives—most of whom turned up dead, if at all. The week before my visit, *desconocidos,* "unidentified men," abducted a young Chimalteco and two men from San Pedro as they stood in line outside a bank in Huehuetenango. Protesting his innocence, townspeople wondered if the youth had fallen victim to the illicit involvements of the other two. The incident made Chimaltecos suddenly aware of their vulnerability. Shortly before I left, a young woman asked me if it were true what she had heard on the radio that soldiers were coming from Nicaragua to start a war in Huehuetenango. "*Qokymeela* [We're going to die]," she feared.

By 1982, guerrillas controlled large parts of Guatemala's western highlands where army patrols simply ceased to go. Uniformed and well-armed ORPA troops briefly occupied Chimbal, blocking roads, cutting the telephone line, and rounding up everyone for a meeting in the town plaza. They told Chimaltecos of their plans for a "government of the poor," with justice and a better life for all Guatemalans—a message undoubtedly lent greater credibility by the fact that the guerrilla leader and many of his companions were Mam-speaking Mayas, not Ladinos. The guerrillas at that time appeared to have a real chance of winning, and some Chimaltecos must have found favor with their revolutionary goals.[15] Nonetheless, with no police station, no nearby Ladino plantations, and no local oppressors against whom to take action, Chimaltecos remained largely quiescent.

Shortly before the presidential elections in March 1982, ORPA recruits from San Pedro burned their town hall in broad daylight and then destroyed Chimbal's a few nights later. Although the guerrillas may have intended this as symbolic liberation from class or government oppression, to many Chimaltecos destruction of the town hall constituted a direct attack on their community and its vital records, including birth and citizenship papers and all-important land titles. Misgivings about the guerrillas, as well as lack of immediate targets for local activism, may have helped spare Chimaltecos the death and destruction that the army soon unleashed on the countryside all around them (cf. Manz 1988; Carmack 1988).

As government control of Guatemala's western highlands deteriorated, a military coup in March 1982 brought to power General José Efraín Ríos Montt, a born-again Christian and "disciplined career

soldier, an authoritarian with dependable anti-communist creden-
tials . . . [who had once been] commander of the country's most
powerful garrison and principal of the military's *Escuela Politécnica*
(Polytechnic School)" (Black et al. 1984: 128). Under his regime, the
army prosecuted a savage counterinsurgency campaign against the
rural, largely Maya population to eradicate its revolutionary sympa-
thies. As army depredations escalated to unprecedented levels, guerrilla organizations found themselves overextended and unable to
protect their support communities from massacre. Maya disillusion-
ment deepened with each new blasted bridge, burned bus, or deserted plantation that resulted from increasingly desperate guerrilla
actions—to say nothing of the army reprisals that such sabotage
provoked.

In July 1982, I received a letter from a Chimalteco friend who
wrote: "[Everyone here] is well. Our only worry is that we're in the
middle of a war. Every day the guerrillas kill people; fifty people died
in Chanjón, where we go down to the highway on our way to Huehuetenango. Here in Chimbal, we finished the new road, and now
there's a bus, but the guerrillas have blocked the road, and the bus
can't leave town because of them. They have also cut down the
power lines, and now there's no electricity in Chimbal either."

When I returned to Chimbal in 1988, Chimaltecos told me that
the army had done nearly all the killing. Although only two or three
people "disappeared" in Chimbal, soldiers in other towns executed
hundreds of people fingered as subversives by local army informers.
Such denunciations often involved personal vendettas or political
feuds rather than revolutionary activism: as one Chimalteco official
said, "*O kyim tuʔn q'ooj tiʔj xuʔj, tiʔj tx'otx', tiʔj okslaal* [(People)
died from fights over women, over land, (even) over religion]." Acting unquestioningly on such accusations, soldiers butchered entire
families to extirpate the "bad seeds." Rather than the result of "some
irrational bloodlust, or because individual field commanders 'lost
control,' or because raw recruits committed excesses as a result of
poor discipline and training" (Black et al. 1984: 120), such savagery
originated in the army's purposive scorched earth policy designed to
isolate the guerrillas from their supporters in the countryside.

At the end of September 1982, the army instituted civil patrols in
Chimbal to combat the guerrillas. Officially called Patrullas de Auto-
defensa Civil (Civilian Self-Defense Patrols), this so-called voluntary
militia required every male between eighteen and fifty to serve a
twenty-four hour shift once every two weeks. Two groups of twenty
men patrolled the main roads day and night, with orders to kill unidentified individuals or be killed themselves by the army. Ostensi-

bly intended to defend towns from guerrilla attack, the patrols effectively controlled both the activities and movements of Guatemala's rural population (cf. Americas Watch 1986). On one hand, refusal to participate, for whatever reason, labeled one a subversive and thus fair game for execution; on the other, participation severely restricted the time that patrollers could spend away from home, even as migrant laborers for Ladino plantations on the coast. Indeed, without proof of participation in a patrol and a pass from the local patrol coordinator, travel became nearly impossible.

Unlike other communities, however, Chimalteco patrols were armed only with machetes and sticks, and local patrol coordinators did not abuse their powers for personal gain (cf. Paul and Demarest 1988). Several Chimaltecos also mentioned that they had never gone on patrol but had paid someone to take their turn, suggesting that Chimalteco patrol coordinators retained a greater degree of autonomy than in other communities. Although the patrols were still officially operating when I visited Chimbal in early 1988, neither guardhouse on the edge of town ever had more than two patrollers, and no one patrolled the roads. In speaking about the patrols, many Chimaltecos characterized them as a defense of their community—not necessarily as support for the army.

Chimaltecos had little good to say about the army. From the fall of 1982 to the spring of 1983, a detachment of "several hundred" soldiers occupied Chimbal, imposing a dusk-to-dawn curfew. With armed soldiers at every corner and machine guns mounted in the bell towers of the church, no one spoke openly in the streets or answered the door after dark, and each morning Chimaltecos anxiously checked to see if family and friends in other parts of town had survived the night. Everyone carried identification papers, even to their fields, for to be caught without them meant instant arrest, if not death. Chimaltecos described most of the soldiers as "rabid," as "animals," as "having no respect for anything." They took food without paying and used the church convent as a barracks. "The commander even slept in the padre's bed!" exclaimed one incredulous Chimalteco. The soldiers took the padre's stove, refrigerator, and even a chalice when they withdrew.

Despite the army occupation, almost no one died in Chimbal, in contrast to all the towns around them. When I asked why, many responded that because they were "good people"—or more precisely, good "Christian believers" of whatever persuasion—they had not denounced one another to the army as people had elsewhere. Others suggested that Santiago, the town's patron saint, had ridden through town on a white horse and driven the army away (see chapter 8). The man who served as provisional *alcalde* following the Ríos Montt coup told me that after the army had apparently killed his brother, he confronted the commander in Chimbal. Taking him by the shoulders, the *alcalde* shouted that the army had no right to kill people indiscriminately and that as a personal appointee and friend of Ríos Montt he would report him to the president. The *alcalde* had long served as coordinator of the Democracia Cristiana party in Chimbal and probably did have ties, if only indirectly, to Ríos Montt, who had run as the DC candidate for president in 1974. The army commander had no reason to know—or care—about this, and almost everyone gave the *alcalde* up for dead. For whatever reason, however, the army spared him and withdrew soon afterwards.

Whether by collective disposition, acts of personal courage, or even divine intervention, Chimbal survived. Perhaps the absence of local oppressors or any substantial Ladino elite kept Chimaltecos from a premature and fatal revolutionary fervor. Perhaps the large face-to-face community in Chimbal with its densely interwoven social networks kept factions from escalating into cycles of denunciations. Or perhaps the still-viable improvisations of subsistence farming, migratory wage labor, and local cash-cropping in coffee kept Chimaltecos from risking a proven—if increasingly precarious—livelihood against the long-term but more problematic gains of revolution.

Far from unscathed, however, Chimaltecos learned better the political dangers of innocent acts and the sometimes deadly consequences that the presence of strangers can bring. They once again fear the power of the state, especially the army, yet ironically, the terrorism of recent years has also taught them more clearly what a just government should be. As the *alcalde* in 1988 said to me, "Things are peaceful here for now. The present government [of Venicio Cerezo, elected in December 1985] that tries to help the poor—this is the kind of government that I approve of, not one that kills its own people." But how long the calm will last, and how enduring the forbearance—or is it resignation?—of Guatemala's rural people will prove, remains unclear.

This chapter began by showing that rituals within the traditional Chimalteco cargo system constituted more than "merely symbolic" expressions of individual prestige, community solidarity, or economic marginality. Instead, I argued that they pertained directly to issues of access to and control of communal lands. The loss of communal land tenure, combined with government encroachments, eventually obviated any felt need for these rituals. At the same time,

however, the indeterminacies and escalating violence of state intervention have undoubtedly encouraged Chimaltecos to maintain the
formalities of cargo service as an expression of local solidarity, if no
longer political sovereignty (see chapter 5).

The contradictions here are obvious: Chimaltecos' quest for a municipal land title expressed their felt local sovereignty but resulted
in acquiescence to state dominion. In attempting to ensure claims to
land through individual titles, Chimaltecos abrogated the administrative sovereignty of the community that served as their basis for political action vis-à-vis the Guatemalan state (cf. Smith 1987; 1990a).
At each stage, political change in Chimbal since the turn of the century has involved responses to external dictates shaped by local circumstances, yet what transpired in Chimbal neither resulted entirely from obeisance to state hegemony nor stemmed exclusively
from resistance to it.

Two points bear reiterating. First, a multiplicity of commitments
and concerns, not some homogenizing conformity, has always characterized Chimalteco political interests both individually and collectively. The old cargo system and the local party politics that sup-
planted it reflect the actions of diverse individuals conditioned by
shared circumstances, history, and conventions, not the dictates of
immutable Chimalteco customs. In other words, absolute political
consensus remains no more indispensable to "being Chimalteco"
than some imaginary cultural conformity: Chimalteco-ness inheres
as much in Chimaltecos' struggles with each other as it does in their
confrontations with outsiders. Second, the intimate relation between local lands, livelihood, and legitimacy suggests that the overt
political sovereignty of Chimbal remains intimately linked to a
more diffuse existential sovereignty comprised of the practical and
conventional strategies of surviving in that place. Thus, despite unequivocal loss of administrative self-determination, the immediacies of Chimalteco life and livelihood sustain a sense of community—nowhere more obvious than in Chimbal's survival of recent
state repression and terrorism. How long these immediacies will continue to hold Chimbal together, however, depends on a volatile political situation presently beyond Chimaltecos'—or anyone else's—
control or understanding.

8

✤ A Quest for Meaning ✤

Chimalteco confrontations with the surrounding world have involved the importunities of Ladino bureaucrats, soldiers, and plantation owners. In recent years, however, contact with the Catholic church and evangelical missionaries has also transformed, as well as reaffirmed, Chimalteco conceptions of themselves and their community. I now turn to effects of these proselytizing redeemers.

Until the mid–twentieth century, Chimbal, like most of Guatemala, endured the neglect of a Catholic church vitiated by the positivist zeal of late nineteenth-century Liberalism (Holleran 1949: 166–199). Far removed from priestly scrutiny, Chimaltecos nurtured their own brand of folk Catholicism. Public rituals in the cargo system invoked local saints and *witz* to legitimize town sovereignty and to sanction the exercise of political authority within its bounds. These cargo rituals constituted what could be called a "cult of community" in Chimalteco religion. This cult, concerned primarily with local administrative affairs, remained outwardly structured by the imposed institutions of colonial Catholic church and postcolonial Guatemalan state.

At the same time, Chimaltecos practiced what I would call a "cult of the soul" that dealt with the care and constancy of their moral "way of being" (see chapter 4). Less overtly structured by colonialist institutions than the cult of community, the cult of the soul involved local concepts of time, causality, and morality as these informed Chimalteco understandings of individual disposition, purpose, fate, and misfortune. Presided over by local shaman-diviners, care of the soul entailed personal rituals of field, forest, and hearth, divination based on the twenty day-names of the traditional Maya calendar, and curing practices to prevent or alleviate afflictions of the soul. Unlike cargoholders administering the cult of community, shaman-diviners in the cult of the soul lacked any formal organization, acting as private practitioners like "medical doctor[s] in a small

village in the United States" (Wagley 1949: 68). The two cults over-
lapped only in the *chmaan tnam*, the most powerful Chimalteco
shaman-diviner, who served as ritual adviser to the *principales* and
senior officials in the cargo system.

Since 1937, the cult of the soul in Chimbal has undergone more
radical change than the cult of community. While the structure and
some rituals of the cargo system survive today, by 1978, when I first
arrived in Chimbal, only two shaman-diviners still practiced—and
always "in secret." During my various stays in Chimbal, I never saw
a shaman-diviner perform *costumbre* in public or a Chimalteco
carry out rituals in his fields. Conversely, during a single afternoon
in the more religiously conservative town of San Juan Atitán, a two
hours' walk over the mountain, I saw three or four Sanjuaneros enter
the church to perform their rituals, carrying offerings of candles and
swinging their censers of smoldering copal incense.

Before examining this marked transformation in the Chimalteco
cult of the soul, two points need preface my discussion: first, although the external agents of religious change in Chimbal have always remained closely associated with the interests of the Guatemalan government, changes in Chimalteco religion have not simply
followed the state-induced political changes discussed in the last
chapter. By its very nature, state sovereignty intrudes and incorporates local polities into its exclusive order, a process exemplified by
recent Chimalteco political history. In contrast, both Catholic and
evangelical missions in Chimbal, at least in recent years, have relied
primarily on conversion by persuasion and inclusion in hopes of establishing a strong, locally based—but ultimately obedient—Christian lay community. This contrast in means, if not ends, relates directly to the recent history of church and state in Guatemala rather
than to intrinsic egalitarian or humanistic tendencies in the Church
itself.

Given the moribund state of the Guatemalan Catholic church
during the late nineteenth and early twentieth centuries, its re-
surgence following the Counterrevolution of 1954 stemmed from
two developments: first, both state and ecclesiastical authorities
came to perceive the Church as a less radical—if not explicitly anti-
Communist—agent of social change; and second, given this need for
a strong church, the sparse Guatemalan clergy had to be augmented
by a significant number of foreign missionaries. Revitalization of
the Catholic church in Guatemala thus resulted in an increased de-
centralization that encouraged a few progressive, mostly foreign,
priests to reconstitute local congregations through social as well as
spiritual programs. Nonetheless, lacking an independent power base

of its own, the Guatemalan church as a whole remained ultimately beholden to government and elite interests within the country, which limited such welfare and community development programs to highly circumscribed local contexts (Adams 1970: chapter 5; cf. Calder 1970). Although my discussion will not specifically concern these issues, recent religious change in Chimbal presupposes these shifting relations between church and state in Guatemala and between national and foreign clergy within the Guatemalan church itself.

A second prefatory point involves my focus on the meaningful aspects of religious change. Without denying the relevance of economic and political considerations, I choose to explore the changing meanings as well as indeterminacies of religious practices in Chimbal because I take these to pertain most directly to questions of local identity raised in this book. Consequently, I turn first to the former role of shaman-diviners in Chimbal and to what I could glean about religious attitudes before the arrival of orthodox Christian missionaries. I then examine how these attitudes both abetted and impeded acceptance of new teachings following missionization during the 1950s. As with political change, I will argue that abandonment of former religious conventions has not necessarily prompted wholesale conversion to new ideologies and practices but instead has left many Chimaltecos in limbo, *sin religión*, "without [formal] religion."

Care of the Soul in Traditional Chimbal

In the past, all Chimalteco men knew the rudiments of *costumbre*, literally "custom" or "tradition" in Spanish but used by the Maya of rural Guatemala to refer to local ritual practices attributed to their ancestors. *Costumbre* entailed an obligation to act "in the spirit of" the ancestors rather than slavishly following their dictates (cf. Warren 1978: 48–50, 66–75)—most concretely in knowing how to pray and how to make proper offerings of copal incense, candles, and sacrificial chickens. As with other skills, Chimaltecos learned *costumbre* by watching their parents perform rituals for clearing, planting, weeding, and harvesting *milpa:* "Youngsters do not memorize such prayers; they learn them after many years of watching and listening" (Wagley 1949: 32). Consequently, as one of Wagley's informants said, "Each man has his own mode of prayer" (1941: 40). That is, the actual performance of *costumbre* remained more important than the specific content of prayers included in it.

Although Chimaltecos apparently exercised a great deal of personal autonomy in religious matters, at crucial stages of the agricultural cycle or during times of misfortune or sickness, they consulted ritual specialists called *chmaan* in Mam, literally "grandfathers." Use of this term alluded in part to the respect accorded to someone of elder or esteemed status, as well as to the fact that these practitioners were mostly older men (cf. Wagley 1949: 68). Chimaltecos recognized two types of *chmaan*, the *chmaamb'aj* or *aj q'iij*, whom Chimaltecos called *chmaan simple* or *chmaan sencillo* in Spanish, "simple or plain *chmaan*," and the more powerful *aj mees* or *nmaq chmaan*, rendered in Spanish as *chmaan grande* "great *chmaan*."[1] The Mam names clearly reflect the different functions and powers of these two practitioners.[2]

Aj q'iij means literally "person of the sun/day(s)/time," referring to this practitioner's esoteric knowledge of the twenty day-names of the traditional Maya calendar (cf. Wagley 1949: 70; Oakes 1951: 248–253; Koizumi 1981: 65–68). Through familiarity with these day-names and their corresponding positive and negative associations, *aj q'iij* directed the *costumbre* of the laity, determining days on which to carry out rituals and begin important projects. They performed prognostications and divinations by "questioning the beans," bright red seeds (*Erythrina corallodendrum*) called *miich* in Mam. One Chimalteco described divinations that he had seen as a boy: the *aj q'iij* piled his *miich* on a cloth, then asked yes-no questions related to his client's concern. Drawing a random handful of beans from the pile at each question, he counted them out in pairs, an even number indicating an affirmative answer, an odd number a negative one. Wagley (1949: 72) noted a second method in which the diviner counted out the beans from a random pile as he named the days of the calendar in order, beginning with the current day. The favorable, unfavorable, or neutral character of the day on which the count ended determined the response to the question.[3]

The *aj mees* represented a much more powerful type of *chmaan*. The term literally means "person of the table," from the Spanish *mesa*, "table," reference to the short-legged wooden tables used by these *chmaan* as altars for their rituals. In addition to the divinatory powers of the *aj q'iij*, the *aj mees* could summon *witz* and talk with them, usually to determine the cause of a client's affliction and to specify the ritual payments to alleviate it. Individuals who consulted an *aj mees* became "children" of that *chmaan's* altar, and when they died their souls went to work for the *witz* who owned this *mees*.

Rituals conducted by *aj mees* invariably occurred at night. The *chmaan* first consumed *aguardiente* offered to the *witz*, in part to allow the *witz* to enter and speak through him (cf. Oakes 1951: 109). After setting up a small enclosure inside his house, the *chmaan* lit candles and burned copal incense on his table altar. Then, covering the enclosure with a cloth or blanket, he would begin to pray. Chimaltecos who had witnessed such rituals always emphasized the incredible number of place names that the *chmaan* recited in invoking the *witz*. Said one man, "He began with the names of mountains across the whole world, then all those in Guatemala, then Ptxon, Pich'jab', and Wile'yil, and finally the great cross in front of the church—then boom! the spirit arrived, and the walls of the house shook like an earthquake. How could he know so many names?" (cf. Oakes 1951: 115ff., 196, 217). Even a confirmed skeptic had to admit that *chmaan* "must have had to study a lot to learn [all those names]."

Witz did not always respond to the call of the *aj mees*, but when one did, it spoke through the *chmaan* in a deep voice and always in Spanish. One Chimalteco described the *espíritus*, "spirits," as small figures about a foot high similar to saints' images in the church. Indeed, several times he referred to these incarnations of *witz* as *saant*, "saint," (from the Spanish *santo*). "Although they may be small," he continued, "they speak with the voice of a large man, and each carries a whip, but the thongs aren't made of leather—they're snakes. If the *chmaan* doesn't behave correctly, the spirit whips him!" (cf. Wagley 1949: 113n; Oakes 1951: 112). A whirring "like the flight of pigeons through the woods" heralded the arrival and departure of the spirit.

In his discussion of *chmaan*, Wagley does not mention any Chimalteco *aj mees*, only *aj q'iij*. At that time, when Chimaltecos needed an *aj mees*, they evidently consulted *chmaan* from San Juan Atitán, especially during the five-day celebration of *twaalaq qmaan*, the Maya New Year.[4] During *twaalaq qmaan*, Chimalteco *chmaan* had to let their *miich* beans "rest" and thus could not perform *costumbre* or divinations for their neighbors. According to Wagley (1949: 111–114), many Chimaltecos performed the New Year's *costumbre* for themselves, but others called upon the services of *aj mees* from San Juan Atitán. Oakes (1951: 100–114) vividly describes an *aj mees* ritual for the *twaalaq qmaan* ceremony that she witnessed in 1946 in La Florida, an *aldea* of Chimbal, but she fails to mention the presence of a San Juan *chmaan*, even though she clearly recognized the difference in dress between the two *municipios* (1951: 104). Chimaltecos informed me, however, that most of the inhabitants of La Florida had immigrated from San Juan Atitán two or three generations before.[5] In 1937, most of them still wore San Juan dress and paid allegiance to the church in San Juan (Wagley 1949: 11), but by 1946 some may have begun to adopt Chimalteco clothing (cf. Wagley 1949: 12). Certainly today, descendants of these immigrants have become indistinguishable from other Chimaltecos, for the most part having taken on Chimalteco dress and customs.

Nonetheless, it appears that this influx of Sanjuaneros may have brought with it the custom of *aj mees* to Chimbal. "Gregorio Martín said that this type of *costumbre* with the help of a San Juanero *chimán* was 'the way of San Juan,' not of Chimaltenango, but he admitted that many Chimaltecos made *costumbre* in this manner. This may well be a San Juan custom which the Chimaltecos have borrowed in recent years" (Wagley 1949: 114). As will be seen, the possibility that *aj mees* had only recently been introduced into Chimbal may have played a role in the subsequent rejection of traditional ritual practices in the community.

Alleviating Afflictions

In the normal course of quotidian life, Chimaltecos resorted to *chmaan* in times of crisis or uncertainty. When misfortune struck— most often illness—Chimaltecos usually first consulted a *xhb'ool*, or herbal curer. In addition to knowing prayers, these women had at their command a fair range of herbal remedies and treatments involving sweatbaths (cf. Recinos 1954: 105–129; Casteñeda Medinilla et al. 1978: passim). As in the neighboring town of Todos Santos (Oakes 1951: 92, 183–184), a tacit division of labor existed between male *chmaan*, who performed divinations and curing rituals, and female *xhb'ool*, who provided herbal cures and often served as *b'itx'-loon*, "midwives."[6] Although Chimaltecos considered certain ailments such as toothaches *iil te dyoos*, "afflictions of God," that simply had to be endured (cf. Wagley 1949: 76), *xhb'ool* treated most physical maladies, including the relatively serious case of *seky'-pajleenin*, "fright," often associated with soul-loss. To cure *seky'pajleenin*, the *xhb'ool* concocted a potion of herbs and *aguardiente*, which she sprayed through her mouth onto the patient's face and body. The alcohol served to heat the patient's blood, returning it to its normal hot state and thus restoring the soul (see chapter 4); no other ritual cure was necessary.[7]

If an affliction persisted despite the ministrations of *xhb'ool*, the patient consulted an *aj q'iij* to determine its spiritual cause. Usually this meant some sin of omission or commission against the spirit responsible for the trouble; one could also inherit such sins from one's ancestors in a potentially infinite regression of possible wrongdoing (cf. Wagley 1949: 76; Koizumi 1981). The *aj q'iij* divined the sin involved and then prescribed the number, location, and days for the *costumbres* in which he would plead with God to intercede on behalf of his client.[8] Interestingly, Chimaltecos considered the *aj q'iij*'s ritual offerings of candles, copal, and prayers neither *chojb'il*, "payments," nor sacrifices, but simply *tnaab'l dyoos*, "things for praying to God."

If the *poom te chmaamb'aj*, "copal of the *aj q'iij*," proved ineffective, victims of persistent misfortune resorted to an *aj mees*. Another round of divination specified the day for the ritual and the proper offerings of copal, candles, and *aguardiente* that the client had to provide. On the appointed night, the *aj mees* summoned the spirit of his *mees* to determine the *chojb'il* that would absolve his client. If the spirit came, it would either demand a certain number of *costumbres* and sacrificial chickens—or in serious cases, a turkey—or it would refuse all payments, thus sealing the client's fate. In either event, the client's soul now belonged to this *witz*, and when he or she died, the *witz* gained another worker for its subterranean plantation. The *chojb'il* of *aj mees* bought only time, never salvation. If the spirit chose not appear, a new round of divination and ritual was performed.

At any time during this process, divinations by a *chmaan* might reveal that the patient would recover only if he "accepted the beans" and became a *chmaan* himself (Wagley 1949: 72–75).[9] Divination could also reveal witchcraft. Chimaltecos described two types of witches to me. Of less danger was the *xhwiin*, a person who could successfully pray for the death of an enemy. "A *xhwiin* is like the brother of a demon [*demonio*]," said one Chimalteco. "Although he can't see it, he can talk to it and ask that someone die." Nonetheless, a *xhwiin* "only talked" and did not perform rituals. Perhaps not surprisingly, when radios first appeared in Chimbal, older townspeople called them *xhwiin*, "speakers of evil."

A much more malevolent practitioner was the *ky'aawil*, who bewitched people by making *qaanb'il*, "askings," that caused victims to sicken and slowly die. Although Chimaltecos were vague about such matters, one described two types of *qaanb'il* to me. The first consisted of a small tin can full of charcoal with a small cross and a broken piece of mirror pushed into the top; the second involved a bundle of candles tied with the leaves of particular plants. Chimaltecos called these *qaanb'il* "*entierras*" (burials) in Spanish because the *ky'aawil* buried them in the cemetery or in some damp muddy place. As the *qaanb'il* disintegrated, the victim would fall ill and eventually die unless the *qaanb'il* was removed and burned (cf. Oakes 1951: 160–169). Only a *chmaan* more powerful than the bewitching *ky'aawil* could prevail upon the spirit of his *mees* to seek out the *qaanb'il* and bring it to him. A Chimalteco who had witnessed one such ritual of countersorcery assured me, "I don't know where it came from, but suddenly there was the *qaanb'il* lying there on the table!" (cf. Oakes 1951: 168–169).

Ironically, even though *chmaan* have fallen into disrepute in Chimbal, *ky'aawil* still wield their hidden malevolence. During my stay, Chimaltecos spoke of one reputed *ky'aawil*. Even skeptics of the old *creencias*, "beliefs," did not scoff at this, and once when I was returning to the town with a young Chimalteco, we slowed our pace to a dawdle so as not to pass this man on the road. Although a convert to orthodox Catholicism, my companion still held the power of sorcery in wary regard. Fear of the jealousy or envy of others—of which the fear of witchcraft is only an extreme expression—remains a potent force in Chimalteco life (see chapter 4).

From these accounts, it would appear that the cult of the soul provided Chimaltecos with an epistemology of afflictions, not a means of salvation. The natural forces that affected the blood, the distant God, the patriarchal saint, the avaricious *witz*, the wicked man—all served to explain life's misfortunes. Using the day-names of the ancient Maya calendar, *aj q'iij* attempted to discern which of these powers gave meaning to enigmatic suffering. Although Chimaltecos did not necessarily treat the twenty days of the traditional calendar as sacred personages in their own right (cf. Wagley 1949: 71), the sound of their names and the word associations that they conjured provided cues from which *chmaan* could derive their prognostications (cf. Tedlock 1982). Perhaps this facility in manipulating and punning on the day-names to create meaningful results from "questioning the beans" accounted for the reputed ability of *chmaan* to "pray better" (cf. Wagley 1949: 72). Quite literally, their eloquence constituted the clearest measure of the efficacy of their rituals.

Within the parameters of possible meaning circumscribed by the count of days, Chimaltecos' recourse to *chmaan* also precipitated a tacit hierarchy of unseen causes. When a layman's normal *costumbre* proved inadequate or the herbal remedies of *xhb'ool* failed to cure an illness, *aj q'iij* appealed to a distant but all-powerful God to intervene in their clients' behalf. If such pleas brought no relief, *aj mees* entered into direct negotiations with nearby *witz* or with Xwaan No'j, the "father of the *witz*" (see chapter 3), to determine the victim's fate. Yet the ultimate—and perhaps most deadly—cause of misfortune could lie in the sorcery of the *ky'aawil*. This hierarchy of causality remained largely tacit in Chimalteco praxis rather than explicit in some overt scale of probable causes. Indeed, I would hazard that it simply reflected the fact that Chimaltecos strove to minimize their contact with the unknown, thereby curtailing ritual expenses and existential risks.

The work of *xhb'ool* or *aj q'iij* cost no more than the price of candles, rum, copal, and the practitioner's fee—"the same as a worker's daily wage," I was told. Conversely, the more costly rituals of *aj mees* also indentured the victim's soul to the *chmaan*'s *witz* with no guarantee of succor. Finally, protection from *ky'aawil* could run as much as Q40 or Q50, while also confirming the malice not of some unseen presence but of one of the victim's neighbors. As the putative agents addressed in ritual became more definite—from distant God to nearby *witz* to human sorcerer—the economic and personal consequences for the victim grew accordingly. Being the most immediate, the *ky'aawil* was the most dangerous, not only because of his potent malevolence but also because his existence repudiated the common sociality within which both victim and villain sought meaning for their lives. The vengeance of God could be inscrutable and yet, by its inscrutability, remain acceptable in a way that the inimical will of one's neighbors, by its intelligibility, could not.

For all the *chmaan*'s efforts, the alleviation of afflictions through *costumbre* ultimately constituted rationalizations rather than a process of causal explanation or a technical procedure for curing. While their rituals reaffirmed the reality of possible causes, *chmaan* could never ascertain an unequivocal cause of any affliction or misfortune because of the multiplicity of forces involved: "sins" were inherited from *qchmaan*, "our grandfathers," or arose from innumerable individual acts and thoughts; the overlapping influences of God, saints, *witz*, demons, and sorcerers remained inextricably entangled; and even countersorcery involved more a blanket defense against *qaanb'il* than ferreting out the identity of the *ky'aawil* involved (cf. Koizumi 1981). At the same time, however, such indeterminate causality also served to confirm its own reality because any particular failure to relieve suffering through appeals to God, bargains with *witz*, or evasion of witchcraft simply meant that the relevant cause lay elsewhere.

In the end, however, conventional forms did establish a basis for interpreting experience and making it meaningful. What transgression might have been committed, which presence offended, which neighbor maligned or thwarted? Through the rituals of *chmaan*, Chimaltecos could seek answers to such questions, but they found neither straightforward explanations nor final remedies. *Chmaan* simply articulated a means by which Chimaltecos created meanings

out of the substance of their own experiences and the shadowy transgressions of their ancestors' past (cf. Wagley 1949: 76).

Missionization: The Maryknoll Fathers, 1945–1980

In 1937, Chimaltecos considered themselves *muy buen católicos*,
"very good Catholics" (Wagley 1949: 50), despite their lack of religious orthodoxy. No resident Catholic priest had ever lived in Chimbal, and sporadic pastoral visits by itinerant priests had done little to
alter their heterodoxy. "Until the Fiesta of Corpus Christi in 1937 a
priest had not visited Chimaltenango in over two years. The Padre at
Huehuetenango has more than twenty municipios under his care.
(Only the government health officer has more.) . . . The Padre, who
was Spanish by birth, complained bitterly of his fate, of the sad state
of the church in Chimaltenango, of the impossibility of making
good Catholics out of barbarians and brutes. His greatest dream was
a parish in Chicago 'where people are rich'" (Wagley 1949: 50n; see
chapter 2). These priests belonged to the Mercedarian Order, carrying out their pastoral rounds from Malacatancito, Chiantla, Cuilco,
Soloma, and Jacaltenango (Oakes 1951: 53).

In the late 1920s, evangelical missionaries also began working in
the Cuchumatán Highlands, meeting with limited success because
Maya believed that they worshiped a different God from Catholics
(Wagley 1949: 73n). Furthermore, these missionaries had the "pleas-
ant habit of telling everyone they met that he was destined directly
for hell-fire, where all his forebears already were. . . . They [were] regarded as the very emissaries of anti-Christ" (LaFarge 1947: 11–12).
In 1937, Wagley noted only three evangelical converts in Chimbal, at least one of whom "suffered socially from his new religion,
and . . . [had] few friends" (1949: 73n).

In 1943, the Catholic church in northwestern Guatemala began to
awake.[10] In that year, two North American Maryknoll missioners[11]
recently repatriated from war-torn China were given permission to
enter "the poor, isolated, and mountainous region of Huehuetenango
for their work" (Calder 1970: 52; my translation). The newcomers
adopted the same tactics as the Mercedarian Fathers before them,
basing themselves in centrally located towns and visiting outlying
municipios as often as schedules and stamina permitted. In 1945, a
lone Maryknoll missioner took up residence in San Ildefonso Ixtahuacán, a large Mam town about six miles southwest of Chimbal.
Working alone until 1951, he rode on horseback throughout the
southern part of the department of Huehuetenango, trying to arrive
on local market days so as to make contact with the greatest number

of people. Because he could spend only a limited time in each community, he tried to work closely with existing church personnel, including the *sacristanes* and *maestros de coro,* "cantors" (*xnaq'-tzoon*).

According to baptismal records, this missioner began regular visits to Chimbal in 1950, coming about four times a year and staying for a day or two. Contact with Chimbal undoubtedly occurred well before this, however, because one Chimalteco showed me a devotional that this priest had given him inscribed and dated in 1946. The priest found Chimbal a well-organized, tightly knit community, and the concentrated population of the pueblo facilitated his pastoral work. Here, as in other towns, the Maryknoll program consisted of three elements. First, a core group of catechists received training in Catholic doctrine (Calder 1970: 88–89). Chimaltecos had apparently preserved much of the old Latin liturgy (cf. Wagley 1949: 86), and the priest's main task lay in revealing to them the significance of the old chants and practices. Second, missioners combatted traditional religion by distributing medicine to draw converts away from the *chmaan.* Initially, this involved drugs for the dysentery and malaria that migrant workers picked up on coastal plantations, but eventually the Maryknolls established clinics throughout rural Huehuetenango (Calder 1970: 83, 101). To further distance catechists from the *chmaan,* Maryknolls also denounced the drinking central to *chmaan* ritual as immoral and wasteful. The final element in the Maryknoll program involved education. By establishing primary schools in the rural areas of Huehuetenango and the Colegio La Salle (a secondary school) in the department capital, Maryknolls sought to overcome the linguistic and cultural barriers that Maya encountered in regular public schools, hoping that education might enable Maya to defend themselves from Ladino exploitation (cf. Calder 1970: 78–79).

In 1953, a Maryknoll priest established pastoral residence in San Pedro Necta, and Chimalteco catechists began to attend training sessions there. Having recently regained their municipal autonomy in 1948 (see chapter 7), however, Chimaltecos evidently hesitated to submit entirely to San Pedro in religious matters. At about this time, Chimaltecos began renovating their church, replacing the old tile roof with corrugated sheet metal and adding two bell towers to the facade—a decade-long project that tacitly reaffirmed their independence from San Pedro. Throughout the 1950s, Chimbal nurtured this autonomy, and the number of converts to orthodox Catholicism continued to grow, no doubt encouraged by the influx of missionaries and resources into rural Guatemala following the Counter-

revolution of 1954 (cf. Calder 1970: 47–59). By 1956, Catholic converts in Chimbal numbered at least one hundred (cf. Wagley 1957:
xxv), and in 1979, a catechist told me that the congregation had
grown nominally to "four hundred couples," although only a small
fraction, mostly women and children, attended church services regularly. In 1988, the number of baptized, practicing Catholics stood at
perhaps five hundred, if as one catechist suggested, one omitted the
one hundred or so who backslid into "drinking *aguardiente*" from
time to time.

Maryknoll activities in Huehuetenango expanded greatly after
1954. In the early 1960s, the Maryknoll mission established a clinic
and later a hospital in San Pedro, then renovated the church building
and convent. Although the priest continued to preach against traditional Maya religion, between 1964 and 1968, Chimbal remained
somewhat shielded from his policies by the presence of the only
resident priest that the community has ever had. Ironically, according to a former Chimalteco catechist who worked closely with him,
this Maryknoll father considered his work in the community primarily that of a linguist rather than a priest. Having previously studied and taught at the Summer Institute of Linguistics, he spent most
of his four years in Chimbal working on a Mam grammar and dictionary and teaching Chimaltecos to read and write their own language
(Lansing n.d.). He also rebuilt and expanded the convent behind the
church and established a small medical clinic in Chimbal. Com-
ments at the end of his grammar make clear that his concerns extended beyond linguistics and religion to community welfare and development. After leaving Chimbal, he helped to found a linguistics
project in Antigua, Guatemala, to promote Maya literacy in their native languages.

The progressive tendencies of the Maryknoll mission in San Pedro
grew during the late 1960s and early 1970s. New priests helped to
found agricultural and savings cooperatives in both San Pedro and
Chimbal, encouraging the use of fertilizers and new crops to improve agricultural production. Many Chimaltecos, catechist and
noncatechist alike, still speak warmly of the Maryknoll priests'
efforts to improve community welfare. "Before the padres came, our
milpas barely grew, and many families had no corn," one catechist
told me. "The padres brought agronomists to show us how to take
better care of our fields. Now every house in Chimbal has corn" (see
chapter 6).

During the 1970s, the Maryknolls also expanded their efforts to
train a Maya lay clergy. By participating in a requisite number of *cur-
sillos*, a combination of instructional courses and religious retreats

The plaza in Chimbal, 1937. Photograph courtesy of Charles Wagley.

The plaza in Chimbal, 1979. The corrugated metal roof and new façade of the church were added during the 1950s along with the garden and cement benches.

(Adams 1970: 298–299), Chimalteco catechists could become "animators" with authority to preach sermons and give communion in their community. Such training apparently further reinforced the Chimalteco catechists' sense of autonomy, so that by the mid-1970s they ceased to attend sessions with the catechists in San Pedro and had the Maryknoll priest duplicate sessions with them in Chimbal instead. In 1980, seven Chimalteco animators presided over the local congregation and served as intermediaries between their community and the priest in San Pedro.

In a very real sense, these men acted as true mediators rather than go-betweens like the local coordinators of political parties (see chapter 7). From the beginning, Maryknoll missioners had relied heavily on local converts, both because of a shortage of mission personnel and because of a desire to create strong leadership within local congregations. The intermittent visits of the priest from San Pedro and the turnover in Maryknoll personnel every few years made the catechists, not the parish priest, the enduring core of the reconstructed Catholic church in Chimbal. No priest could dictate doctrine or policy to the catechists without undermining the credibility of the Church's efforts to foster local leadership. Such action could also jeopardize his primary access to the community, especially if the catechists disagreed with changes that he wanted to make in mission policy or programs. This could occur especially when a new priest attempted to change the policies of his predecessor.

Catechists readily availed themselves of their autonomy as brokers. During my 1978–1980 fieldwork, this was apparent in the contrast between local fact and fancy about the Maryknoll priest in San Pedro. A few Chimaltecos—mostly noncatechists—initially told me that this priest was "very strict" and that he had forbidden many traditional rites during the celebration of Holy Week and other fiestas. I fostered the image of a narrow-minded, overzealous missionary. When I actually met this priest, however, I found him quite the opposite. Contrary to the suspicions of some Chimaltecos, he expressed a strong preference for Chimbal over San Pedro; only the logistical demands of San Pedro's much larger and dispersed populace and the relative inaccessibility of Chimbal kept him from moving his parochial residence up the mountain. He also found much of traditional Chimalteco theology "fairly acceptable" and had long urged a dialogue between the catechists and more traditional Chimaltecos. Although he had found the traditionalists amenable, he encountered strong opposition from the catechists.

The tension between priest and catechists found overt expression during the traditional Thursday night procession of Holy Week that

I witnessed in 1979 and 1980 (see chapter 5). The catechists opposed it—and most other processions—because of the drinking and carousing associated with it. Actually, as described earlier, two processions took place—one the raucous *baile de torritos,* "dance of the little bulls," the other a solemn and sacred homage to Christ and the Virgin Mary. Nonetheless, the *martoon* still portioned out shots of *aguardiente* to participants in the second procession as it moved through its fourteen stations, prompting the catechists' disapproval. I was surprised when the Maryknoll priest, whom I had just met, joined the procession and gave every indication of approving what I found to be a beautiful ceremony. At several stations, however, the marimba player—the only Chimalteco who knew the sacred *son* played during the processions of Holy Week—quit the procession and left the cantors to sing unaccompanied. I later learned that he had recently accepted Catholicism and participated in the procession reluctantly, possibly because the priest did. The other catechists refused to follow the priest's example and shunned the procession, while also disapproving of his participation.

Such acts of tacit reconciliation on the priest's part did little to disabuse Chimaltecos of their image of him as a "strict man," an impression the catechists cared not to dispel. Indeed, by preserving a certain distance between priest and community, the catechists could effectively exercise power in both directions. To most Chimaltecos, the Maryknoll priest in San Pedro constituted the principal religious authority in the community. At the same time, he worked almost exclusively through the catechists and, in his words, "never actually got very close to the people." Consequently, in the eyes of most Chimaltecos, the catechists' direct access to the priest imbued their actions with the legitimacy of official Church doctrine and policy, even when the priest saw these tendencies as counterproductive to the integrity of the community as a whole. In other words, to the community at large, the catechists carried out what the priest decreed, but perhaps more importantly, whatever the catechists carried out became, by implication, what the priest had decreed.

As long as the priest could ill afford to alienate his most direct contacts with Chimal, the catechists effectively retained a meaningful degree of local autonomy within the new Catholic orthodoxy. At least a few catechists clearly recognized where their power lay: Maryknolls who expressed interest in learning to speak Mam prompted concern from certain catechists over this perceived threat to their brokerage between priest and community. Although thoroughly reconstructed, the Catholic church in Chimbal remained unquestionably Chimalteco.

Evangelicals in Chimbal

The Maryknoll Fathers have not been the only missionaries at work in rural Guatemala. As mentioned before, evangelical missionaries began proselytizing in the Cuchumatán Highlands during the 1920s, but Chimaltecos did not begin converting in any number until the 1940s. At about that time, a missionary of the fundamentalist Central American Mission established himself in the nearby town of San Sebastián Huehuetenango. He had worked in the area since 1934 and had translated the New Testament into Mam (Sywulka 1966; Sociedad Bíblica en Guatemala 1968). Through periodic visits to Chimbal, he gained a small group of converts that grew steadily. By the time that Wagley briefly visited Chimbal in June 1956, "[on] Sunday the songs could be heard of fifty or sixty evangelicals who met for services in a small house that temporarily [served] as their place of worship" (1957: xxv; my translation). In 1988, one church member put evangelical numbers at about 500 in the municipio as a whole, and the 300 members of the congregation in the town center had begun to outgrow the church that they had built a decade before.

During the late 1970s, other evangelical sects proliferated in Chimbal, but only one grew to more than a few families. In addition to the Central American Mission, small gatherings of Adventists and Pentecostals began to meet at the homes of individual members. Irregular visits by itinerant preachers occasioned daylong meetings punctuated by spirituals adapted from the Mexican ranchera music so popular in rural Guatemala. Often heard late into the night or early in the morning, the poorly amplified voice of the preacher, usually a Ladino or Maya from another municipio, would echo through the streets and then rise into an off-key wail of song and salvation. From 1978 to 1981, several pairs of Mormon missionaries, both North American and Guatemalan, also sought—unsuccessfully—to establish a church in Chimbal.[12]

During the 1980s, splits within the ranks of the catechist leadership led one dissident to found a new "Church of the Pilgrims." With thirty or forty members in 1988, it represents by far the largest sectarian group in Chimbal. Its founder—a forceful, charismatic former church leader—had long served as the Chimalteco coordinator for the Democracia Christiana Party (DC). His political involvements finally ran him afoul of both the Ladino bishop in Huehuetenango and fellow catechists in Chimbal. In explaining why they had "expelled" him, he cited doctrinal grounds—especially his opposition to the Church's tacit sanctioning of drunken public celebrations for the saints—but the differences appeared as much personal and political as theological. Evidently, the Ladino bishop had always thought him too independent and too outspoken for an Indian, and his fellow catechists perhaps feared that his excessive influence might threaten their own autonomy. Always well liked and respected by previous Maryknoll missioners, he may have felt doubly betrayed when the new Maryknoll priest in 1983 confronted him with an "are you with us or against us" ultimatum. Obviously angered by this lack of support, he left the Church.[13]

I have the impression that local factionalism and interpersonal differences underlie much of the increased sectarianism in Chimbal. The highly fragmented evangelical churches apparently do not represent any direct outgrowth of the born-again Christianity espoused by President Efraín Ríos Montt at the height of Guatemala's counterinsurgency war during the early 1980s (see chapter 7). Despite the factionalism, however, relations between Chimalteco evangelicals and Catholics appear nonmilitant, although evangelicals criticize Catholics more than Catholics do them. Evangelicals neither drink nor participate in fiestas. They call Catholic processions of the saints "idol worship" and fiestas nothing but excuses for drinking and dissipation. "How could such idolatry and drunkenness be a religion?" asked one evangelical. Consequently, evangelicals make no contributions for the ritual paraphernalia used during fiestas.[14] For these converts, the only valid religious acts are prayer and song. It remains unclear whether their strictures against drink and ritual expenditures imply, as Annis (1987: 87, 142) has speculated, an anorexic self-denial intended to control one's life in an increasingly uncontrollable world. Whatever the reason for their abstemious nature, however, it would have to apply equally to local orthodox Catholics, because Chimalteco catechists have adopted the same disapproval of drinking and public ritual expenditures.

Indeed, despite their professed differences, very little separates evangelical from orthodox Catholic converts (cf. Koizumi 1981: 170–172). Evangelicals have their distinctive habit of addressing each other as *hermano*, "brother," and *hermana*, "sister," but evangelicals and strict catechists alike neither drink nor take part in rituals for the saints. Nonetheless, because these Catholics belong at least nominally to the same, if now-revitalized, church as the traditional people, they must steer a narrow course between doctrinal orthodoxy and local precedents.[15] Whether the catechists like it or not, many unreconstructed Chimaltecos still profess first loyalty to the Catholic church. Too vehement an attack on traditional church rites in Chimbal might not only alienate these "informal" Catholics but also motivate them to abandon Catholicism altogether for the evangelical fold. At the same time, if catechists take too lax a stance against the "evils" of traditional religion, they leave themselves vulnerable to charges from evangelicals of idol worship and excess, again perhaps discouraging potential converts to Catholicism. Ironically, without the threat of evangelical defections, the catechists might have long ago closed the doors of their church to all but the most orthodox, yet evangelical criticism also leaves them ambivalent about their own association with the church of their forebears, since the past remains associated with the sinfulness of unsaved ancestors.[16]

Beyond precipitating an increasingly diverse religiosity within the community, then, the rise in evangelical conversions since the 1950s suggests that the erosion of traditional Chimalteco religion did not simply result in the triumph of some new orthodoxy. Instead, the success of catechists against the *chmaan* apparently created a vacuum that left other Chimaltecos open to choose which—if any—new religion to accept. Some converted to Catholicism, while others turned to evangelicalism. Many Chimaltecos, however, despite their neglect of traditional practices and a professed first loyalty to the Catholic church, even today remain uncommitted. As one middle-aged Chimalteco put it, "Perhaps it is better with God. Perhaps I will accept religion, but if I do, it will be the Catholic church because it was the first; it is the only true Church in the world."

The ascendancy of new religions in Chimbal has apparently resulted more from successful campaigns against traditional Chimalteco *costumbre* than from acceptance of what reformers had to offer in its stead. While the inherent indeterminacies of the Chimalteco cult of the soul may have left traditional religion vulnerable to religious alternatives, the deeper problem of meaning with which *chmaan* once grappled but could never resolve still persists. For many Chimaltecos, the new religions have proven equally problematic, leaving many of them *sin religión*, "without religion." It remains to examine how—and why—this should be so.

Initial Conversions

Upon his brief return to Chimbal in June 1956, Wagley immediately noticed the absence of public *costumbre.*

> I had not seen, during the first three days of my visit, even one *chimán* going into the church with his censer to perform *costumbre.* . . . Gregorio Martín, my old friend, told me that the priests in San Pedro Necta (of the Maryknoll mission) had forbid-

den the *chimanes* to perform *costumbre* in the church. Continuing, Gregorio surprised me by adding that he no longer believed in *chimanes*, nor did the majority of young people. Francisco Aguilar said that if he got sick, he would not consult any *chimán*. "Now we have medicine [remedios]," he said. "Why should anyone call a *chimán*?" Others had not stopped believing in the powers of the *chimanes*, and it was said that some of them still performed their *costumbres* and curing rituals late at night outside of the town at mountain shrines; however, for such activities, they hid themselves from the priests as well as from the orthodox Catholics, since the latter would have informed the priests. (Wagley 1957: xxv; my translation)

When I asked Chimaltecos about religious changes in the community, they usually attributed them to the Maryknoll priests: "When the padres came, many *costumbres* died." "The priests prohibited the cantors from singing responses at funerals because they always got drunk." "The priests barred the marimba from the church because of the drinking that always went along with it." "The priests taught us that the *chmaan* were only deceiving us with their false rituals." Chimaltecos also frequently cited the introduction of Western medicine by the Maryknolls as a reason for abandoning the *chmaan*.

These commonly held Chimalteco notions, however, contain two inconsistencies. First, older Chimalteco catechists maintained that they, not the Maryknoll priests, carried out religious reform in Chimbal. This makes sense, given the paucity of Maryknoll personnel during their early years in Huehuetenango and the rejection of *chmaan* that Wagley noted in Chimbal by 1956. Quite clearly, once the Maryknolls recruited a core group of catechists, these Chimaltecos vigorously prosecuted what one Maryknoll priest likened to me as a "holy war" against the *chmaan*. In part, this involved gaining control of the church building itself. As mentioned earlier, by the early 1950s, the catechists had begun extensive renovations on the church, including a new roof and facade, and removal of the interior rear balcony where drunken marimba musicians had played during fiestas. By making this project a community-wide effort, catechists mobilized the tacit support of traditionalists who had yet to accept formal Catholicism. At the same time, the project also denied practicing traditionalists access to the church for their celebrations. It also undoubtedly served to identify catechist reforms with the renewed civic pride of Chimbal's recent emancipation from San Pedro rule (see chapter 7). If nothing else, catechist renovation of the church demonstrated that new ways in religion, as in politics, could bring tangible results.

The catechists also strove to extirpate what they saw as idolatry in public Chimalteco life. Sometime in the mid-1950s, they managed to burn the *caja real*, "royal coffer," a wooden chest entrusted to the *alcalde* containing "all the old documents of the pueblo," as one former catechist told me (cf. Oakes 1951: 66–67). "They dumped out the old books, all tied up in *petates* [straw mats], and then burned them to prove that they held no power. The catechists burned the *caja real* because the people treated it as an idol and performed *costumbre* for it." The eclipse of ritual responsibilities in the cargo system following the advent of political elections for *alcalde* and high-ranking *regidores* also clearly expedited catechist designs on the *caja real* (see chapter 7). Despite their boldness, however, the catechists evidently still claimed that they burned the *caja* at the urging of the Maryknoll priest in San Pedro, perhaps invoking the authority of the priests to sanction a potentially unpopular action. Perhaps too, such exculpation led other Chimaltecos to accord to the priests responsibility for bringing religious changes to Chimbal.

A second, more intractable problem in Chimalteco perceptions about religious change lies in the pace with which these changes took place. If medicine played an important role in the downfall of *chmaan*, as Chimaltecos frequently told me, it did so long before the Maryknolls established clinics in Chimbal and San Pedro during the 1960s. As mentioned before, medicine dispensed by the early missioners consisted of little more than aspirin and treatments for dysentery and malaria. This suggests that Chimaltecos may have been questioning the efficacy of *chmaan* well before the Maryknolls arrived, and the introduction of even limited Western medicines sufficed to depose them.

Indeed, Chimalteco attitudes toward *chmaan* were waning even in Wagley's time. As early as 1937, Chimalteco men expressed embarrassment at carrying a censer in public *como un viejo*, "like an oldster," leaving their wives to perform most family *costumbre* at church and shrines without them (Wagley 1949: 73, 112). Few Chimalteco men aspired to the role of *chmaan* because of the prohibitions involved: "It contributes little to their economic status, and, further, it forces continence on them for much of the year, since no *costumbre* can be performed if the *chimán* has had access to his wife the previous night" (Wagley 1949: 72). Chimaltecos may have thus still professed faith in the practices, but they had already acquired a certain latitude in their religiosity that subsequent changes undoubtedly informed but by no means wholly engendered (cf. Wagley 1949: 20n). The ability of many Chimaltecos to live today *sin religión* would seem to reinforce this supposition.

Three other factors appear to have contributed to the rapid decline of traditional religion in Chimbal. First, Chimalteco catechists encountered relatively little institutionalized opposition to their appropriation of the local church. Chimbal lacked the elaborate *cofradías* found elsewhere—hierarchically organized religious brotherhoods dedicated to particular saints, which often possess their own images and chapels. Instead, public religion in Chimbal had long centered on the church itself: in 1937, only four Chimalteco *martoon*, "stewards," cared for all the saints in the church, and at no time since the arrival of the Maryknolls have there been more than seven. Given their structural marginality within the Chimalteco cargo system as a whole (see chapter 5), the *martoon* represented a minimal institutional interest in controlling the local church, and once the catechists had usurped the building itself, traditionalists had no other formal institutions to sustain them. In contrast, Maya towns with more elaborate *cofradías*, especially those in the midwestern highlands of Guatemala, often opposed Catholic missionization much more vigorously (cf. Mendelson 1965; Reina 1966; Calder 1970: 96–101; Warren 1978). The Mam towns that today remain more religiously conservative have apparently always maintained more well developed religious organizations.[17]

Second, in addition to the vulnerability of local church organization, the catechists may have triumphed by successfully identifying their reforms with existing holy places and familiar ritual practices. That is, Maryknoll priests revealed to them the significance of a Catholic liturgy already extant in Chimbal. The first Maryknoll priest perhaps inadvertently initiated this strategy when he taught early converts the meaning behind the Latin liturgy that Chimalteco cantors and *sacristanes* had long repeated but little understood. What had been merely rote adherence to external form took on greater depth and meaning. Better yet, these newly revealed truths lay inextricably bound to familiar local practices. Catechists could thus appeal not merely to the dictates of an intrusive Catholic orthodoxy but also to established precedents in the church of their ancestors. Armed with the newly revealed significance of long-accepted practices, the catechists could act even more self-righteously as the redeemers of past iniquities in their community's church.[18]

A third, and largely unintentional, fact may have also contributed

to Maryknoll efforts to attract initial converts. As white foreigners
rather than Ladinos, Maryknoll missioners neither encountered the
immediate ethnic hostility of Mayas nor had to overcome Ladino
stereotypes of "backward Indians." They did have to allay Maya
fears of their foreign appearance and distant origins (cf. Oakes 1951:
33), but two things worked in their favor. First, they were Catholic
priests, not evangelical missionaries, and second, they demanded
very little in the way of provisions during their pastoral visits. They
did not even charge for baptisms and masses, as the Mercedarian Fathers had (cf. Wagley 1949: 50n, 121; Oakes 1951: 53; LaFarge 1947:
80). As foreign missionaries, Maryknolls drew support from their
home dioceses in the United States and remained financially independent of the communities where they worked in ways that the
Guatemalan national clergy could not (cf. Calder 1970: 59–62).

    These differences favorably impressed Chimaltecos. Indeed, Chi-
maltecos often expressed their preference for gringos over Ladinos.
As one said, "Ladinos speak too fast, and when we don't understand
them right away, they insult us. Gringos speak slower and have more
patience." During the 1960s and 1970s, Maryknoll efforts to learn
Mam and to preach in it won further approval, despite the misgivings of certain catechists. In contrast, the Maryknoll priest in San
Pedro Necta in 1980 told me that a Guatemalan Ladino priest who
once worked in the parish had had difficulties, feeling that Chimaltecos were "immoral" and "too independent." In later years, Maryknoll community development programs also helped attract converts, but initially, the humanistic, relatively egalitarian attitudes of
the American Maryknoll missioners themselves may have made
Chimaltecos more receptive to the teachings of these new and decidedly different kinds of priests.[19]

    The coincidence of a number of historical factors thus facilitated
Maryknoll success in Chimbal. The creeping erosion of traditional
ways, the waning authority of cargo rituals to legitimize community
sovereignty, the vulnerability of Chimalteco church organization,
revelations about the true meaning of religious forms, and the arrival
of foreign missionaries who nonetheless belonged to the Catholic
church all enabled Chimalteco catechists to appropriate the physical center as well as moral high ground of religious life in Chimbal
and so effectively challenge the *chmaan*. With so much of public
religion thus firmly in their hands, the catechists besieged the traditionalists with increasingly vigorous opposition.[20] This confrontation and the reaction that it eventually engendered in the community must be examined in greater detail.

The *Chmaan* as *Choolil*

Religious change in Chimbal, whether Catholic or evangelical, entailed two phases. Missionaries first recruited a core group of local
adherents, who then proselytized within the community. Initial
Catholic converts found strength in the newly revealed meaning of
old practices; evangelical converts saw fit to reject these practices
altogether. In either case, converts had to convince others of the
truth of their revelations. For the catechists, direct contact between
the Maryknoll priest and the community remained too sporadic and
brief to inspire mass conversion. Consequently, catechists interpreted and implemented Maryknoll mission policy on their own, en-
gendering the autonomy that still leads to occasional tensions between them and the priest. In prosecuting their holy war against the
chmaan, catechists chose to fight primarily on pragmatic rather
than theological grounds, focusing on what they saw as the two fundamental abuses of *costumbre:* drinking and wasting money on
pointless rituals (cf. Warren 1978: 99).

Catechists argued that expenditures for *costumbre* outweighed
any tangible return, whether in curing or divination. Their arguments obviously had their intended effect because older Chimaltecos repeatedly told me that they had lost faith in *costumbre* because
chmaan had only "deceived" people. As one nonconvert observed,
"If the *chmaan* had been true, they would have been gladly given
their tortillas [payment], but many times they just drank their *tragos*
[literally, "swallows" (of *aguardiente*)] and didn't do a thing." Another elderly Chimalteco proudly recounted how he had completed
his cargo service as first *regidor* in 1952 when the office still required "over Q200 in expenses," but he concluded by saying, "*Kukx
teen costumbre; minti? iil ti?j* [Let *costumbre* be! There's no need
for it]." "Before, when we went to *chmaan*," he continued, "sometimes they would say that the sick person would live, other times
that they would die. Sometimes the *chmaan* were right, sometimes
they were wrong. They didn't know. That's why the catechists taught
us that they only deceived people." I later learned that this man's
grown daughter had died in 1961 after he had allowed only a *chmaan*
to treat her illness. Even his lifelong commitment to traditional ritual and religion could not blind him to what he eventually came to
perceive as the deceitful inefficacy—intentional or not—of the
chmaan. His personal tragedy did not lead him to convert immediately to the religion that had revealed the folly of his faith in
chmaan, perhaps because this would have denied him the solace of

accepting his—and his daughter's—fate. Only at the end of 1980, at the age of seventy-three, did he and his wife accept baptism into the Catholic church.

Another skeptic remarked that a *chmaan*, hidden in the enclosure surrounding his *mees* altar and covered with a blanket in a darkened house, could easily fake an encounter with his spirit (cf. Oakes 1951: 204–208). "Once, when I was young," this man went on, "I went to a *chmaan* with my mother because one of her cousins was sick. He got under his blanket and began calling the *witz*. I don't know how he knew so many names! Then he changed his voice and began speaking in Spanish. The *chmaan* called me by my older brother's name since he had accompanied my mother on her previous visit. When I told the 'spirit' that I wasn't my brother, he said that I should have more respect!" This man showed me how *chmaan* made the whirring sound that signaled the arrival and departure of the spirits by twirling a small stick with strips of leather attached to it called *alas de Dios*, "wings of God" (*wi'y* in Mam). Despite this skepticism and deprecation of the few *chmaan* left in Chimbal, many of these same Chimaltecos assured me that in the past there had been true *chmaan* with real power and faith, but they had all died *ojtxe*, "long ago."

Several factors appear to have aided the catechists in successfully maligning the *chmaan*. First, as mentioned before, the practices of Chimalteco *aj mees* may have actually come from San Juan early in this century, and catechists perhaps played on Chimalteco fears of foreign sorcery to discredit these "ways of San Juan" and, by association, all other *costumbre* (cf. Wagley 1949: 114). Chimaltecos had long feared sorcerers from neighboring towns, claiming that although Chimalteco *chmaan* lacked knowledge of such evils, sorcerers infested nearby San Juan Atitán and Colotenango (Wagley 1949: 77–78; cf. Koizumi 1981). Certainly, the ability of *aj mees* to make pacts with *witz* and to counter witchcraft smacked more of sorcery than the simple divinations of *aj q'iij*.

A second factor aiding the catechists involved Chimalteco conventions that left *aj mees* highly vulnerable to accusations of being *choolil*, "murderers," in league with *witz* (see chapter 4). Although the two callings opposed one another in Chimalteco conceptions, *aj mees* and *choolil* shared many characteristics. Both trafficked with *witz* regarding others' misfortunes: the *aj mees* ostensibly prayed for his fellow Chimaltecos, while *choolil* preyed upon them, carrying their victims' heads to bloodthirsty *witz* in exchange for money. Furthermore, both acted in socially anomalous contexts—the *aj mees* conjuring up *witz* during rituals late at night when Chimaltecos usually slept, the *choolil* making pacts with *witz* while wandering through the wilds far from the pueblo. Even more damning for *aj mees*, the actions of both practitioners ultimately benefited the *witz: choolil* supplied them with heads; *aj mees* provided them with souls, since even a successful cure condemned the patient to long servitude with the spirit "owner" of the *aj mees*'s altar. That is, in defending Chimaltecos from the machinations of both *witz* and malevolent fellow mortals, *aj mees* could only negotiate *chojb'il*, "payments," that postponed—but never forestalled—the inevitable triumph of the *witz*. Even within established Chimalteco conventions, then, the transformation of *aj mees* into *choolil* only required that Chimaltecos come to interpret such expiation as collusion with *witz* instead of subservience to them.

In addition to the historical and conventional vulnerability of Chimalteco *chmaan*, a third factor contributing to the success of the catechists involved the introduction of Western medicine. Because alleviating afflictions constituted a primary function of traditional Chimalteco religion, the first Maryknoll missioner to work in Chimbal distributed medicines specifically "to draw people away from the *chimanes*," as he told me. This allowed converts not only to challenge *chmaan* ritual on the practical grounds of being a needless expense but also to offer something tangible in its stead. Although unimpressive compared to the Maryknoll medical programs that came later, even simple remedies enabled catechists to argue that if these cures belied the prognostications of *chmaan*, then the entire process of ritual expenditures only further victimized those it purported to relieve. The efficacy of alternative remedies did not have to be absolute in order to impugn the self-confirming, but contingent, powers of *chmaan*.

Nonetheless, medicine alone could not discredit the *chmaan*. Chimaltecos had long recognized that sickness involved natural causes, but "even though a person will ask for and take a *remedio* (medicine), the Chimalteco believes that some supernatural cause is at the base of his misfortune" (Wagley 1949: 75). Catechists thus had to counter the epistemology of the *chmaan* as well. To a certain extent, they again paralleled Chimalteco conventions, this time the *aj q'iij*'s ritual appeals for God's protection. Rather than *costumbre*, catechists stressed the importance of personal prayer in seeking God's mercy. God did not "eat" offerings of candles or copal, turkey eggs or chickens. Instead, God saw into people's thoughts and knew their hearts when they prayed. Catechists emphasized the primacy of internal spiritual attitude over external ritual acts (cf. Warren 1978: 103–104), a shift doubtlessly influenced by the priest's revelations to them of the "deeper" meanings of Catholic liturgy. Finally, catechists argued that *witz* represented nothing more than incarnations of the devil himself. Since God had no need for ritual offerings, *costumbre* could only serve the devil. Not only was *costumbre* wasteful in practical terms, but it also actually worked against the sufferer's spiritual interests and intentions.

The practical and theological arguments of the catechists eventually engendered the disdain that most Chimaltecos presently hold toward *chmaan*. Ironically, *chmaan* proved more vulnerable to accusations of what they were not—that is, curers in a technical sense—than to attacks on the epistemology and practices that they used to explain, but not necessarily to cure, afflictions. In fact, the catechists held a number of assumptions in common with the *chmaan*. For them, as for the *chmaan*, the ultimate power to heal lay with God. Similarly, rather than denying the reality of *witz*, catechists identified them as minions of the devil, a suspicion that Chimaltecos may have already held (cf. Wagley 1949: 56n). In other words, in challenging the practical efficacy of *chmaan* rituals, catechists disputed not the validity of unseen agency but the motivations and demands of human practitioners. Once the possibility of more effective cures made their rituals problematic, *aj mees*, and by association, *aj q'iij*, metamorphosed into *choolil*—at best the unwitting cat's-paws of *witz*; at worst, deliberate frauds profiteering from the afflictions of others. By 1979, a young Chimalteco who had recently converted to Catholicism could say unequivocally, "*Chmaan* today don't know how to cure. They only perform sorcery to kill people or to get money. I don't know where the money comes from, but it's only used for evil. They only use it to buy *aguardiente*." Through youthful eyes, the transformation of *chmaan* into *choolil* appears complete.[21]

Today, although older townspeople still burn candles to Santiago in the church, *costumbre* for curing has disappeared completely from public life. Instead, Chimaltecos have developed an almost religious faith in pills and injections, frequently resorting to medicine without necessarily heeding the exhortations of the catechists to accept orthodox Catholicism. This hardly means that Chimaltecos now unequivocally believe in Western medicine. The vagaries of diagnosis, cursory consultations with Ladino physicians or self-trained local "barefoot doctors," and the cost of inappropriate drugs or unnecessary injections can quickly dampen Chimalteco enthusiasm if relief is not forthcoming. Chimaltecos often note that because doctors do not understand things like *seky'pajleenin* or *kyq'iq'*, "chills" (literally, "wind" in Mam, *aire* in Spanish, that enters the body and causes sickness), their drugs seldom cure such maladies. Nonetheless, ever pragmatic in matters of survival, Chimaltecos try different remedies—especially a drug that has proven effective in the past. When the magic of pills and injections fails, however, they freely resort to *xhb'ool*, the traditional herbal curers and midwives whose skills remain highly respected in Chimbal.[22] While the downfall of *chmaan* and *costumbre* clearly increased Chimalteco awareness of alternative modes of curing, it neither led to wholesale conversion to orthodox Catholicism nor resulted in blind acceptance of Western technology.

At the same time, protracted illness still carries strong moral import in Chimbal, and groups of catechists visit sick neighbors to persuade them that faith in God will cure their afflictions. As with the former recruitment of *chmaan*, sickness constitutes a primary mode of contemporary religious conversion. One convert told me: "About four years ago I was sick for three months. I didn't have any strength and I didn't want to do anything. I barely had the strength to get up to sit by the fire. I went to a doctor in Huehuetenango, but he didn't help. Finally, the catechists came to visit me, and they said that God was the only cure. I listened to them, and within a week I began to get better. I recovered only because of my prayers to God." An older catechist described how he and several other Chimaltecos had visited an ailing *chmaan* in a nearby hamlet of San Juan Atitán. They argued that his rituals were futile—and therefore foolish—and that the demands of his *mees* altar were a thing of the devil rather than of God. According to the catechist, after several visits, "he finally broke up his *mees* and threw it away."

For these converts, the alleviation of afflictions now rests ultimately with God. "Only God is the medicine, only God," said one, meaning that without prayers to God, medicines have no potency. Like laymen's prayers in the past, these supplications contain nothing esoteric, consisting primarily of rapid repetitions of "*Qmaan dyoos, qmaan jesu kriisto, qmaan espíritu santo* [Our Father God, Our Father Jesus Christ, Our Father Holy Ghost]" and pleas such as "*Chintq'aanme dyoos* [Cure me, God!]." The invalid recites such prayers before taking the medicine, and although brief, the act is by no means perfunctory. Dispensing with *chmaan* as ritual mediators, converts relate more directly to God, yet this relationship has become increasingly intangible. Where saint and *witz* once demanded the concrete recognition and attention of conventionalized social interlocutors, God demands the simple—but infinitely more difficult—spiritual act of faith.

The Elusiveness of Meaning

In analyzing religious change in a neighboring Mam *municipio*, Junji Koizumi (1981) clearly demonstrates that conversion there often reflected tenets of traditional Mam religion rather than total acceptance of a new ideology. Religious change remained dialectical rather than linear, embedded in an inconclusive praxis of inquiry, interpretation, and doubt. The demise of traditional religion in Chimbal reveals the same process. On one hand, historical and social structural factors contributed to the changes that took place: the relative dearth of religious cargos and the preservation of much of the old Latin liturgy, the lack of formal institutions linking *chmaan* in the cult of the soul, the possible introduction of foreign ritual practices from San Juan Atitán, the arrival of active, humanistic Catholic missionaries—all hastened the collapse of traditional religion. On the other hand, the triumph of new religions in Chimbal also depended on the reinterpretation rather than eradication of former religious conventions: long-standing church liturgy acquired meaning beyond its mere performance; *chmaan* became vilified as a kind of *choolil*; "magical" medical remedies replaced formulaic *costumbre*; personal supplications to God superseded the *naab'l*, "things for praying," of the *aj q'iij* and the *chojb'il* of the *aj mees*. Thus, despite the unquestionable transformation of local institutions, much religious innovation in Chimbal developed from, and in this way reaffirmed, preexisting Chimalteco conventions.

Continuities in Chimalteco religion persist, despite the protestations of catechist and evangelical alike and the repression suffered during the Guatemalan army's counterinsurgency campaigns of the early 1980s (see chapter 7). When I visited Chimbal in January 1988, I was surprised at the prevalence and intensity of religious concerns within the community. Many people asked if I had become a "believer," and the phrase "*o ʔkx tu ʔn dyoos* [only by (the grace of) God" punctuated many conversations. More concretely, during the year before my visit, the catechists had organized and carried out construction of a new wooden ceiling for the church. The project had involved nearly four hundred days of donated labor and over Q4,300 in donations from baptized and unbaptized Catholics alike. According to one Chimalteco, the carpenter who supervised the work had followed a design that had come to him in a dream. Equally impressive, Catholic youth groups had burgeoned, with over eighty girls and a hundred boys, and young men had formed six bands complete with guitars, trumpets, and electric bass and organ to play *ranchera*-style religious songs during church services.

A Chimalteco catechist and his family, January 1988.

During the ceremonies to dedicate the new ceiling, sermons by Chimalteco animators echoed two themes. First, they likened their ancestors' building of the church in Chimbal to King David's building of the Temple in Jerusalem. Then the animators drew parallels between the newly completed ceiling and the original efforts of these first Chimaltecos. They emphasized that their efforts could not match the accomplishments and sacrifice of the ancestors who, few in number, had built the church only by working day and night. The new ceiling remained a mere embellishment to ancestral achievements. In modeling their actions on the past, the animators rhetorically conflated biblical king with Chimalteco ancestor, Church universal with ancestral church in Chimbal. Eliding for the moment associations between ancestors and iniquitous *costumbre*, they accentuated positive continuities with the local past, specifically embodied by the seemingly ageless church building itself. In so doing, they legitimized the catholicity of the Chimalteco church while reaffirming its inherent Chimalteco-ness.

The ruthless counterinsurgency measures of the Guatemalan army severely tested Chimalteco faith and endurance, but townspeople repeatedly told me in 1988 that their religiosity, regardless of church affiliation, had saved them from the jealousy and envy that had caused people elsewhere to denounce each other to the army as "subversives." Two older Chimaltecos separately and spontaneously recounted how the army occupation of the town had ended in 1983: one night, a civil patrol on the San Pedro road met an imposing figure on a white horse who told them to turn back. When the Chimaltecos told him that they were under pain of death to carry out their patrol, he led them back to town himself. When the soldiers tried to shoot him, their rifles misfired, and the horseman rode up the steps of the church and disappeared inside. The next night, the army commander, "a hot-headed man," led the patrol himself, and they again encountered the man on the white horse, this time at the edge of town just above the cemetery. The commander tried to shoot him, but the horse reared and knocked him down the hill into the cemetery, and again the horseman rode into town and entered the church. The horseman returned a final time to confront the army commander, warning that if any Chimaltecos were killed, he would kill the soldiers: he, not they, best protected Chimbal. The next day, according to the story, the army withdrew.

The horseman, of course, was Santiago—not just the wooden image in the church but "the spirit of Santiago," charged by God to protect the community. Regardless of what actually happened, and the creeping disenchantment of Chimalteco life, Santiago still embodied a way of meaningfully representing—perhaps even explaining—enigmatic events and the reality of local sovereignty, solidarity, and luck.

At the same time, real changes in religious conventions have undeniably occurred. In preaching against *chmaan* and *witz*, catechists succeeded in reducing the dialectical nature of Chimalteco religious conventions to diametric oppositions. In the past, deities had represented a mix of positive and negative qualities, of both benevolence and selfish disregard for mortal concerns. Ritual relations with saint and *witz* strove to balance these opposites, in the process substantiating the need for a similar equanimity in human social relations (see chapters 3 and 4). Both catechists and evangelicals, however, now dichotomize the cosmos into that which is "good"—and therefore godly—and that which belongs to the devil. They have reduced saint and *witz* to analytical dualisms that hold importance not as social interlocutors but as moral—or immoral—exemplars. Religion must now be found in private faith rather than public acts, in personal purity rather than animate images.[23]

This loss of social scale, and the necessity of confronting deities as abstractions, has perhaps discouraged many Chimaltecos from converting to some form of orthodox Christianity, even though most have overtly forsaken the *chmaan*. Equally daunting, some evangelicals see only a wrathful God, a fact brought home to me when I heard one convert thunder to a sick Chimalteco, "Pain and sickness are the whips of God to punish and drive out the evil in us, even in our thoughts! Search for proper medicines, but you must pray to God." This polarization of good and evil in religious conventions paradoxically demands that Chimaltecos make a greater personal commitment than ever before to an increasingly impersonal, unknowable God, while conversely, the devil lurks close at hand, ready to bring down God's wrath on all at any time.

It is important to note, however, that few Chimaltecos agonize over such metaphysical dilemmas in their daily lives. Even sectarian disputes remain relative rather than absolute. Neither the disdain of evangelicals for Catholic ritual nor the intransigence of catechists toward traditionalists has yet split the community into mutually exclusive factions. As I heard one Chimalteco evangelical say to a Catholic neighbor, "There are many ways to God, but only one God." Both espouse a similar theology: have faith in God and go to heaven, or live sinfully and burn in hell. For all Chimaltecos, regardless of religious affiliation, the path of righteousness still largely follows the earthly dictates of *naab'l*—their "soul" or moral "way of being"—that oblige them to act toward one another in recognizable and understandable ways, not simply according to some absolute standard of good and evil. Whatever the other commandments from church and conscience, exemplary Chimaltecos still honor a morality predicated on the transparency of this-worldly rather than otherworldly souls. They remain engaged in the continuously negotiated social reality conventionalized by *naab'l* that has for so long defined them as a community (see chapter 4).

Yet Chimaltecos must also grapple with realities that have changed irrevocably. Local conventions alone no longer suffice to interpret the totality of Chimalteco experience. Rather than conventionalizing immorality in the form of *witz* and fearing strangers as possible visitations of these brooding presences, Chimaltecos now have frequent enough contact with outsiders to perceive them in human—if no less ambivalent—terms. Similarly, rather than trusting to *swert,* "fate" (from the Spanish *suerte,* "luck"), many Chimaltecos now speak of having *xiimb'itz,* "thoughts"—or more specifically, "plans." Life consists of making decisions, not merely discovering and acquiescing to one's fate. As one man put it, "There are people in Chimbal now who know more of the world than just this pueblo, and they want more than what they find in it." At the same time, old boundaries and barriers persist. One catechist observed, "All people in the world are of the same spirit, but Ladinos used to think that Indians were merely animals without souls [he used the Spanish word *alma*]. There are some Ladinos today who have realized that everyone—Indians and Ladinos alike—are the same. But there is still exploitation. . . ."

Witz no longer walk abroad in the world, but Ladinos still do; ritual relations with Santiago may no longer conventionalize the moral obligations of being Chimalteco, but the tacit dictates of *naab'l* still do; and familial and community responsibilities may no longer shape all the possibilities of Chimalteco ambition, but Chimalteco rootedness in their place of birth still does. Chimaltecos must now steer their own life courses: *aj q'iij* no longer reassure with their divinations, yet Chimaltecos recognize that the solace the *aj q'iij* once offered frequently proved empty, leaving them to discern for themselves the meaning of their fate. For Chimaltecos today, this meaning lies not in their own or their ancestors' past sins but in the outcome of their present *xiimb'itz,* their future hopes and plans for *chunqlaal,* "life." In attempting to escape the moral fatalism of the past, however, Chimaltecos have perhaps inadvertently become hostages of the future—and thus all the more vulnerable to the oppressors who would exploit them and the reformers, redeemers, and revolutionaries who purport to save them.

9

✛ *Conclusion* ✛

This study began with two questions. First, how do the people of Santiago Chimaltenango define their ethnic distinctiveness? And second, what is the relationship between this enduring ethnic identity and changes that have occurred in Chimalteco life during the last century? In answering the first question, I focused on the conventionally constructed rather than institutionally structured aspects of Chimalteco identity. I argued that Chimaltecos' ideas about themselves begin with quotidian routines and the seasonal round. Townspeople conventionalize their identity in terms of how they make their world work given where they live, what they must do to survive there, and who they must enlist to do so. Saint and *witz*, souls and soul-loss, mutual obligations and public recognition—all demonstrate how closely "being Chimalteco" depends on being in Chimbal. There Chimaltecos pursue their common—if not always compatible or even constant—concerns and commitments. These ongoing interactions engender the sense of community that lies at the heart of their ethnic distinctiveness. This identity presumes neither enduring uniqueness nor compulsive conformity. Instead, Chimaltecos are Chimalteco because they are born in Chimbal, live in Chimbal, and do what Chimaltecos do, whatever this might be or become.

As tautological as this sounds, Chimaltecos are not free simply to invent their own identity. History constrains them, especially the colonial heritage of Guatemala that glorifies the Maya past yet denigrates contemporary Maya as "uncivilized Indians." The material, social, and spiritual immediacies of local life also constrain what it means to be Chimalteco. Far from an arbitrary act of individual or collective will, Chimalteco identity reflects the culturally defined ways and means available to them; the attitudes, actions, and interests of those around them; and the ever-shifting predicaments facing everyone. Consequently, the first question posed by this study concerning the nature of Chimalteco ethnic identity necessitates the second question of the relationship between this identity and the changing circumstances of its expression.

The second half of the book thus documented certain economic, political, and religious changes that have occurred in Chimbal during the twentieth century. Although never passive tokens in these events, Chimaltecos have often had few options. A burgeoning population on a limited land base has indentured them to labor and commodity markets outside the community. The Guatemalan state has usurped their autonomy while repressing local political and economic activities. And catechists as well as evangelicals have successfully overthrown the old shaman-diviners, even though otherworldly Christian salvation remains no less problematic.

Where possible, however, Chimaltecos have seized upon cash-cropping in coffee, local party politics, and the redemptive promise of new religions, provoking disparities in wealth, ambition, and belief that have broadened—at times confounded—what it is that Chimaltecos do. Nonetheless, the place where they do it still endures. Successful Chimaltecos seldom choose to leave town but maintain a locally respectable, if more comfortable, style of living. Poorer Chimaltecos migrate seasonally to the plantations on the Pacific coast or depart periodically to work small plots of corn and coffee in nearby *municipios*, but they leave Chimbal permanently only as a last resort. All simply aspire to make their lives better. Although outwardly transformed, local continuities in place, people, and premises clearly persist through two dialectically related processes.

On one hand, the exigencies of life have progressively blurred the boundaries of Chimbal. Most men now dress in a generalized *campesino* fashion, and only Chimalteco women and older men retain their distinctive handwoven garb. Cargoholders have become civil servants of the national government, Catholic and evangelical converts espouse a universal Christianity, and elders lament the creeping Hispanicisms in the Mam of younger Chimaltecos. Workers migrate to the plantations, while their richer neighbors venture to the cities as merchants to replenish their stock for resale in local markets. Even the humblest Chimaltecos own radios that link them to the national society, if only for the music rather than the news bulletins in staccato Spanish that often prompt a marked drop in the radio's volume. A few television sets even flicker here and there, although they still nonplus viewers uncertain about the boundary between actuality and entertainment. In many ways, contact with the larger world breeds a sense of impending dissolution of Chimalteco culture.

On the other hand, Guatemalan national society also heightens Chimaltecos' awareness of their distinctiveness. They enter the Ladino world as strangers confronted by indifference in the cities, by economic exploitation on the plantations—and everywhere by racial discrimination and deprecation of their uncivilized ways. Even encounters with other Maya only accentuate the different languages and customs that separate them. Sometimes Chimaltecos themselves circumvent this larger world: town officials win back from the government Chimbal's status as a *municipio;* a few educated Chimaltecos become teachers in distant towns; local coffee growers secede from the Ladino-controlled cooperative in San Pedro; town merchants break the monopoly that Ladino and other Maya vendors once held in the weekly market; and catechists actively mediate priestly authority in the community.

Just as Guatemalan society erodes community boundaries, its anonymous prejudices accentuate the familiarity of Chimbal, even though no magical affinity—not even the presumed constancy of Chimalteco souls—guarantees the good faith of neighbors simply because they are Chimalteco. While permanence and proximity often do make neighbors willful competitors, propinquity also enables Chimaltecos to expect moral correctness from each other. Within the community, persistent bad faith readily engenders resentment, gossip, and eventual avoidance—a dangerous sanction in an uncertain world. Inescapable local reputation thus defines who to trust and how far. In contrast, the anonymity, the inconstancy—at times the outright villainy—of the Ladino world offer little in place of this common, if circumscribed, humanity. The relative dearth of Ladinos in Chimbal only sharpens the ethnic nature of this contrast.

At the same time, because Chimalteco identity remains dialectical rather than merely oppositional, it changes as the social and material conditions of the community change. In the past, notions of community presumed an inclusive, largely tacit sense of Chimalteconess embedded in a localized but far from isolated social existence. *Naab'l* defined community membership in terms of a collective "way of being" predicated on individual observance of social expectations. Such normality, however, involved not simply compulsive cultural conformity but recognizable improvisations on the changing circumstances of life. Here again, the relative absence of Ladinos in the community clearly enabled Chimaltecos to take up Ladino-like activities such as cash-cropping, party politics, and religious reconstruction without immediately becoming identified with local oppressors.

Economic, political, and religious changes have slowly altered this local identity. As Chimaltecos venture ever more routinely outside their community, encounters with Maya from other towns, overseers on Ladino plantations, Ladino shopkeepers in the cities, and Guatemalan soldiers rooting out suspected subversives on streets and buses prompt a more personal, individualized experience of otherness. Their Chimalteco-ness has become as much a nexus of personal traits, such as parentage, physiognomy, and place of birth, as the shared basis for social interaction within a circumscribed time and place. While an inclusive, interactional definition of identity has yet to change to an exclusive, essentialist one, models for such atomism already exist in the town: economic innovations demand individual initiative, party politics highlight individual politicians and voter choice, and religious conversion hinges on personal conscience.

Short of wholesale destruction of the town, however—or a revolutionary transformation in Guatemalan society as a whole—Ladinos will continue to class all Chimaltecos pejoratively as "Indians," whether rich or poor, impassive or activist, Christian or traditionalist. So categorized by others, Chimaltecos will likely continue to live according to the conventions of identity and community described in this book. Patterns of work and weather; the existential sovereignty of people and place; the prudence of minimizing risks before maximizing gains; the obligations as well as rewards of enduring acquaintance; the local fostering of trust, decency, and hope—none of these remain unique to Chimbal, but when fleshed out by individual Chimalteco lives, they take on a compelling familiarity that once experienced remains unmistakably Chimalteco.

At the beginning of this book, I asserted that close attention to the "existential sovereignty" of Chimalteco life—that is, to the realities of place, people, and premise—would help clarify Chimalteco and, more broadly, Maya motivations for living in ethnically distinct communities. I also argued that it could provide insight into how larger global realities take shape within particular times and places. In this regard, I have tried to confront at least two "empty centers" in Maya and Guatemalan studies, one ethnographic and the other analytical.

Ethnographically, the empty center that I have tried to plumb lies in reconciling Maya ethnic solidarity with the intrinsic antipathies of so-called peasant communities. That is, how do apparently enduring Maya identities abide within the self-interested envy, suspicions, and "limited good" that have come to characterize post-Redfieldian views of peasant life? I have tried to show in this book that resolving this dilemma demands more than choosing one view over the other, because both are true. Like all peoples, Maya are by turn nasty and nice, opportunistic and inveterate. Their communities encompass individual interests and common commitments, short-term contingencies and long-term considerations. Neither primordial cultural patterns or pernicious peasant marginality sufficiently explain how these conflicting personal, local, and ethnic realities shape Maya communities—or why Maya live in them at all. Answers to these questions lie in the more general problem of social cooperation itself.

In his book *The Evolution of Cooperation* (1984), Robert Axelrod argues that in the absence of an overarching central authority, cooperation between purely self-interested parties depends on repeated interactions. "As long as the interaction is not iterated, cooperation is very difficult. That is why an important way to promote cooperation is to arrange that the same two individuals will meet each other again, be able to recognize each other from the past, and to recall how the other has behaved until now. This continuing interaction is what makes it possible for cooperation based on reciprocity to be stable" (1984: 125). Axelrod goes on to observe that chances of stable cooperation are further enhanced by "making the interactions more durable, and by making them more frequent" (1984: 129). That is, the longer a relationship presumably extends into the future, the greater its potential benefits. The temptation to cheat or defect diminishes as perceived long-term advantages come to outweigh the short-term gains of doing less than one's fair share. Similarly, by making interactions more frequent, the future rewards of cooperation become more immediately relevant to present decisions of whether or not to cooperate.

Finally, Axelrod notes, "A good way to increase the frequency of interactions between two given individuals is to keep others away. . . . [A]ny form of specialization tending to restrict interactions to only a few others would tend to make the interactions with those few more frequent. This is one reason why cooperation emerges more readily in small towns than in large cities" (1984: 130). Not incidentally, such circumstances also make local reputation increasingly effective in identifying cheaters and forestalling deceitful behavior. If partners punish known cheaters by refusing to interact with them, habitual offenders can soon find themselves with no other partners to dupe and must either mend their ways or leave the group.

Given these considerations, community becomes not just a convenient locus for social cooperation but a necessary correlate of it.

The ethnic "specialization" of Maya communities also clearly conditions social cooperation. It promotes "iterated," long-term interactions, which invest present behavior with future considerations,
intensify the sanction of local reputation based on past behavior,
and impede cheating within local bounds. While itself almost a
truism, the association between shared identity and social cooperation underscores the emergent nature of Maya communities: in
regulating interactions between parties, community defines less an
absolute institutional order than a nexus of contingent strategies of
social cooperation. Consequently, just as cooperation tempers—but
never eliminates—other individual interests and antipathies, bonds
of local identity neither deny nor override enduring differences in
Maya communities. They represent but one of the centripetal as
well as centrifugal pressures that shape community boundaries.

At the same time, the ethnic specialization of Maya communities
does more than merely localize social cooperation. It also sanctifies
community boundaries in the sense developed by Roy Rappaport
(1979a, 1979b): the saints, ancestors, and souls that objectify local
Maya identities remain purely conventional and thus unfalsifiable,
inasmuch as no one can prove that they do not exist. As long as
Maya take them to be meaningful, these images of common origins
and essences lend their aura of self-evident truth to whatever local
practices and expectations that become associated with them. As a
sanctifying principle, Maya identity presumes neither absolute accord nor strict adherence to ancestral ways, only a mutual engagement that makes possible—without ever guaranteeing—common
social purpose.

In answering the ethnographic question of why Mayas should live
in ethnically distinct communities, I would argue that they continue to do so based on the formal prerequisites of cooperation that
Axelrod so elegantly outlines, conditioned by the practical, conventional, and historical realities discussed in this book. That these
communities should also accommodate equally real divisions and
disaffections, and often express them in ever-changing institutional
and conventional forms, attests less to their waning Mayaness—or
to their disintegration as communities—than to their intrinsic, contingently cooperative nature.

Such a strategic, cooperative approach to community pertains
equally to the second, analytical empty center addressed in this
book concerning the conjunction of local and global influences in
Maya life. As noted at the outset, treatments of the Maya of Guatemala tend to take one of two complementary tacks. On one hand,

cultural essentialists stress local attitudes, values, and behavior as the core of Maya distinctiveness; they predict that as acculturation alters these, the Maya will disappear. On the other hand, colonial historicists argue that the past and present political economy of Guatemala confirms the colonialized Indianness of contemporary Maya life; when oppression disappears from Guatemalan society, so will Indianness—and with it the Maya. Ironically, culturalist predictions have proven wrong, but for the right reasons: acculturation has not eviscerated Maya communities, but they endure precisely because local values and social morality survive the passing of particular institutions and practices. In contrast, historicist explanations are right, but for the wrong reasons: oppression and inequality do cause Maya communities to persist, but such iniquity alone did not create them. Maya have always created themselves—if not exactly as they wanted, then neither entirely as others intended.

As I have argued in this book, the emergent continuities of Maya community mediate this disjunction between culturalist and historicist considerations. On one hand, the existential sovereignty of community derives from the local contingencies of social cooperation and cultural conventions; on the other, it also presupposes the global encompassments of ecology, history, and hegemony. That I have focused on a single community such as Santiago Chimaltenango thus involves no denial of global processes, only the assumption that such conditions must always find articulation in particular times and places: although perhaps "ultimately determinant," global events and interrelationships by definition remain incontiguous and thus often amorphous. At the same time, however, the human collectivities of particular times and places also evince the indeterminate immediacies of individual sensibilities, perceptions, and opportunities. As itself a contingent interface between them, community concretizes—and thereby clarifies—these elusive realities.

The approach taken here may seem somewhat at odds with current theoretical fashions in anthropology, which at times appear to polarize analysis between global structures and local meanings, political economy and cultural deconstruction. I have taken this tack, however, because I still see the challenge of anthropology to lie precisely in combining local and global views into meaningful, multidimensional portraits of human proclivities and possibilities. Consequently, I have tried to show how the Maya of Santiago Chimaltenango actively engage the world through local realities that are as tangible and objective as the larger global situations that encompass them. In the process, I have also tried to demystify Chimalteco culture as strategic expressions of community identity rather than mistakenly reify it into the essence of this identity—or community—itself.

Ultimately, all these ruminations on ethnographic and analytical empty centers pale before the intractable political empty center that afflicts Guatemala. Torn between rich and poor, Indian and Ladino, revolutionary left and anti-Communist right, Guatemala in recent years has aggravated rather than assuaged these differences. Despite military ascendancy over guerrilla insurgents and "pacification" of the countryside that supported them, political killings and disappearances continue to terrorize any who take exception to the status quo; despite the first civilian presidency in over twenty years, the Guatemalan army still constitutes the real power in the nation; despite the economic pressures of a burgeoning population and monocrop export dependency, counterinsurgency warfare has left the rural poor more destitute, more dislocated, more dominated than ever before.

One may well ask whether intellectual musings or social scientific research retain any relevance whatsoever under such circumstances. I would argue that they do, if only to correct overly simplistic interpretations of events there. Despite the clear injustices, the struggle in Guatemala reflects not simply good versus evil but deeply entrenched, contending interests. In its own eyes, the Guatemalan state represses not out of sheer malevolence but because its operatives see no alternative to their vision of national security, development, and progress. Similarly, the peoples of Guatemala resist not out of revolutionary idealism but because they too see no alternative to lives of small promise impoverished further by the fears of those who would rule them. To misconstrue these contending interests only obfuscates more complex—and thus equivocal—truths, something that already happens all too often in Guatemala itself.

In this book, I have tried to show that the Maya of Santiago Chimaltenango, although victimized by history and circumstance, live more than as victims; although painfully aware of the injustices in their lives, they struggle on as pragmatists, not ideologues. In this sense, Chimaltecos survived the widespread death and destruction of the 1980s through careful consideration of their interests as both individuals and a community. While perhaps listening to the guerrillas more than they will ever admit now, Chimaltecos also perceived that the risks of revolution far outweighed its promise. With as little as they had, they still felt they had too much to lose. While such reckoning obviously serves the present status quo in Guatemala, it makes Chimaltecos neither hopeless reactionaries nor willing dupes of a terrorist state.

Nearly five hundred years of ongoing conquest have left the Maya of Guatemala culturally transformed and ethnically beleaguered, yet the centuries have also instilled in them habits of survival that if pushed too far might well metamorphose from time-tested local parochialisms into a more generalized, perhaps even revolutionary, activism. Such developments, however, will come in Maya time, in Maya ways—not at the urgings of leftist vanguards or even the outrages of right-wing death squads.

Myriad empty centers pervade Guatemalan life. This study neither resolves nor explains away any of these voids, but it does suggest that at one such center, the people of Santiago Chimaltenango still abide the distances in their lives through the mutual presence once invoked by their old shaman-diviners, *qejo oto²ya tzaluu²,* "We who are here. . . ."

✠ *Notes* ✠

1. Introduction

1. Of course, Wolf originally intended his model of the closed corporate peasant community as a Weberian ideal type designed to identify the socio-economic processes underlying the persistence of ethnically distinct "Indian" communities. Unfortunately, the closed corporate peasant community has become canonized for many Mesoamericanists as a substantive archetype of insular localism, shared poverty, and cultural conformity. It has wrongly become a standard against which the "community-ness" of actual communities is measured empirically rather than being situated conceptually on a continuum between "open" and "closed" configurations (cf. Wolf 1955).

2. More recently, Adams has noted that ladinization also involves Ladino acceptance, not simply acts of Indian will: "For an Indian to lose Indian identity—to become a ladino—two things must happen. The Indian must, for whatever reason, find it undesirable to be an Indian, and the ladinos with whom the Indian associates must also desire or at least accept it. While some Indians may feel that there are advantages to becoming ladino . . . there is rarely any complementary reason leading ladinos to accept them. Thus mestizos in Guatemala and other Latin American countries are still often referred to as indios [a pejorative term for "Indian"] irrespective of the traits and desires of the individuals" (1988: 283).

3. Douglas Brintnall (1980) and Waldemar Smith (1975) have both criticized Colby and van den Berghe's approach. Brintnall (1980: 311–313) argues that the static nature of their model blinds them to the transformational changes in "race relations" between Mayas and Ladinos that has occurred in recent years. Brintnall's analysis, however, overdraws the shift from paternalistic to competitive "race relations" between "Indians" and Ladinos. Moreover, Brintnall comes close to Colby and van den Berghe's notion of a "dual monism" of enduring ethnic boundaries when he identifies Mayas and Ladinos—quite rightly, I think—as "social races" defined by parentage and cultural inheritance that persist despite changing social, political, and economic relations between them. Smith (1975) in turn castigates Colby and van den Berghe for stressing "mentalistic or emic" determinants

of Maya ethnicity. Although he argues that "modernization" in the Maya town of San Pedro Sacatepequez—which he equates with acculturation to Ladino ways—follows from economic change, Smith also notes that local ethnic distinctions between Maya and Ladino persist despite both acculturation and economic change—just as Colby and van den Berghe predict. The "acculturated" Maya of San Pedro choose to identify themselves as *civilizados*, "civilized ones," or *guatemaltecos*, "Guatemalans," rather than as Ladinos (Smith 1977: 56, 121–122; cf. Hawkins 1984). Obviously, material or institutional changes in San Pedro alone fail to explain ethnic perceptions, attitudes, and actions and, even less, how "emic" models might affect these changes in the first place.

4. In his study of San Antonio, for example, Annis (1987) illustrates the tendency—and its pitfalls—of reducing detailed local ethnography to all-encompassing global explanations. On one hand, he provides a very insightful analysis of "*milpa* logic" as a local form of production that serves to "optimize inputs" of otherwise marginal household labor and resources rather than "maximize output" of marketable commodities (Annis 1987: 31–38); on the other, he characterizes this "approach to production" in terms of past and present colonialist domination, exactions, and depredations (cf. Annis 1987: 17, 34, 51). This leap to global explanations, however, overlooks the possibility that such optimizing strategies may also represent intrinsic features of localized, noncapitalist economies, a point raised, for instance, in Marshall Sahlins's (1972) discussion of the "domestic mode of production" or in Michael Taussig's (1980) analysis of the confrontation of "use value" and "exchange value" economies. In other words, without denying the importance of colonial encompassments, other explanations of "Indian production" might temper the exclusive—or even final—determinism of historicist formulations.

5. At the time, the Guatemalan quetzal was on par with the U.S. dollar. See chapter 6, note 3.

2. Santiago Chimaltenango

1. *Tierra fría*, literally "cold country," lies above 5,000 feet with an average temperature of 10°–17° C (50°–65° F) (Recinos 1954: 83). In Guatemala, altitude most directly determines climate.

2. In Guatemala, where there are no marked seasonal differences in temperature, early Spanish colonists came to call the wet season that runs from May to October "winter" (*invierno*) and the dry season between November and April "summer" (*verano*), a practice still followed today.

3. William Sherman (1979: 328) points out that slavery, tribute, and forced labor all existed in Central America before the Spanish conquest, but in a letter to Sherman, historian Benjamin Keen writes, "I am convinced that Spanish demands for labor and tribute were immeasurably greater than before the Conquest, simply, aside from other reasons, because pre-Conquest tribute demands were limited by the capacity of the native ruling classes to consume the fruits of tribute and labor, whereas the Spanish demands,

aimed at the accumulation of wealth in monetary form, were quite unlimited" (quoted in Sherman 1979: 456n2).

4. A *fanega* equals 116 pounds.

5. AGI:AG = Archivo General de las Indias [Seville], Audiencia de Guatemala; the number refers to the *legajo*. I thank Drs. Christopher Lutz and William Swezey, directors of the Centro de Investigaciones Regionales de Mesoamérica (CIRMA) in Antigua, Guatemala, for making available to me transcriptions of this document.

6. *Congregaciones* were often located in or near pre-Hispanic towns, but I have been unable to find mention of Chimbal before the Spanish conquest. Recinos (1954: 428–437, 476, 478, 485) lists eleven pre-Hispanic towns in the northern Mam area, many of which later became *congregaciones*. They include Chinabajul (modern Huehuetenango), Zaculeu (archaeological ruins near Huehuetenango), Malacatán (Malcatancito), Mazatenango (San Lorenzo), Chicol (an *aldea* of Santa Barbara), Toj Hoj (San Sebastián Huehuetenango), a site near modern Colotenango, (San Ildefonso) Ixtahuacán, (San Andrés) Cuilco, (Todos Santos) Cuchumatán, and a site near present-day San Martín Cuchumatán. Miles (1965: 277) also notes (San Pedro) Necta on a map but gives no further reference (but cf. p. 285).

7. A century later, Fuentes y Guzmán (1972: 24, 26) reports populations of two hundred tributaries and eight hundred total inhabitants for Chimbal, and three hundred tributaries and twelve hundred inhabitants for San Juan Atitán. Given the general decline in Maya numbers throughout the sixteenth and seventeenth centuries, such growth could have only resulted from resettlement, suggesting that *congregación* in these two towns took place after the 1549 assessment. Nonetheless, the round figures of these mid-seventeenth-century counts and the perfect ratio of 1:4 between tributaries and inhabitants make them suspect. A 1740 census putting Chimbal at thirty-one tributaries, and San Juan at twenty-five (Olaverreta 1935: 17), reinforces the suspicion that these two towns always remained small. Despite Fuentes y Guzmán's figures, I would favor a late 1540s date for *congregación* in Chimbal.

8. See Sherman (1979: 5–6) for more conservative, but equally calamitous, estimates.

9. Although the Cuchumatán Highlands missed "many of the major military, political, and cultural intrusions from Mexico" during pre-Hispanic times (MacLeod 1973: 32; cf. Miles 1965: 278), the last Mam ruler, Caibil Balam, nonetheless mustered twenty-one thousand warriors to oppose the Spanish invasion, evidence of a populous, centralized, stratified state society (Fuentes y Guzmán, cited in Recinos 1954: 478, 485, 489; cf. Lovell 1982: 104–107 for a discussion of the reliability of these figures). The Spanish initially tried to rule through the Maya *señores naturales*, "native lords" (Sherman 1979: 271–272), but fears of native-led revolts, brutal treatment by the conquerors, and the conflicting demands of Crown, Church, and their own subjects, had ruined the native aristocracy by the end of the sixteenth century (MacLeod 1973: 140–141; Sherman 1979: 277–303).

10. Lovell's careful archival research shows that Spanish acquisition of

land in the Cuchumatán Highlands focused on the rich pastures of Los Altos de Chiantla north of Huehuetenango, and on the temperate slopes to the west near Jacaltenango and Santa Ana Huista (1985: 119–137). Chimbal sits on the high, broken terrain in between, and pressure on Maya landholdings there grew only during the eighteenth century, due as much to population growth as to Spanish encroachments (Lovell 1985: 129–130).

11. Unrest in Maya communities throughout the colonial period consisted of outbursts against local abuses that appealed to a distant, paternalistic Crown for redress. Such local disturbances never escalated into revolutionary challenges to the colonial order itself (cf. Taylor 1979: 145; Bricker 1981: 83–84).

12. These figures come from two baptismal books currently kept in the parish church in San Pedro Necta, Huehuetenango, the first from June 1663 to September 1730, the second from November 1730 to April 1766.

13. These figures come from the *Libro de difuntos de este pueblo de Santiago Chimaltenango* (1678–1723), found in the parish records in San Pedro Necta, Huehuetenango.

14. Inga Clendinnen (1990: 93) suggests that when native peoples called Spaniards "gods," they were referring not to their divinity but to their "weirdness"—that is, to their penchant for doing things that no ordinary, or perhaps normal, human being would dare. Spanish conceit, however, probably preferred to take this as attribution of a more familiar godhood.

15. In analyzing the conquest of Central Mexico, Inga Clendinnen (1990) argues that the opposition between Spaniard and native may have been forged as early as Cortés's campaign against Tenochtitlán, the Aztec capital. She maintains that during the struggle, each side's constant misreading of the other's conventions of war engendered not just mutual antipathy, but incomprehensibility. The Aztecs came to despise the cowardly Spaniards for refusing to place themselves at risk like true warriors, instead killing from afar with harquebus and crossbow, siege and starvation. Likewise, the Spaniards came to abhor the Aztecs' "inhuman" refusal to surrender after all had been obviously lost. This "fierce and unnatural cruelty" that the Spaniards perceived in the Aztecs—and during the final brutality of the siege certainly in their native allies and perhaps in themselves as well—"divided Spaniards from Indians in new and decisive ways. . . . Once that sense of unassuageable otherness has been established, the outlook is bleak indeed" (1990: 123). Pedro de Alvarado's experiences with Cortés at Tenochtitlán undoubtedly colored his actions and attitudes during the conquest of Guatemala a scant three years later in 1524 (cf. Kelly 1971: 135–150).

16. Van Oss and MacLeod differ in their interpretations of the persistence of ethnically distinct Maya populations in western Guatemala. Van Oss gives priority to the missionary friars and their efforts to foster local Maya economies that would ensure their ecclesiastical autonomy. MacLeod tends to see Maya survival as a function of Spanish entrepreneurial interests: on one hand, Indians survived in the western highlands where lands were too cold and remote for commercial purposes; on the other, acculturative Spanish demands on native land and labor varied directly with the boom and bust

cycles of various cash crops, such as cacao, cochineal, and indigo. Despite their difference in focus, however, both imply the same underlying point: colonial strategies of exploitation, whether temporal or ecclesiastical, molded themselves to conditions of the native population itself.

17. In a recent paper, historian Christopher Lutz (n.d.) argues that the term "Ladino" only came into usage with the homogenization of mestizos (Indian-Spanish) and mulattos (black-Spanish) during the eighteenth century. Until that time, "mestizo" continued to be a significant social category in colonial Guatemala.

18. The Guatemalan census bureau officially defines ethnic status as "the social valuation that the person has in the place where he was censused, since in rural areas and small villages there is a certain local awareness that classifies a person as Indian or non-Indian" (DGE 1968: 37; my translation)—presuming, of course, that Indians always live in "rural areas and small villages." Additional criteria include use of traditional Indian dress, Indian language, and footwear (DGE 1977: xxx), since Ladinos never go barefoot and seldom wear sandals, whereas Indians commonly do both. Beyond such official niceties, Ladinos continue to identify someone as Indian if they know—or suspect—that his or her parents still live as Indians, regardless of that person's Ladino dress, language, and livelihood. Maya also acknowledge innate distinctions, especially in cases of mixed marriages, although for them comportment rather than parentage most clearly marks ethnic identity (see chapter 4).

3. The Conventions of Community

1. Even Chimalteco families who now live and work permanently outside Chimbal retain a house in the pueblo if they can afford to do so and often keep some land in the town. Over the last fifteen to twenty years, a number of Chimaltecos have bought land and moved to the neighboring community of La Democracia. There, in the lower-lying hot lands near the Mexican border, they grow corn and coffee. Nonetheless, most of these expatriates maintain close ties with Chimbal, through relatives who remain in the town and through periodic visits "home," particularly for the major fiestas.

2. Of course, this local universe of concentric spatial categories is encompassed by a wider field of activities extending to other Maya communities, to Ladino towns and cities, and to the plantations of Guatemala's Pacific coast. Chimaltecos, however, conventionalize such interactions in moral rather than in spatial terms, a topic to be broached later in this chapter and analysed more fully in chapter 4.

3. This tendency to evaluate space in relation to time finds clear expression in the formal terms of Mam cardinal directions, which translate literally as "in" (east), "out" (west), "up," and "down." Space in Mam cosmology appears to be modeled directly on the sun's apparent passage through the heavens; spatial directions resemble vectors rather than fixed points in some abstract space; and these directional vectors in turn are defined in ref-

erence to time, which consists of the sun's diurnal and annual movements above and below the plane of the earth's surface. For a more detailed discussion of Mam and Maya cosmology, see Watanabe (1983).

4. Chimaltecos often leave the pueblo long before dawn to walk to distant fields or to depart on long journeys, suggesting that their vague night uneasiness reflects not a superstitious fear of the dark but what Chimaltecos normally do. Here again, experiential and conceptual factors coincide to shape the cultural meaning of space and time. Experientially, early morning forays into field and forest commonly occur without mishap. Conceptually, the sun has passed the nadir of *tk'u?j aq'b'il*, "midnight"—literally, "stomach of the night"—and the imminent yet still unseen dawn presages the expansion of Chimalteco cultural space. Conversely, in the dead of night, what happens outside is not properly of human concern, either experientially or conceptually.

5. Recinos (1954: 135) identifies the tree from which copal is taken as *Bursera bipinnata*, but Valladares (1957: 148) attributes it to *Cuphorbia heprophylla*.

6. It is interesting to note that both the nearby mountains and the more distant volcanoes have female *witz* occupying the westernmost peak, again a possible reflection of the association in many Maya cosmologies of west with femaleness, darkness, and the waning heat of day (cf. Thompson 1970: 196; Gossen 1974: 42–43). Wagley's informants said that Rosnaa was also female (1949: 59), but I could not verify this. In any case, all these volcanoes lie to the south of Chimbal and hold associations with death and the afterlife, tacitly reflecting Gossen's finding that south in Chamula cosmology relates to the underworld, night, and the dormant period of the agricultural cycle at the winter's solstice (Gossen 1974: 33; Wagley 1949: 60, 67).

7. While repudiation of saint and church as images of conquest may simply suggest the successful encompassment of Chimaltecos by a colonialist hegemony, I have argued elsewhere that Chimalteco devotions—to Santiago in particular and Maya saint worship in general—evidence a self-determined localism neither dictated nor desired by global interests or intents (Watanabe 1990).

8. Santiago and Santa Ana also make annual visits to San Juan Atitán and Ixconlaj, a hamlet of the neighboring community of Colotenango, accompanied by Chimalteco civil and religious officials. Just as local processions express Santiago's sovereignty over Chimbal, these longer excursions reaffirm municipal boundaries vis-à-vis surrounding communities (see chapter 5).

9. For a review and discussion of the extensive literature on these "owners of the mountains" and their relation to Maya saints and ancestors, see Watanabe (1990).

10. This, of course, is historically and not just mythically true. Historian William McNeill (1976) suggests that Old World infectious diseases may have constituted a primary reason why the peoples of Mesoamerica so readily embraced the saintly protectors of their conquerors. "First, Spaniards and Indians readily agreed that epidemic disease was a particularly dreadful

and unambiguous form of divine punishment. . . . Secondly, the Spaniards were nearly immune from the terrible disease that raged so mercilessly among the Indians. They had almost always been exposed in childhood and so had developed effective immunity. Given the interpretation of the cause of pestilence accepted by both parties, such a manifestation of divine partiality for the invaders was conclusive. . . . The situation was ripe for the mass conversions recorded so proudly by Christian missionaries" (McNeill 1976: 183–184). If the Maya did not at first accept the saints out of love, they may have learned to do so out of fear or desperation. Perhaps the coercion evident in Santiago's mythological incorporation into the community echoes the trauma of this initial accommodation.

4. The Conventions of Morality

1. Perhaps not surprisingly, Maya in other communities associate words—or more generally, speech—with notions of "soul." I examine the relation of Chimalteco *naab'l* to Maya "souls" later in this chapter, but for now suffice it to note that Gossen (1975: 450) reports that in Chamula the *ch'ulel*, "inner soul," is said to reside as an invisible essence on the tip of the tongue. Similarly, residents of the Tzeltal community of Amatenango say that a mute child has had its soul stolen (Nash 1970: 283). Among the Tz'utujil Maya of Santiago Atitlán, Mendelson describes the local concept of *nuwal* as "a thing that separates a man from all other men, the pure spirit of God and also a prayer that a man has inside him" (1965: 91; my translation).

2. In its simple transitive form, *na-* means "feel, perceive": *ma t-na-a xjaal che?w*, "The person felt cold." Used in its antipassive form with the relational noun *-u?n*, *na-* means "remember": *na-a-n w-u?n-i*, "I remember." Intransitivized as *na-a-?n*, it means "guess": *ma na-a-?n-a*, "You guessed." The intransitivized form of *naab'l, nab'liin*, means "behave": *ba?n na-b'l-ii-n xjaal*, "The person behaves well." Used as a simple antipassive, *na-a-n, na-* means "pray": *ma chin na-a-n-i*, "I prayed" (cf. England 1983: 99–102, 110; dashes in the Mam transcriptions indicate morpheme boundaries, following the conventions used by England). More idiomatically, *teen t-naa-b'l-a*, "Be careful!" translates literally as "Let there be [present] your *naab'l*!" Similarly, "assume or suppose" is rendered as *tu?j q-naa-b'l-a qa*—literally, "in our *naab'l* 'if' . . ." (i.e., "We assumed that . . ."}.

In Tzotzil, a Maya language spoken in Chiapas, Mexico, Laughlin (1975: 246) finds the transitive verb *na?*, undoubtedly cognate with the Mam root *na-*, which similarly means "know, remember, miss [as in 'long for'], calculate, realize, regret, be accustomed to, think." It can also mean "pray" in the sense of "remembering Our Lord."

3. This general association between the hotness of the blood and perceptual sensitivity provides a cultural explanation of why Maya shamans consume large amounts of alcohol during rituals: they are heating their blood in order to "see" better (see chapter 8; cf. Vogt 1976: 27, 35–38).

4. *Seky'pajleenin* represents the Chimalteco version of the "folk ill-

ness" *susto* commonly found throughout Mesoamerica. Extensive research on *susto* by Arthur Rubel, Carl O'Nell, and Rolando Callado-Ardón (1984) reveals that in Oaxaca, Mexico, individuals afflicted with soul-loss suffer not only from greater "social stress" associated with inadequate performance of social roles but, as the Chimalteco pattern would suggest, from greater organic disorders as well, both in number and seriousness (1984: 71–72, 84, 114). Furthermore, far from being "malingerers," *asustados* exhibit a stronger positive correlation between the "gravity" (how life-threatening) and "severity" (how incapacitating) of their illnesses than do ailing individuals without *susto* (1984: 105–106). Although irreducible to any specific clinical disorder or constellation of disorders (1984: 97–98), *susto* clearly reflects a higher—and to the authors, an unexpected—organic disease burden in individuals who suffer from it. Indeed, several Chimaltecos themselves associated *seky'pajleenin* with "malnutrition" or "anemia."

5. Roger Keesing (1982: 46–49) makes an analogous argument concerning the Oceanic concept of *mana*, as used by the Kwaio of the Solomon Islands. Rather than denoting some mystical power conferred on something from the outside, *nanama*, the Kwaio equivalent of *mana*, refers to a thing's "natural" state of being, of "working" properly. When Kwaio ancestors watch over their descendants and their efforts, they do so not by infusing them with some mystical ingredient but by protecting them in ways that "allow their natural fulfillment" (1982: 47). I would suggest that a similar "de-objectification" would benefit anthropological understandings of Mesoamerican concepts of soul and soul-loss.

6. In this same vein, Tzotzil Maya in Zinacantán also recognize a correspondence between souls and sociality but without a lexical distinction between the soul's metaphysical and social aspects. The same word *ch'ulel*, derived from the adjectival root *ch'u*, "holy," refers to the "inner soul" as well as to "dreams," "ritual speech," and "sense," as in "Don't you have any sense?" (Laughlin 1975: 139).

7. This discussion of the emergent yet canonical qualities of Chimalteco souls parallels Warren's (1978: 56–57, 67–73) analysis of *costumbre*, "ritual, custom, tradition," in the Kaqchikel town of San Andrés Semetabaj. Following David Schneider, she argues that *costumbre* canonically represents, on one hand, blood relatedness to the community's ancestors, who first established local cultural practices, and, on the other, a "code for conduct" predicated on respect for living elders and intergenerational cooperation. In actual practice, however, *costumbre* emerges more in reference to ancestral precedents rather than as slavish replication of them: in celebrating *costumbre*, the "goal of community groups [i.e., *cofradías*, "religious brotherhoods"] is not to challenge different [individual] wills or to force consensus, but rather to create an environment in which individuals with different *voluntades* ["wills"] may 'unify and understand each other'" (Warren 1978: 71). This kind of pragmatic flexibility within a presumed ancestral canon suggests a certain formal similarity between Mam and Kaqchikel conceptualizations of morality, although the explicit cultural notations differ: for Chimaltecos, notions of "soul" have come to conventionalize affini-

ties of blood and behavior, while *costumbre* now refers specifically to traditional ritual practices that they no longer observe (see chapter 8).

8. One wealthy Chimalteco, whose father was a Ladino, and a full-blooded Chimalteco who taught the bilingual first grade in the municipal school both carried the nickname *moos*, "Ladino," because neither spent much time in their fields. The tacit censure applied more to their livelihood than to their wealth or profession because another well-off Chimalteco, also half Ladino, escaped such disapprobation because he still worked his *milpa* alongside the *mozos*, "laborers," that he hired.

9. During the late 1970s, only two Ladino families native to Chimbal lived in the community, and by 1988 one of these families had moved away. Together with the school teachers, postmistress, nurse, drivers for local truck owners, and family dependents, perhaps forty Ladinos lived in the town center (cf. DGE 1977; 1984).

10. Like the women's blouse, the traditional men's shirt and woolen jacket had true sleeves and a stand-up collar.

11. When asked the reason for this change in men's dress, Chimaltecos often said that manufactured clothing was more comfortable and cheaper: one merchant reasoned that a Q2.00 shirt twenty years before had cost twenty days' labor on the plantations, while at the daily wage of Q2.50 in 1979, even a Q7.00 shirt required only three days' work. Other Chimaltecos pointed to increased labor migration during the 1950s and 1960s as an explanation, saying that they adopted Ladino dress on the plantations because of the hot climate and to avoid Ladino harassment. Men gradually took to wearing Ladino clothes back in Chimbal as well. This last argument rings false as a general explanation, since men from the neighboring town of San Juan Atitán still wear distinctive, handwoven clothing, even though they have been among the most frequent migrants to the Pacific coast since the 1930s (cf. Wagley 1941: 56n). Nonetheless, the stability in women's dress and the age-grading reflected in the loss of men's dress suggest that the nature and degree of social activity outside the community, to say nothing of accustomed habit, probably play an important role in individual decisions about dress. Indeed, older Chimaltecos are more likely to don Ladino clothes for trips to Huehuetenango or Guatemala City and resume traditional dress in Chimbal. Conversely, when petitioning government officials for construction of a new road into Chimbal, one middle-aged Chimalteco wore the traditional clothes that he had given up in daily life to emphasize that he came representing his community.

12. The process of learning by observation is common in Maya communities throughout Guatemala. Even in a textile factory, Manning Nash (1967: 35–37) noted that K'iche' Maya learned to operate machinery this way. A new worker observed an experienced loom operator for several weeks with no questions asked or instruction given. When the apprentice said she was ready, "the machine she had been observing for six weeks was turned over to her and she operated it, not quite as rapidly as the girl who had just left it, but with skill and assurance" (Nash 1967: 36).

13. In Chimbal, women, and to a lesser extent men, have little use for the

basic education that they receive. Children are required by Guatemalan law to complete six years of primary school, but few Chimaltecos ever do. Those who actually finish seldom master more than the rudiments of arithmetic and reading and writing Spanish. Some Chimaltecos blame the Ladino school teachers, saying that they promote students each year regardless of their proficiency so that their "clean" record will gain them better jobs in the city. While obviously untrue of all teachers, many Chimaltecos question the use of such a limited education. Those who value education and aspire to send their children to secondary school in Huehuetenango see it not as a way out of "Indian backwardness" but as a means of better "defending" themselves from the machinations of Ladinos (cf. Smith 1977: 76).

14. Wolf (1955: 459) defined such "*defensive ignorance,* an active denial of outside alternatives" (original emphasis), as a characteristic of the "closed corporate peasant community" (cf. Wolf 1957), but he interpreted this pattern of cultural exclusion primarily in economic terms of minimizing local consumption, thus reducing not only local dependency on external sources of income but also internal social differentiation. Without denying Wolf's point, I would argue for an equally important moral dimension to such exclusions, given that they tacitly establish the "ground rules" of proper behavior within the local community. Redfield (1941: 134, 344) favored such a moral interpretation of local conformity, but he saw the lack of cultural alternatives in such "folk communities" as largely a function of their relative isolation and intrinsic homogeneity. I would follow Wolf in seeing the need for such "moral closure" as a response to outside intrusions rather than as the self-sustaining equilibrium that Redfield envisioned.

5. The Conventions of Responsibility

1. Until 1976, *consejales* served for only two years, but after the elections that year, their terms were extended to four. The description presented here depicts municipal government as of about 1980. During the army's counterinsurgency campaigns of the 1980s, local governments were radically restructured, co-opted by the military, or abolished altogether when their towns effectively ceased to exist (cf. Manz 1988), although Chimbal suffered much less than elsewhere (see chapters 7 and 8).

2. Wagley's informants placed the *alguaciles* on the civil side of the hierarchy and the *escuelix* (*ixhkweel*) on the religious side (Wagley 1949: 82, 84). Linguistically, this makes more sense, given that *alguacil*, from the Arabic *al-wazir*, "[the] vizier" (Pagden 1987: 527), originally referred to a local constable. Similarly, Frank Cancian (1967: 285), in his review of Mesoamerican cargo systems, identifies *alguacil* as a low-level civil cargo analogous to *miyool* in Chimbal rather than as a religious one. Nonetheless, June Nash (1970: 216) notes that *alguaciles* in Amatenango have also metamorphosed into ritual assistants. The transposition in Chimalteco perceptions of these low-ranking cargos perhaps reflects changing perceptions of the duties that each entails (see note 6, below).

3. The *aldea* of Ixconlaj lies over two hours' walk from Colotenango,

which sits on the far side of the Pan American Highway. In actual distance, it is closer to both Chimbal and San Pedro Necta. Recently, the inhabitants of Ixconlaj have begun asserting their autonomy from Colotenango by building a small chapel and by exchanging saints with Chimbal, a mode of social differentiation also reported in Chiapas (cf. Wasserstrom 1978).

4. Waldemar Smith (1977: 5–6) suggests that changing economic circumstances, whether for better or worse, produce two possible transformations in individual sponsorship of community fiestas. Short of abolishing such sponsorship altogether, communities may form what he calls "appended" systems, in which more sponsors share the costs, or they may opt for systems of an "administered" type, which involve the formation of permanent brotherhoods to organize fiestas. Chimaltecos appear to have combined both strategies by having more *martoon* administer community-wide sponsorship of fiestas. The administered aspect of the cargo may have originated in the collections that *martoon* used to make from the community to pay for the masses said when the Catholic priest made a rare visit from Huehuetenango (cf. Wagley 1949: 83).

5. In Spanish, Chimaltecos refer to this animal as a *gato de monte*, possibly a type of small fox (cf. Recinos 1954: 145).

6. As mentioned earlier, Chimaltecos now define the duties of *alsiil* as a religious rather than civil cargo, contrary to what Wagley found in 1937. Nonetheless, the duty of *alsiil* to "capture" new cargoholders reinforces the suspicion that these might have originally been civil cargos, although the purely ceremonial function of such responsibilities may explain their present transformation into religious ones. By the same token, *ixhkweel*, the young boys who care for the village plaza, may rightfully constitute religious cargos, because the *pixhkaal* (*fiscales*) whom they assist serve as church officials in other Maya communities (cf. Oakes 1951: 55; LaFarge 1947: 82; Tax 1953: 10). Here again, the secular duties of sweeping the marketplace and maintaining the small garden in the plaza may account for their transformation into civil cargos in Chimbal.

7. This by no means represents a full account of Holy Week in Chimbal. Rituals traditionally include the dance with Judas on Wednesday night and a passion play on Thursday that lasts all day with "apostles" dressed in white tunics (appropriately, Judas alone of the apostles wears dark glasses), *soldados*, "soldiers," in blackface and sunglasses who capture Jesus, and two "thieves," also in blackface, who "steal" bread from people. On Thursday night, the bull dance and procession take place, followed on Friday by the "crucifixion" of Christ and the two thieves. Friday night, the *waakx*, "bulls," dance again, and on Saturday the *sqatx ti cheej* (*corrida de cintas*) takes place, a horse race that formerly involved galloping full-tilt down the main street of the town while attempting to rip the heads off live chickens hanging from a rope strung across the street (cf. Wagley 1949: 116–117; Oakes 1951: 209–210). Today Chimaltecos use ribbons instead of chickens. On Easter Sunday morning, young men and boys dressed as women, animals, and Maya of neighboring communities dance in front of the western *ttxaʔnja* shrine, where the images of Christ and Mary have been taken by the *martoon*.

Many of the older dancers, called *b'iixil b'uʔxh* in Mam, "worn-out or wasted dancers," make lewd gestures and call suggestively to the audience, while three *maaʔyil*, men masked as two male figures and one female, dance sedately in front of the saints (cf. Wagley 1949: 117). As always, the *martoon* are there to measure out shots of *aguardiente* to the other cargo officials and to the *maaʔyil*. At the end of the morning, when drunkenness has exceeded the capacity to dance, the images of Christ and Mary are returned to the church after being greeted by Santiago and Santa Ana in the plaza. On the following evening, the *miyool* burn Judas.

While cargo officials take part in many of these activities, most participation appears to be on an individual basis. Indeed, due to "lack of interest," Chimaltecos did not perform the passion play in 1980, and several predicted that the custom would soon be lost. Actual cargo duties consist of the dance with Judas, the various processions, and attending the *maaʔyil* dancers on Easter morning.

6. From Livelihood to Labor

1. I choose here to retain Chimalteco measures for ease of comparison with Wagley's calculations and to keep already-rough estimates from suffering the added inaccuracies of rounding off or the false precision of decimal point conversions to acres or hectares. The basic land measure in Chimbal is the *cuerda* of 25 *varas* square. A *vara* equals about 33 inches, making the *cuerda* in Chimbal about 70 (68.75) feet on a side. There are roughly 9.22 *cuerdas* in an acre, 22.75 *cuerdas* in a hectare. Conversely, a *cuerda* equals about 0.11 acres, or 0.044 hectares. To add further to the confusion, 16 *cuerdas* make up a *manzana* (about 1.73 acres, or 0.70 hectares), and 64 *manzanas* comprise a *caballería* (about 111 acres, or 45 hectares). The census bureau in Guatemala uses the *manzana* as its basic unit of land measure.

2. At this time, long before construction of the Pan American Highway in the 1950s, Chimbal stood on the main trail between Huehuetenango and the hot lowlands to the west, and older Chimaltecos still recall the long strings of "a hundred or more mules" that passed through the town laden with coffee on its way to market.

3. Until the 1980s, the Guatemalan quetzal was on par with the U.S. dollar. In the early 1980's, inflation and devaluation pushed the quetzal to as low as Q3.80 to the dollar; at the beginning of 1988, the exchange rate stood at Q2.50 to the dollar and since then has hovered between that and Q5.00 to the dollar.

4. In the 1979 agricultural census, Chimaltecos reported planting an average of just under 17 *cuerdas* of *milpa* per household. Those owning less than 16 *cuerdas* (31 percent) planted an average of 8.2 *cuerdas* of *milpa*; those with more, 20.8 *cuerdas* (DGE 1983). Embedded in these figures, however, lies a clear discrepancy in corn consumption between 1937 and the late 1970s that cannot simply reflect changes in Chimalteco diet. Based on direct statements and inferences from harvest yields, an "average" Chimalteco today consumes about 525–550 pounds of corn annually. Conversely,

Wagley's calculations of Chimalteco land needs, cited earlier, imply an annual corn consumption of 800 pounds per person. This appears high, even by Maya standards: June Nash (1970: 60) and Raymond Stadelman (1940: 193) report yearly consumption rates near 700 pounds per person, but Redfield and Villa Rojas (1934: 56), Manning Nash (1967: 51), and Sol Tax (1953: 165–167) suggest amounts closer to 600 pounds. The latter two towns engaged extensively in cash-cropping and wage labor, which may have increased the amount of purchased foods in their diets, but Wagley's figures still fall on the high end of the scale. I suspect that Wagley's informants overestimated the corn that they produced, inadvertently inflating what they consumed each year. Indeed, due to increasing land shortages, many Chimaltecos in 1937 had to plant the same fields many years running, with an unavoidable decrease in productivity from the 100 pounds per *cuerda* that they took as given (cf. Wagley 1941: 31, 51–54). Perhaps a more realistic average yield would have been about 75 pounds per *cuerda*, dropping yearly corn consumption closer to 600 pounds per person. This by no means invalidates Wagley's synchronic analysis of Chimalteco land tenure and use, since it simply suggests that Chimaltecos produced less but also ate less. Diachronically, however, it dramatizes the improvement in land productivity in recent years.

5. Three factors make precise measurement of corn production difficult. First, corn yields vary from year to year. Drought can stunt the crop, as it did in 1987; overabundant rains can wash out fields or rot the corn stalks; whirlwinds can level a *milpa* at any time. In 1979–1980, when I made most of my observations, no major disasters blighted Chimalteco fields, but neither were they bumper-crop years; they may thus perhaps be taken as generally representative, although yields are never guaranteed. Second, the exact size of any *milpa* remains secondary to its topography, soil quality, and altitude, as these directly affect how much that field will produce. Thus, Chimaltecos will often only approximate the size of their fields. Third, harvests are measured by *xyub'*, "net bag," or by *cheej*, "muleload," not by weight. A net bag can hold anywhere from 50 to as much as 100 pounds of dried corn on the cob, and a muleload consists of two net bags. Since the dried ears yield about 100 pounds of shelled corn for every 125 pounds still on the cob (cf. Stadelman 1940: 116), a conservative estimate would be that an average muleload amounts to about 100 pounds of shelled corn.

Using this very approximate conversion factor, I offer the following estimates of Chimalteco land productivity from harvests in which I actively participated in 1979 and 1980: a Chimalteco harvested 10 large net bags from a plot of 5–6 *cuerdas*. Since he had the bags carried back to town on a pickup truck rather than by mule, they were larger than average, weighing upwards of 80–90 pounds each. This suggests a yield of between 100–150 pounds of shelled corn per *cuerda*. Another family with whom I worked from planting in May 1979 to harvest in late January 1980 harvested 35 muleloads from four locales totaling 18–21 *cuerdas*. Because some of these loads fell under 100 pounds, I opt for the lower production estimate of about 160 pounds per *cuerda*. Finally, a man told me that in 1978 he had harvested

75 muleloads from 40 *cuerdas*, or about 190 pounds of shelled maize per *cuerda*. Despite the blatant imprecision of these figures, the general consensus on corn production from many different Chimalteco men and the relative consistency between individuals' estimates of *milpa* yields and my own observations of their harvests makes an average land productivity of 150 pounds per *cuerda* appear reasonable.

6. One example suggests the new pattern of Chimalteco land use. A man owned about 280 *cuerdas* of land, nearly all of it self-acquired. Of this, he planted about 15 *cuerdas* in *milpa* each year to feed his wife and four children still at home (ages 14, 10, 7, and 2). He also had about 20 *cuerdas* of land in coffee, half of it producing in 1979. He rented another 15 *cuerdas* of land to neighbors or men from San Juan Atitán, charging two days' labor for each *cuerda* (Wagley [1941: 76] notes that in 1937, Chimalteco landlords rented 10 *cuerdas* of land for eight days' work a year). The man explained, "If I rented my land for cash, a man could earn the rent in a few days on the plantations and then have the use of my land for the rest of the year. It's better that I receive some of his labor in my own fields." At that time, wages in Chimbal stood at Q1.25 a day, and twice that on the plantations. The remaining 200 or so *cuerdas* of his land he fallowed "to grow firewood."

7. It is impossible to say to what extent Chimaltecos underreport land in official censuses because no figures exist on how much municipal land is actually arable. Certainly, the extremely high, broken terrain makes much of it unproductive, if not completely unarable, and my own rough estimates from 1:50,000 topographic maps suggest that less than a third of Chimalteco land falls on the more sheltered valley slopes below about 7,200 feet (2,200 m). Land totals reported in Wagley's census (1941: 72) and the national agricultural censuses of 1964 and 1979 (DGE 1968; 1982) reflect a relative consistency: 25,688 *cuerdas* in 1937, 27,600 *cuerdas* in 1964, and 26,085 in 1979. This represents about 11.5 square kilometers or approximately one-third of the township's total area. Given the coincidence between topography and reported landholdings, the property that Chimaltecos publicly claim may thus closely reflect the land that they deem most worth owning, if not all that they actually control.

8. This dramatic rise in profits from coffee had more to do with devaluation of Guatemala's national currency than with any jump in coffee prices (see note 3), although when converted into dollars, 1987 coffee sales still represent a fourfold increase over 1979 receipts.

9. This would appear to corroborate Carol Smith's (1984a; 1990a) findings in Totonicapán where artisans prefer to hire local workers at higher wages than they would have to pay outsiders in order to preserve political solidarity within the community. Nonetheless, when I visited Chimbal in 1988, I noted that a number of Chimaltecos appeared to be hiring men from the neighboring town of San Juan Atitán to work in both their coffee groves and *milpas*. Long known as land-poor (cf. Wagley 1941: 56n), and lacking even the small parcels of coffee land that Chimbal boasts, Sanjuaneros depend heavily on wage labor and itinerant peddling to make ends meet. This might indicate that Chimalteco landlords are resorting to "foreign" labor to

reduce the costs of neighborliness incurred with workers from their own town, but until further research can be done, this remains purely speculative. If so, this still differs from Totonicapán because it involves day-laborers, not apprentices or journeymen. The more incidental relationship here between employers and employees may make such practices less threatening to community solidarity than in Totonicapán.

10. My reasoning rests on estimates by Chimalteco growers of their annual production costs, ignoring for the moment initial capital investments: 1 *cuerda* of mature, healthy coffee produces between 1.5 and 2 *quintales* of dried coffee a year but also requires 1–2 *quintales* of fertilizer. Taking the higher figures, 2 *quintales* of dried coffee means picking about 900 pounds of coffee berries—in other words, about twelve days' labor at the more relaxed local quota of perhaps 75 pounds per worker per day. Producing 1 *quintal* of coffee thus entails the cost of 1 *quintal* of fertilizer plus six days' wages and rations (roughly the equivalent of perhaps 10 pounds of corn). This represents a high estimate of costs, since many growers use less fertilizer and not all feed their workers for the entire day, especially those with groves close to the town. On the other hand, some growers hire workers to help weed, fertilize, and maintain their groves as well as to process the picked coffee, and food for "resident" workers includes staples other than corn, such as sugar, salt, beans, and beverages. Given this rough conversion formula, actual costs and net income for specific years can be estimated. For example, in 1979, fertilizer cost Q12.00 a *quintal*, corn Q8.00 a *quintal*; coffee sold for about Q60.00 a *quintal* (after transport costs); and the daily wage in Chimbal stood at Q1.50. One *quintal* of coffee thus cost Q12.00 for fertilizer, Q9.00 (Q1.50 × 6) in wages, and Q.80 in rations, yielding a net income of about Q38.00 per *quintal* of coffee sold. Recalling that Chimaltecos need 5–7 *quintales* of fertilizer to make their *milpas* sufficiently productive, in 1979, a Chimalteco had to sell at least 2 *quintales* of coffee simply to feed his family. Other expenses for food staples, clothing, tools, kerosene or electricity, transportation, medicine, and additional hired labor to help with *milpa* work all quickly mount, in 1979 prices, to perhaps Q500.00–600.00 a year for an average-size family. This would mean selling another 15 *quintales* or so of coffee, suggesting a round figure of about 10 *cuerdas* of mature coffee for economic self-support. By early 1988, inflation had doubled the price of fertilizer (Q26.00), corn (Q20.00), and labor (Q3.00) in Chimbal, but devaluation of the Guatemalan quetzal had more than tripled the local price of coffee to Q200.00. Despite inflation, then, net income per *quintal* of coffee had risen to over Q150.00. While a boon to coffee growers, higher prices had of course made it much harder for those without coffee to become growers. Even worse, real income for wage earners had fallen—that is, in 1979 about five and one-third days of local work bought a *quintal* of corn, while in 1988, it took six and two-thirds days to earn the same.

11. This steady rise in wages occurred well before the now-famous CUC (Comité de Unidad Campesina) strike on the Pacific coast in May 1980, which succeeded in nearly tripling the legal minimum wage in Guatemalan

agriculture to Q3.20 a day. As Black, Jamail, and Chinchilla (1984: 100–102) argue, however, the impact of the strike was primarily political, since Chimalteco workers—and others, I would assume—had already been earning close to, if not more than, the new minimum wage before it took effect. Similarly, in a study of working conditions on Guatemalan plantations at the end of the 1970s, Jude Pansini (1980: 208–213) noted the abysmally low net income that workers reported from migratory wage labor, but he also cited a Maya worker and a plantation owner who both explained that workers never told the truth about how much they earned. He added, "[This] opinion is important owing to the implications mentioned by many social scientists . . . that Indians have an excellent commercial sense and tend not to make transactions that are not beneficial" (1980: 211; my translation).

12. When Wagley first visited Chimbal in 1937, the town had no weekly market (Wagley 1941: 21). A Chimalteco who was a boy in 1943 described to me the first Friday market in April of that year (cf. Wagley 1949: 123). On that day, the *alcalde* had a marimba play in front of the town hall to attract a crowd, but "the people were afraid and nobody came." The *miyool* went out into the streets and seized two Colotecos who were selling *panela* (unrefined sugar) door to door and sat them down in the plaza. Still no one came, "and the poor Colotecos didn't sell anything!" The Chimalteco officials finally bought up the unhappy vendors' wares and urged them to return the following Friday. A week later, five Colotecos arrived to sell sugar, chickens, and eggs, and a few Chimaltecos came in from outlying hamlets because they had heard of the market. "Everyone had a good time, and that's how the market began here in Chimbal." Although market day crowds have grown since those early days, the market still begins and ends early, running only from about 7:00 A.M. to noon each Friday.

7. The Struggle for Sovereignty

1. A central problem in the anthropology of Mesoamerican cargo systems has been to explain the purpose of cargo rituals and the massive expenditures associated with them. Most interpretations tend to ignore the manifest political functions that these rituals might fulfill in favor of their possible latent economic or social consequences. Localized community studies tend to stress the integrative nature of the rituals: cargo expenditures maintain community solidarity by leveling wealth differences (Wolf 1959: 115–116) or by legitimizing social and economic stratification within the community (Cancian 1965; Brintnall 1979). Conversely, historical or regional studies stress the role that cargo expenses play in draining local resources into the hands of Ladino elites (Harris 1964) or in channeling marginal economic resources into "merely symbolic" local prestige (W. Smith 1977). While this is not the place to discuss the relative merits and shortcomings of these theories (cf. Greenberg 1981; Chance and Taylor 1985), such explanations fix the rationale for cargoholding atomistically in individual quests for prestige within the local community or globally in the inequalities of Mesoamerican

economy and society without sufficient regard for political issues of legitimacy and sovereignty.

2. This is not to say that Ladino merchants failed to profit from local ceremonial life, only that they did so more from the annual cycle of religious fiestas than from cargo rituals per se. While cargoholders had to buy skyrockets and candles for the processions of the saints during local fiestas, most other expenses involving Ladino merchants were incurred by private individuals, not cargoholders. The greatest cost involved renting costumes for a colonial pageant dance that Chimaltecos once performed—and revived in 1985—during the fiesta of Santiago (Wagley 1949: 105–106). Moreover, Maya always spent money at holiday markets, which Ladino merchants once dominated directly but now do so primarily as wholesalers to Maya peddlers. Local bootleggers also profited by selling *aguardiente* during fiestas, while labor recruiters often filled their quotas by advancing wages to drunken Maya in return for future work contracts (Wagley 1941: 74; 1949: 107–108).

3. Wagley reports that these divinations at times more closely reflected the preferences of the *chmaan tnam* than those of the gods, suggesting that the real power to choose officials lay with the *chmaan tnam*. Divinations, however, could approve more than one candidate, leaving the *principales* to make the final selection (Wagley 1949: 85–86, 88).

4. Individuals often exchanged labor (*yaab'in* in Mam)—a practice still found in Chimbal—or loaned land in return for work, but the labor capacity of individual households traditionally determined the size of Chimalteco landholdings (Wagley 1941: 61, 72n). Wagley suggests that the concept of wage labor was introduced into Chimbal after migratory work on coffee plantations began in the late nineteenth century, although Chimaltecos must have known wage labor outside the town as early as the sixteenth century from such things as *repartimiento* labor drafts (Sherman 1979: 117, 198–199, 339). In any event, before the advent of local wage labor, Chimalteco men evidently relied on their own labor and that of their sons for working their fields, and ideally the *alcalde* maintained the correspondence between individual landholdings and family size.

5. In this regard, Manning Nash (1970) has argued that the use of cargo service to define community boundaries may have originated in response to external encroachments on Maya lands beginning in the middle years of the nineteenth century. Evidence from Oaxaca, Jalisco, and central Mexico also suggests that intensification of local cargo systems occurred during the upheavals of the nineteenth century, as communal property came under increasing attack from the Mexican government (Chance and Taylor 1985). Jan Rus and Robert Wasserstrom (1980) report a similar elaboration of cargo systems in Chiapas but not until the twentieth century. In a parallel development, Chester Lloyd Jones (1940: 159) cites evidence suggesting that early in this century, Maya communities in Guatemala may have also expanded the number of positions in local cargo systems so that more individuals could claim exemption from forced labor due to "community obligations."

6. Communities in this region still fell victim to the infamous *fincas de mozos*—in the words of historian David McCreery (1988: 244), "farms which produced workers" instead of crops. According to this system, Ladino plantation owners acquired large tracts of commercially useless land in highland communities and rented parcels to local subsistence farmers in return for seasonal labor on their lowland coffee and sugar plantations. Although Chimbal managed to avoid such expropriations, the neighboring town of San Juan Atitán still harbors a sizable, heavily forested, largely unused tract of land that Chimaltecos say belongs to "a finca." Census figures for San Juan indicate a single holding of 720 *manzanas* (roughly 506 hectares) that comprises nearly a quarter of the town's declared landholdings (DGE 1982).

7. AGCA:ST = Archivo General de Centroamérica, Sección de Tierras, located in Guatemala City.

8. There are major discrepancies regarding the exact area of Chimbal. Basing his calculations on a government map made in 1930, Wagley (1941: 56) gives the municipal area as 158 *caballerías*, 40 *manzanas*, almost precisely the figure in Ordoñez's original survey. Recinos (1954: 314), however, says that Chimbal possesses 119 *caballerías*, 59 *manzanas* of *ejido*, "plus 58 *caballerías* that subsequently have been added." The former figure obviously reflects the *baldíos* according to Ordoñez's calculations, but the latter is in error, possibly a reference to the 38 *caballerías* of Chimbal's original *ejido.* Conversely, Gall (1980: 686) gives 17 square kilometers as the area, including only Chimbal's *ejido* lands. From my own estimates, derived from 1:50,000 topographic maps drawn in 1959 and a sketch map used by census-takers during the 1979 agricultural census, I calculate that the actual area of Chimbal is close to 35 square kilometers. This is noticeably less than the land included in the 1891 title, but I cannot account for this difference.

9. Figures given by parish priests toward the end of the eighteenth century show considerable consistency. In 1770, there were 451 Chimaltecos, more than two-thirds of them living in the surrounding mountains (AGI:AG 928.2: 77; see chapter 2). In 1779, the population of Chimbal stood at 484, but after the smallpox epidemic between April and September of the following year, it dropped to 405 (Lovell 1988: 250, figure 3, 252–253, cuadro 2). Joseph Domingo Hidalgo, writing in the *Gaceta de Guatemala* on November 13, 1797, put Chimalteco numbers at 502 (cited in Gall 1980: 687). Figures for much of the nineteenth century are lacking, but the national census of 1880 includes 770 Chimaltecos (cited in Gall 1980: 687), although this is undoubtedly low. The department of Huehuetenango was not directly enumerated by census-takers, but the population was estimated from births and deaths recorded in the Civil Registry, a procedure likely to produce low estimates due to underreporting of these events in remote Maya communities such as Chimbal (Arias de Blois 1982: 157, 159). If this figure, however, approximates the population of the town center of Chimbal, where records may have been more accurately kept, the distribution between "urban" and "rural" Chimaltecos reflected in later censuses (DGE 1923; 1968; 1977;

Wagley 1941: 9) suggests that the population of Chimbal in 1880 may have been closer to 1,300. In 1893, Chimbal reputedly had 1,345 inhabitants; in 1921, it had 1,491 (DGE 1923).

10. It might be argued that alienation of land, not population pressure, created Chimbal's growing land problem. Indeed, Wagley states that even in 1937 the problem lay less in an absolute shortage of land than in its unequal distribution (Wagley 1941: 72–75, 82). Nonetheless, two conditions suggest that local pressures on communal land tenure preceded or coincided with the individualization of property associated with Liberal land legislation. First, given Wagley's calculations on land needs (an absolute minimum of 120 *cuerdas* per household) and availability (25,688 *cuerdas* of arable land) (1941: 55, 72–73; see chapter 6), municipal lands could support about 214 households, or a total population of just over 1,000. Census data from the late nineteenth century (see note 9 above) suggest that land pressure in Chimbal may have antedated the 1877 land reforms. Second, Carol Smith (1984b: 203–204; cf. LaFarge 1940: 285–286) has argued that reduced tribute and labor demands during the mid-nineteenth-century regime of Rafael Carrera engendered increasing economic differentiation in Maya communities. If true, this may have also led to widening disparities in communal landholdings well before Liberal land reforms.

11. Unfortunately, even these records have been lost due to guerrilla actions that burned the town halls in Chimbal and other Maya communities in the department of Huehuetenango shortly before the presidential election of 1982. According to the municipal secretary in 1980, records for years preceding 1948 were sent to Guatemala City in the early 1950s in response to a request by the Archivo General de Centroamérica, but these documents remain uncataloged and therefore unavailable (cf. Lutz and Weber 1980: 276–277, 281). Wagley noted that prior to 1935, when there had still been a municipal secretary in Chimbal, "many men registered their holdings and obtained through him bills of sale in cases of transfer" (1941: 64). Copies of these documents presumably still exist somewhere in the AGCA.

12. Historical demographers estimate that the 1950 census closely approximates the size of the native population in highland Guatemala just before Spanish contact in about 1520 (Veblen 1982: 85–88, 98; Lovell and Swezey 1982: 81–82). Veblen argues: "According to the native documents, the nearly constant warfare of the late pre-Hispanic period was at least partially caused by overcrowding and the need for more land to sustain the growing population. As [Sherburne] Cook has suggested for central Mexico, on the eve of the Spanish conquest the Mayan population of highland Guatemala may have been on the verge of contraction due to years of demographic strain on the land" (1982: 98). Thus the 1950 population of Chimbal may represent an upward limit to the carrying capacity of local lands, given traditional methods of swidden agriculture. Only the introduction of chemical fertilizers and cash-cropping in coffee during the 1960s eased these demographic constraints somewhat (see chapter 6).

13. In most civil disputes, the *alcalde* designated the *síndico* and two *xtool* (*regidores*) to investigate the matter. The cost of this commission—in

the late 1970s, Q1.50 for the *síndico* and Q1.25 for each *xtool*—had to be paid by the offending party. To avoid the risk of paying these fees, disputants often preferred to settle out of court. The only serious criminal case that occurred while I was in Chimbal involved a drunken fight in which a person was wounded with a machete. The *alcalde* eventually prevailed on both parties to agree to the assessment of a large fine.

14. ORPA stands for Organización del Pueblo en Armas (Organization of the People in Arms), along with the Ejército Guerrillero de los Pobres, (Guerrilla Army of the Poor, or EGP), one of Guatemala's principal guerrilla organizations. A card that a Chimalteco passed on to me carried the ORPA logo of a smoking volcano and read, "We fight the army and landowners who bomb our villages. No youth should let himself be taken by the army. Soldier, policeman, the struggle of the rich is lost. Don't let them make you a murderer."

15. Much of this account comes from interviews conducted in early 1988, long after the guerrillas had lost the armed struggle for much of western Guatemala. Few Chimaltecos would have openly expressed even a passing former interest in such a lost cause. From recurring patterns in different accounts, it became clear to me that townspeople had come to a general consensus about the war and their involvement in it, making it virtually impossible to discern what contemporary attitudes and reactions had been. Several Chimaltecos, however, left the distinct impression that they had listened seriously to what the guerrillas had had to say and approved of it, at least in principle. Others roundly condemned the guerrillas for the hardships and violence that their actions had precipitated.

8. A Quest for Meaning

1. In contrast, Oakes (1951: 90) reports that in the neighboring Mam town of Todos Santos, "*aj ij*, 'young sun,'" referred to a novice *chmaan*, compared to "*chimanes baj*, ones 'who know.'"

2. Although I was unable actually to observe traditional Chimalteco religious practices, I gathered accounts of various rituals from Chimaltecos who had attended them as youngsters. These descriptions agree closely with Wagley's material on agricultural rituals (1941: 32–33, 34–40), divination (1949: 71–72), and curing (1949: 75–78). Maud Oakes's description of a New Year's ceremony (*twaalaq qmaan*) in Chimbal in 1946 (1951: 100–114) and her more extensive research in Todos Santos also corroborate what I was told, as does Junji Koizumi's (1981) study of contemporary religion in a nearby Mam town. Although minor variations occur, the general patterns of *costumbre* appear to be quite consistent throughout the northern Mam region.

3. Koizumi (1981: 63–70) presents a detailed description of divination in a nearby Mam town, which suggests that "questioning the beans" in Chimbal probably also involved other complicated repetitions and manipulations in the counting procedure. Furthermore, Barbara Tedlock's (1982: 107–131) work on K'iche' divination clearly indicates that mnemonics and

punning determine the interpretation of day-names within any given divination; the names themselves do not necessarily hold specific denotative significance. Koizumi's data suggest that this was—and remains—true in Mam divination as well.

4. Literally translated, *t-waa-laq q-maan* means "our father's plateful of food [i.e., tortillas]" or more elegantly, "an offering of tortillas for our father." In the nearby Mam town where Koizumi did his research, this celebration is called *twalb'q'ii*, "food for the year" (1981: 52), suggesting that "our father" in Chimbal refers to *qmaan q'iij*, "our father sun/day/time" (cf. Watanabe 1983: 716).

5. Richer Chimaltecos evidently loaned or gave land to poor Sanjuaneros during the early decades of this century in return for serving in their stead on the forced labor gangs that were common before Ubico's labor "reforms" of the 1930s (cf. Wagley 1949: 102; Jones 1940). San Juan Atitán has always been land-poor in comparison to Chimbal, but even then, Chimaltecos were careful to sell or exchange only their least productive land on the high ridge between La Florida and Bella Vista, where most San Juan immigrants now live.

6. Oakes (1951: 105, 114) mentions a female *chmaan* in Chimbal, but she was most likely a *xhb'ool*, not unlike the *pulsera*, "pulser," known to Oakes in Todos Santos who, in addition to being a midwife, "had an amazing knowledge of herbs, of the calendar, and of all *costumbres*," although she apparently was not a *chmaan* (Oakes 1951: 184). I never heard Chimaltecos speak of women *chmaan* in Chimbal.

7. Chimaltecos still practice this cure, and *seky'pajleenin* is a common diagnosis of illness, especially in children.

8. In Todos Santos, Maya made a distinction between the municipal religious officials, who actually "prayed," and the *chmaan*, who could only "plead and beg" (Oakes 1951: 59–60).

9. Divinations for a female patient would sometimes reveal that a close male relative had to become a *chmaan* to prevent her death (Wagley 1949: 73).

10. Except where noted, the information on Maryknoll activities in Huehuetenango and Chimbal comes from an interview with the first Maryknoll missioner to work in the Mam area and from conversations and correspondence with the Maryknoll priest who lived in the parish seat of San Pedro Necta from 1974 to early 1983.

11. The term *missioner* is one that Maryknolls use to refer to themselves.

12. By 1979, the Mormons were "talking to" about twenty families, although, by their own admission, they had yet to baptize anyone or to attract any prominent Chimaltecos, something they deemed necessary to give their church local "respectability." Ever pragmatic, a few Chimaltecos commented drily about the heavy tithes that church membership would entail.

13. I believe that the priest erred here and actually precipitated the split through his desire to "know where [this catechist] stood." In communities such as Chimbal, conflicts may often smolder interminably, but open rifts occur only if provoked. Given their embeddedness and interdependencies

within the town, Chimaltecos can rarely afford to burn their social bridges behind them in such all-or-nothing fashion.

14. During one fiesta, two Chimaltecos pointed out an evangelical merchant who had set up his stall in his customary place in the holiday market. Neither man was a catechist, but both agreed that the evangelical should not have done so because the market was an integral part of the celebrations that his church so vehemently condemned.

15. For instance, one year during my stay in Chimbal, the procession of Santiago and Santa Ana that closes the celebration of Corpus Christi (see chapter 5) did not take place. Some Chimaltecos cited heavy rains that day as the reason, but others complained of the "lack of interest" due to catechists' disapprobation of processions. The following year, however, the procession occurred as usual.

16. In discussing the potential problems of religious conversion in the Q'anjob'al town of Santa Eulalia, Oliver LaFarge (1947: 81) observes: "The task confronting a priest who wished to revive true Christianity among these people is made almost overwhelming by the fact that they are not merely non-Christians but non-Christians who believe themselves to be the only maintainers of pure Christianity. It would unquestionably be easier to convert them to a new religion or at least to a new and entirely different denomination." The catechists appear to have disabused most Chimaltecos of the notion that the traditional religion was authentic Catholicism. As one middle-aged man said, "Before, there was no religion in Chimbal, only *costumbre.* Over in San Juan *costumbre* continues; there's no religion there." Nonetheless, catechists cannot afford to ignore the appeal of evangelicalism as a new—and possibly more authentic—religion, untainted by practices of the past.

17. In the community where Koizumi did his work, fifty-six *martoon* served in eight groups, each charged with celebrating one of the eight major fiestas of the year (1981: 15). In Todos Santos, Oakes noted thirteen *rezadores,* "prayermakers," and the *Chimán Nam* assisted by four *mayores* (1951: 55). Both these *municipios* remain noted for their cultural distinctiveness as well as their decidedly insular nature.

18. Concerning a similar religious transformation effected by a vigorous priest, LaFarge (1947: 80–81) reports: "When I was at Jacaltenango in 1927, the Prayermakers dominated the religious scene, both Christian and Indian. There was a definite arrogance in their carriage. I was interested and amused to see that in 1932 they were definitely serving the priest in many minor capacities, attended mass regularly, and had been trained by him in the proper moments for rising, kneeling, and crossing themselves, so that they served as guides to the rest of the congregation."

19. Although I would argue that ethnicity represented an important element in subjective Chimalteco perceptions of and reactions to Maryknoll missionization, the actual humanistic behavior and attitudes of the priests, regardless of their national or ethnic origin, unquestionably proved equally important. As LaFarge (1947: 80) noted regarding a Mercedarian priest in northern Huehuetenango: "At Jacaltenango in 1932 there was a most re-

markable man, the Padre Ybisate. This priest had completely broken through the traditions, visiting his missions without warning or fanfare and demanding no more for himself, either there or in the home village, than was necessary to maintain life. He was an unfailing source of astonishment to the Indians, who were beginning vaguely to feel that he was admirable, not merely foolish."

20. In comparison, Tedlock (1982: 25, 35–36) notes that the K'iche' "shaman-priests" of Momostenango also serve as lineage heads, giving them both ritual and political power. In Chimbal, *chmaan* held no such position or authority.

21. June Nash (1970: 242–250) notes a similar transformation of curer into witch in the Tzeltal community of Amatenango, but there the metamorphosis resulted from struggles for political power between civil authorities and curers in the town. Similarly, Warren (1978: 75–77) describes two kinds of traditional practitioners in the Kaqchikel town of San Andrés Semetabaj that closely reflect Mam distinctions between *aj q'iij* (*ajg'ij* in Kaqchikel) and *aj mees* (*ajitz*), but she characterizes both as "sorcerers"— the first a "sorcerer of the day," the second a "sorcerer of evil." I suspect that this characterization results from the active presence in San Andrés of Catholic Action catechists since the early 1950s with whom she appears to have had closest contact during her fieldwork.

22. According to Chimalteco conventions, modern drugs are "magical" because they lack the physical properties of "heat" found in traditional remedies such as sweatbaths, poultices, and alcoholic potions that counteract the supposedly "cold" state of *yaab'il*, "sickness" (Watanabe 1981b). *Xhb'ool* probably escaped the disapprobation of the catechists because they had no magic to offer, only the expertise of conventional Chimalteco common sense.

23. Tedlock (1982: 40–44) reports a similar effort by catechists in the K'iche' *municipio* of Momostenango. Traditionalists, however, object to the radical separation of spiritual God and material earth "that leads, as they point out, to the confusion of the very earth itself with the devil" (1982: 42). Instead they have developed a "counter-catechism" consisting of *Tiox*, "God," which encompasses the Catholic Trinity and the saints; *Mundo*, "the World," meaning the material world as a whole; and *Nantat*, "the Ancestors," in both their spiritual and material aspects. Chimalteco traditionalists have yet to articulate a comparable ideology.

✠ *Glossary* ✠

aanma: Soul, from the Spanish *alma* or *ánima*, "soul."

aguardiente: A raw, often bootleg, sugarcane rum.

aj mees: Literally "person of the table," a shaman-diviner possessing a small tablelike altar consecrated to a particular spirit owner of the mountains (*witz*); a kind of *chmaan*.

aj q'iij: Literally "person of the sun/day/time," a calendrical diviner; a kind of *chmaan*.

alcalde: Town mayor, highest civil official of a *municipio*.

aldea: Hamlet, outlying settlement of a *municipio*.

alsiil: Low-ranking Chimalteco religious cargo charged with "capturing" the incoming cargoholders during each year's change-of-office ceremony, from the Spanish *alguacil*, "constable."

baldío: Unclaimed public land that Maya communities came to hold by usufruct during colonial and early republican times but which they often lost to government and commercial agricultural interests toward the end of the nineteenth century.

caballería: Unit of land equal to about 111 acres, or 45 hectares.

cabecera: Literally "head town," municipal seat of a *municipio*.

cacique: Local political leader or boss.

campesino: Rural dweller, small farmer.

cantina: Bar, informal drinking establishment.

cantón: Ward or neighborhood, subdivision within a *municipio*.

censo enfitéutico: Annual rent formerly paid by residents of a town for usufruct rights to local communal lands, often used by towns to meet taxes imposed by the state.

chirimía: Double-reeded woodwind instrument played on ceremonial occasions, especially processions, often accompanied by a drum.

chmaamb'aj: Generic Mam term for folk Catholic religious practices and practitioners.

chmaan: Literally "grandfather," shaman curer and calendrical diviner.

chmaan tnam: Literally "shaman of the town," the shaman-diviner who served as ritual adviser to local civil and religious officials.

choolil: Murderer who trades the heads of his victims to mountain spirits for material gain, *cholero* in Spanish.

CIRMA: Centro de Investigaciones Regionales de Mesoamérica, Center for Regional Studies in Mesoamerica, located in Antigua, Guatemala.

cofradía: Religious brotherhood dedicated to a particular saint in the local Catholic church; in Maya communities, membership normally rotates on an annual basis.

colonial historicism: Scholarly perspective that reduces Maya cultural distinctiveness to an artifact of colonialist domination, either as an imposed instrument of economic marginalization and political subordination or as a mechanism of peasant resistance to capitalist depredations.

comerciante: Merchant or traveling peddler.

community: Conjunction of people with a place that engenders interpersonal familiarity and social identity based on common commitments, concerns, and ways of dealing with these to survive in that place.

congregación: Colonial resettlement of the scattered Maya population into nucleated Spanish-style towns intended to Christianize, civilize, and control them more easily; consequently such settlements themselves.

consejal: Town councilman elected every four years as part of the "municipal corporation" that governs a *municipio*.

convention: Regular pattern of interaction between individuals of a community that makes particular events and actions recognizable while also drawing on such instances of use to substantiate its meaningfulness; an enactment of a people's culture.

copal: Pungent pine pitch incense used in Maya religious ceremonies.

costumbre: Literally "custom" or "tradition," specifically Maya folk Catholic rituals, especially offerings of prayers, candles, copal, and the sacrifice of chickens or turkeys to God, saints, or mountain spirits.

CUC: Comité de Unidad Campesina, Committee for Peasant Unity, a revolutionary organization of the rural poor active beginning in the 1980s.

cuerda: Basic unit of land measure, in Chimbal equal to about 0.11 acres, or 0.044 hectares.

cultural essentialism: Scholarly perspective that defines Maya ethnicity in terms of specific cultural or institutional attributes, implying that any waning of these attributes indicates a loss of Mayanness and subsequent acculturation to Ladino ways.

DC: Democracia Christiana, the Christian Democracy party, a centrist, reformist political party.

DGE: Dirección General de Estadística, the Guatemalan Census Bureau.

EGP: Ejército Guerrillero de los Pobres, Guerrilla Army of the Poor, a militant revolutionary organization of the 1970s and 1980s.

ejido: Inalienable common land allotted to Maya communities during the colonial period and administered by local officials.

encomendero: Holder of an *encomienda*.

encomienda: A colonial grant giving Spanish settlers rights to the tribute and initially the labor of Maya from specified towns in return for which recipients were obliged to Christianize and civilize their charges, from the Spanish *encomendar*, "entrust."

existential sovereignty: The sense of place and propriety that grows out of everyday activities and interactions; the practical, largely tacit basis for community.

finca: A large farm, in Guatemala usually a commercial plantation growing coffee or cotton for sale on the international market.

gringo: White foreigner.

huipil: Handwoven woman's blouse.

iipin: Strength, physical vitality.

indio: Derogatory term for Indian.

juuris: Monster or demon, probably from the Spanish *judio,* "Jew," so characterized by colonial Catholic priests as the killers of Christ.

ky'aawil: Sorcerer.

Ladino: Spanish-speaking mestizo identifying in dress and outlook with Guatemalan national society rather than a local Maya culture or community.

likaal: Town mayor, from the Spanish *alcalde,* "mayor."

manzana: Unit of land consisting of 16 *cuerdas,* roughly 1.73 acres, or 0.70 hectares; the basic unit of measure used in Guatemalan agricultural censuses.

marimba: Large wooden xylophone with resonators below each bar played by three or four musicians, the musical instrument of choice in Chimbal especially during public celebrations.

martoon: Local religious official charged with care of saints' images in the church, from the Spanish *mayordomo,* "steward."

mayor: Town clerk.

Mesoamerica: Cultural area extending from just north of the Valley of Mexico south to the western regions of Honduras and El Salvador where the "high civilizations" of native Mexico and Guatemala developed in pre-Hispanic times.

milpa: Corn field.

miyool: Town clerk, from the Spanish *mayor,* "clerk."

moos: Ladino.

mozo: Hired laborer.

municipio: Administrative and territorial jurisdiction usually consisting of a town center (*cabecera*) and outlying settlements (*aldeas*), which for the Maya also constitutes an ethnic community with distinctive dress, speech, and customs.

naab'l: A person's "way of being" that involves perceptual sense and social sensibility, individual perspicacity and recognition of locally acceptable conventions of behavior; analogous to notions of "soul" in black culture in the United States.

natural: Native, term that Maya often use to refer to themselves when speaking Spanish.

niiky': A person's nature, expressed in his or her disposition, abilities, and effect on others.

ORPA: Organización del Pueblo en Armas, Organization of the People in Arms, a revolutionary guerrilla group of the 1980s.

patrón: Boss, landlord, protector.

PID: Partido Institucional Democrático, The Institutional Democratic Party, the political party of the Guatemalan military.

político: Politician.

PR: Partido Revolucionario, The Revolutionary Party, founded following the Revolution of 1944 but co-opted by the military after the Counterrevolution of 1954.

principal: Town elder who has passed cargos on all levels of the local civil-religious hierarchy and safeguards the conduct of public affairs in the community.

quetzal: The Guatemalan national currency, on par with the U.S. dollar until the early 1980s, since when it has fluctuated between Q2.50 and nearly Q5.00 to the dollar.

quintal: 100 pounds.

regidor: Town councilman.

repartimiento: Colonial system of forced labor in which a specified number of Maya from a given community had to work for Spanish settlers on a rotating basis.

Santiago: Saint James, saintly protector of the Spanish *conquistadores* and consequently patron saint of many towns they founded, usually depicted as Santiago Matamoros, "St. James the Moorkiller" astride a white horse with sword raised to drive out the Moors from Spain and by extension to subdue the natives of the New World.

syncretism: Process of cultural change in which elements from distinct traditions are combined to form a new culture unlike its predecessors.

taajwa witz: Spirit owner or master of the mountain, often characterized as powerful Ladinos holding plantations, large herds of animals, and chests of money inside their mountains but also associated iconographically with the snakes, clouds, and lightning of pre-Hispanic rain gods.

ttxaʔnja: Literally "edge of the houses," the two shrines at the eastern and western entrances to the town; referred to in Spanish as *calvario*, "crossroad" or "Calvary."

witz: Mountain, also the spirit owner said to live inside any prominent peak; often short for *taajwa witz*.

xtool: Town councilman, *regidor* in Spanish.

xtxuun: A thin corn gruel spiced with cinnamon, drunk on public ceremonial occasions.

✛ References ✛

Adams, Richard N. 1956. La ladinización en Guatemala. In *Integración social en Guatemala*, vol. 1, ed. Jorge Luis Arriola, pp. 215–244. Seminario de Integración Social Guatemalteca, pub. 3. Guatemala City: Tipografía Nacional.

———. 1970. *Crucifixion by Power: Essays on Guatemalan National Social Structure, 1944–1966*. Austin: University of Texas Press.

———, ed. 1972 [1957]. Political Changes in Guatemalan Indian Communities: A Symposium. In *Community Culture and National Change*, pp. 1–54. Middle American Research Institute, pub. 24, New Orleans: Middle American Research Institute, Tulane University.

———. 1988. Conclusions: What Can We Know about the Harvest of Violence? In *Harvest of Violence: The Maya Indians and the Guatemalan Crisis*, ed. Robert M. Carmack, pp. 274–291. Norman: University of Oklahoma Press.

Americas Watch. 1986. *Civil Patrols in Guatemala*. New York and Washington: The Americas Watch Committee.

Annis, Sheldon. 1987. *God and Production in a Guatemalan Town*. Austin: University of Texas Press.

Appelbaum, Richard P. 1967. *San Ildefonso Ixtahuacán, Guatemala: Un estudio sobre la migración temporal, sus causas y consecuencias*. Cuadernos del Seminario de Integración Social Guatemalteca, no. 17. Guatemala City: Editorial José de Pineda Ibarra.

Archivo General de Centroamérica (AGCA). Guatemala City. Todos Santos y Chimaltenango, amparo en sus tierras (1670). Sección de Tierras (ST), *paquete* 1, no. 1.

———. Pueblo de Chimaltenango: Medida de sus ejidos (1891). Sección de Tierras (ST), *paquete* 12, no. 2.

Archivo General de las Indias (AGI). Seville, Spain. Chimaltenango y Atitlan . . . (1549). Audencia de Guatemala (AG), *legajo* 128, folio 128 verso.

———. Respuesta del cura de Gueguetenango . . . (1770). Audencia de Guatemala (AG), *legajo* 928, tomo 2, folios 76–79.

Arias, Arturo. 1990. Changing Indian Identity: Guatemala's Violent Transition to Modernity. In *Guatemalan Indians and the State: 1540 to 1988*, ed. Carol A. Smith, pp. 230–257. Austin: University of Texas Press.

Arias de Blois, Jorge. 1982. Mortality in Guatemala towards the End of the Nineteenth Century. Trans. John D. Early. In *The Historical Demography of Highland Guatemala,* ed. Robert M. Carmack, John Early, and Christopher Lutz, pp. 155–168. Institute for Mesoamerican Studies, pub. 6. Albany: Institute for Mesoamerican Studies, State University of New York.

Axelrod, Robert. 1984. *The Evolution of Cooperation.* New York: Basic Books, Inc.

Barth, Fredrik. 1969. Introduction. In *Ethnic Groups and Boundaries: The Social Organization of Culture Difference,* ed. Fredrik Barth, pp. 9–38. Boston: Little, Brown, and Company.

Bellah, Robert N., Richard Madsen, William M. Sullivan, Ann Swidler, and Steven M. Tipton. 1985. *Habits of the Heart: Individualism and Commitment in American Life.* Berkeley and Los Angeles: University of California Press.

Black, George, Milton Jamail, and Norma Stoltz Chinchilla. 1984. *Garrison Guatemala.* New York: Monthly Review Press.

Borhegyi, Stephen F. 1965. Settlement Patterns of the Guatemalan Highlands. In *Archaeology of Southern Mesoamerica,* Part 1, ed. Gordon R. Willey, pp. 59–75. Vol. 2 of *Handbook of Middle American Indians.* Robert Wauchope, gen. ed. Austin: University of Texas Press.

Bossen, Laurel Herbenar. 1984. *The Redivision of Labor: Women and Economic Choice in Four Guatemalan Communities.* Albany: State University of New York Press.

Bricker, Victoria Reifler. 1973. *Ritual Humor in Highland Chiapas.* Austin: University of Texas Press.

———. 1981. *The Indian Christ, the Indian King: The Historical Substrate of Maya Myth and Ritual.* Austin: University of Texas Press.

Brintnall, Douglas E. 1979. *Revolt against the Dead: The Modernization of a Mayan Community in the Highlands of Guatemala.* New York: Gordon and Breach.

———. 1980. A model of changing group relations in the Mayan Highlands of Guatemala. *Journal of Anthropological Research* 36(3): 294–315.

Bunzel, Ruth. 1952. *Chichicastenango: A Guatemalan Village.* Publications of the American Ethnological Society, no. 22. Locust Valley, N.Y.: J. J. Augustin.

Calder, Bruce Johnson. 1970. *Crecimiento y cambio de la iglesia guatemalteca, 1944–1966.* Estudios Centroamericanos del Seminario de Integración Social Guatemalteca, no. 6. Guatemala City: Editorial José de Pineda Ibarra.

Cancian, Frank. 1965. *Economics and Prestige in a Maya Community: The Cargo System in Zinacantan.* Stanford, Calif.: Stanford University Press.

———. 1967. Political and Religious Organizations. In *Social Anthropology,* ed. Manning Nash, pp. 283–298. Vol. 6 of *Handbook of Middle American Indians.* Robert Wauchope, gen. ed. Austin: University of Texas Press.

Carmack, Robert M. 1981. *The Quiché Mayas of Utatlán: The Evolution of a Highland Guatemala Kingdom.* The Civilization of the American Indian Series, vol. 155. Norman: University of Oklahoma Press.

————, ed. 1988. *Harvest of Violence: The Maya Indians and the Guatemalan Crisis.* Norman: University of Oklahoma Press.

————, and Francisco Morales Santos, eds. 1983. *Nuevas perspectivas sobre el Popol Vuh.* Guatemala City: Editorial Piedra Santa.

Casteñeda Medinilla, José, Francisco Rodríguez Rouanet, Gladys Aceituno de García, and César Oswaldo García Cordón. 1978. Aspectos de la medicina popular en el área rural de Guatemala. *Guatemala Indígena* 13(3–4).

Chance, John K., and William B. Taylor. 1985. Cofradías and cargos: An historical perspective on the Mesoamerican civil-religious hierarchy. *American Ethnologist* 12(1): 1–26.

Cherry, Colin. 1966. *On Human Communication: A Review, a Survey, and a Criticism.* 2d ed. Cambridge, Mass.: MIT Press.

Clendennin, Inga. 1990. Cortés, Signs, and the Conquest of Mexico. In *The Transmission of Culture in Early Modern Europe,* ed. Anthony Grafton and Ann Blair, pp. 87–130. Philadelphia: University of Pennsylvania Press.

Colby, Benjamin N., and Pierre L. van den Berghe. 1969. *Ixil Country: A Plural Society in Highland Guatemala.* Berkeley: University of California Press.

Crapanzano, Vincent. 1980. *Tuhami: Portrait of a Moroccan.* Chicago: University of Chicago Press.

Currier, Richard L. 1966. The hot-cold syndrome and symbolic balance in Mexican and Spanish folk medicine. *Ethnology* 5(3): 251–263.

Davis, Shelton. 1970. Land of our ancestors: A study of land tenure and inheritance in the highlands of Guatemala. Ph.D. diss., Department of Social Relations, Harvard University.

Dirección General de Estadística, Guatemala (DGE). 1923. *Cuarto censo de población.* Guatemala City: Ministerio de Fomento.

————. 1953. *Sexto censo de población: 18 abril de 1950.* Guatemala City: Ministerio de Economía.

————. 1968. *II censo agropecuario de 1964,* tomo I. Guatemala City: Ministerio de Economía.

————. 1971. *II censo agropecuario de 1964,* tomo II. Guatemala City: Ministerio de Economía.

————. 1977. *Los censos de 1973: Octavo de población, tercero de habitación.* Guatemala City: Ministerio de Economía.

————. 1982. *III censo nacional agropecuario de 1979,* vol I, tomo I. Guatemala City: Ministerio de Economía.

————. 1983. *III censo nacional agropecuario de 1979,* vol. II, tomo I. Guatemala City: Ministerio de Economía.

————. 1984. *Censos nacionales: IV habitación, IX población de 1981.* Guatemala City: Ministerio de Economía.

Douglas, Mary. 1966. *Purity and Danger: An Analysis of the Concepts of Pollution and Taboo.* London: Routlege and Kegan Paul.

Early, John D. 1982. Some Demographic Characteristics of Peasant Systems: The Guatemalan Case. In *The Historical Demography of Highland Guatemala,* ed. Robert M. Carmack, John Early, and Christopher Lutz, pp. 169–

181. Institute for Mesoamerican Studies, pub. 6. Albany: Institute for Mesoamerican Studies, State University of New York.

Edmonson, Munro S., trans. 1971. *The Book of Counsel: The Popol Vuh of the Quiche Maya of Guatemala.* Middle American Research Institute, pub. 35. New Orleans: Middle American Research Institute, Tulane University.

England, Nora C. 1983. *A Grammar of Mam, a Mayan Language.* Austin: University of Texas Press.

Elliott, J. H. 1986. Cortés, Velásquez and Charles V. In *Hernán Cortés: Letters from Mexico,* trans. and ed. Anthony Pagden, pp. xi–xxxvii. New Haven, Conn.: Yale University Press.

Falla, Ricardo. 1971. Juan el gordo: Visión indígena de su explotación. *Estudios Centro Americanos* 26(268): 98–107.

Farriss, Nancy M. 1984. *Maya Society under Colonial Rule: The Collective Enterprise of Survival.* Princeton, N.J.: Princeton University Press.

Foster, George. 1944. Nagualism in Mexico and Guatemala. *Acta Americana* 2(1–2): 87–103.

———. 1965. Peasant society and the image of limited good. *American Anthropologist* 67(2): 293–315.

Fox, John W. 1978. *Quiche Conquest: Centralism and Regionalism in Highland Guatemalan State Development.* Albuquerque: University of New Mexico Press.

Friedlander, Judith. 1975. *Being Indian in Hueyapán: A Study of Forced Identity in Contemporary Mexico.* New York: St. Martin's Press.

Fuentes y Guzmán, Francisco Antonio de. 1972 [1690]. *Obras históricas de don Francisco Antonio de Fuentes y Guzmán, tomo III: Recordación florida.* Biblioteca de Autores Españoles, vol. 259. Madrid: Ediciones Atlas.

Gall, Francis. 1980. *Diccionario geográfico de Guatemala, tomo III.* 2d ed. Guatemala City: Instituto Geográfico Nacional.

———. 1983. *Diccionario geográfico de Guatemala, tomo IV, de la letra t a la z.* 2d ed. Guatemala City: Instituto Geográfico Nacional.

García Añoveras, Jesús M. 1980. La realidad social de la diócesis de Guatemala a finales del siglo XVII. *Mesoamérica* 1(1): 104–173.

Geertz, Clifford. 1973. Religion as a Cultural System. In *The Interpretation of Cultures,* pp. 87–125. New York: Basic Books.

Gibson, Charles. 1964. *The Aztecs under Spanish Rule: A History of the Indians of the Valley of Mexico, 1519–1810.* Stanford, Calif.: Stanford University Press.

———. 1966. *Spain in America.* New York: Harper Torchbooks.

Gillin, John. 1948. Magical fright. *Psychiatry* 11 (November): 387–400.

Glassie, Henry. 1982. *Passing the Time in Ballymenone: Culture and History of an Ulster Community.* Philadelphia: University of Pennsylvania Press.

Gossen, Gary H. 1974. *Chamulas in the World of the Sun: Time and Space in a Maya Oral Tradition.* Cambridge: Harvard University Press.

———. 1975. Animal souls and human destiny in Chamula. *Man* n.s. 10(3): 448–461.

Greenberg, James B. 1981. *Santiago's Sword: Chatino Peasant Religion and Economics.* Berkeley and Los Angeles: University of California Press.

Guiteras-Holmes, C. 1961. *Perils of the Soul: The World View of a Tzotzil Indian.* New York: The Free Press of Glencoe, Inc.

Guzmán-Böckler, Carlos, and Jean-Loup Herbert. 1970. *Guatemala: Una interpretación histórico-social.* Mexico City: Siglo Veintiuno Editores.

Handy, Jim. 1990. The Corporate Community, Campesino Organizations, and Agrarian Reform, 1950–1954. In *Guatemalan Indians and the State: 1540 to 1988,* ed. Carol A. Smith, pp. 163–182. Austin: University of Texas Press.

Harris, Marvin. 1964. *Patterns of Race in the Americas.* New York: Walker and Company.

Hawkins, John. 1984. *Inverse Images: The Meaning of Culture, Ethnicity, and Family in Postcolonial Guatemala.* Albuquerque: University of New Mexico Press.

Hill, Robert M., II. 1986. Manteniendo el culto de los santos: Aspectos financieros de las instituciones religiosas del altiplano colonial maya. *Mesoamérica* 7(11): 61–77.

———, and John Monaghan. 1987. *Continuities in Highland Maya Social Organization: Ethnohistory in Sacapulus, Guatemala.* Philadelphia: University of Pennsylvania Press.

Holleran, Mary P. 1949. *Church and State in Guatemala.* New York: Columbia University Press.

Hunt, Eva. 1977. *The Transformation of the Hummingbird: Cultural Roots of a Zinacantecan Mythical Poem.* Ithaca, N.Y.: Cornell University Press.

Immerman, Richard H. 1982. *The CIA in Guatemala: The Foreign Policy of Intervention.* Austin: University of Texas Press.

Ingham, John M. 1970. On Mexican folk medicine. *American Anthropologist* 72(1): 76–87.

Jones, Chester Lloyd. 1940. *Guatemala, Past and Present.* Minneapolis: University of Minnesota Press.

Kaufman, Terrence. 1974. *Idiomas de Mesoamérica.* Seminario de Integración Social Guatemalteca, pub. 33. Guatemala City: Editorial José de Pineda Ibarra.

Keen, Benjamin. 1971. *The Aztec Image in Western Thought.* New Brunswick, N.J.: Rutgers University Press.

Keesing, Roger M. 1982. *Kwaio Religion: The Living and the Dead in a Solomon Island Society.* New York: Columbia University Press.

Keil, Charles. 1966. *Urban Blues.* Chicago: University of Chicago Press.

Kelly, John Eoghan. 1971 [1932]. *Pedro de Alvarado, Conquistador.* Port Washington, N.Y.: Kennikat Press.

Koizumi, Junji. 1981. Symbol and context: A study of self and action in a Guatemalan culture. Ph.D. diss., Department of Anthropology, Stanford University.

Kramer, Wendy, W. George Lovell, and Christopher H. Lutz. 1991. Fire in the Mountains: Juan de Espinar and the Indians of Huehuetenango, 1525–

1560. In *Columbian Consequences*, vol. 3, ed. David Hurst Thomas, pp. 263–282. Washington, D.C.: Smithsonian Institution Press.

LaFarge, Oliver. 1940. Maya Ethnology: The Sequence of Cultures. In *The Maya and Their Neighbors*, ed. Clarence L. Hay, Ralph L. Linton, Samuel K. Lothrop, Harry L. Shapiro, and George C. Vaillant, pp. 281–291. New York: D. Appleton Century Company.

———. 1947. *Santa Eulalia: The Religion of a Cuchumatán Indian Town.* Chicago: University of Chicago Press.

Lansing, Donald, M.M. n.d. Introducción al Mam de Santiago Chimaltenango. Mimeographed manuscript in Santiago Chimaltenango.

Laughlin, Robert M. 1975. *The Great Tzotzil Dictionary of San Lorenzo Zinacantán.* Smithsonian Contributions to Anthropology, no. 19. Washington, D.C.: Smithsonian Institute Press.

Lovell, W. George. 1982. Collapse and Recovery: A Demographic Profile of the Cuchumatán Highlands of Guatemala. In *The Historical Demography of Highland Guatemala*, ed. Robert M. Carmack, John Early, and Christopher Lutz, pp. 103–120. Institute for Mesoamerican Studies, pub. 6. Albany: Institute for Mesoamerican Studies, State University of New York.

———. 1983a. Landholding in Spanish Central America: Patterns of ownership and activity in the Cuchumatán Highlands of Guatemala, 1563–1821. *Transactions of the Institute of British Geographers*, n.s. 8(3): 214–230.

———. 1983b. Settlement change in Spanish America: The dynamics of *congregación* in the Cuchumatán Highlands of Guatemala, 1541–1821. *Canadian Geographer* 27(2): 163–174.

———. 1985. *Conquest and Survival in Colonial Guatemala: A Historical Geography of the Cuchumatán Highlands, 1500–1821.* Kingston and Montreal: McGill-Queen's University Press.

———. 1988. Las enfermedades del Viejo Mundo y la mortandad indígena: La viruela y el tabardillo en la Sierra de los Cuchumatanes, Guatemala (1780–1810). *Mesoamérica* 9(16): 239–285.

———, and William R. Swezey. 1982. The population of southern Guatemala at Spanish contact. *Canadian Journal of Anthropology* 3(1): 71–84.

———, Christopher H. Lutz, and William R. Swezey. 1984. The Indian population of southern Guatemala, 1549–1551: An analysis of López de Cerrato's *Tasaciones de tributos*. *Americas* 40(4): 459–477.

Lutz, Christopher H. n.d. Evolución demográfica de la población no indígena. In *Dominación española: Desde la conquista hasta 1700.* Vol. 2 of *Historia general de Guatemala*, ed. Jorge Luján Muñoz. In press.

———, and Stephen Weber. 1980. El Archivo General de Centroamérica y otros recursos investigativos en Guatemala. *Mesoamérica* 1(1): 274–285.

McCreery, David. 1988. Land, labor, and violence in highland Guatemala: San Juan Ixcoy (Huehuetenango), 1893–1945. *Americas* 45(2): 237–249.

———. 1990. State Power, Indigenous Communities, and Land in Nineteenth-Century Guatemala, 1820–1920. In *Guatemalan Indians and the*

State: 1540 to 1988, ed. Carol A. Smith, pp. 96–115. Austin: University of Texas Press.

MacLeod, Murdo J. 1973. *Spanish Central America: A Socioeconomic History, 1520–1720*. Berkeley and Los Angeles: University of California Press.

McNeill, William. 1976. *Plagues and Peoples*. Garden City, N.Y.: Anchor Books.

Maldonado Andrés, Juan, Juan Ordóñez Domingo, and Juan Ortiz Domingo. 1986. *Diccionario mam: San Ildefonso Ixtahuacán, Huehuetenango, mam-español*. Guatemala City: Universidad Rafael Landívar.

Manz, Beatriz. 1988. *Refugees of a Hidden War: The Aftermath of Counterinsurgency in Guatemala*. Albany: State University of New York Press.

Martínez Peláez, Severo. 1979 [1971]. *La patria del criollo: Ensayo de interpretación de la realidad colonial guatemalteca*. 6th ed. San José, Costa Rica: Editorial Universitaria Centroamericana.

Menchú, Rigoberta. 1984. *I . . . Rigoberta Menchú: An Indian Woman in Guatemala*. Ed. Elisabeth Burgos-Debray; trans. Ann Wright. London: Verso.

Mendelson, E. Michael. 1965. *Los escándolos de Maximón: Un estudio sobre la religión y la visión del mundo en Santiago Atitlán*. Seminario de Integración Social Guatemalteca, pub. 19. Guatemala City: Tipografía Nacional.

Miles, S. W. 1965. Summary of Preconquest Ethnology of the Guatemala-Chiapas Highlands and Pacific Slopes. In *Archaeology of Southern Mesoamerica, Part One*, ed. Gordon R. Willey, pp. 276–287. Vol. 2 of *Handbook of Middle American Indians*. Robert Wauchope, gen. ed. Austin: University of Texas Press.

Modiano, Nancy. 1973. *Indian Education in the Chiapas Highlands*. New York: Holt, Rinehart and Winston, Inc.

Moore, Alexander. 1979. Initiation rites in a Mesoamerican cargo system: Men and boys, Judas and the bull. *Journal of Latin American Lore* 5(1): 55–81.

Mörner, Magnus. 1967. *Race Mixture in the History of Latin America*. Boston: Little, Brown, and Company.

Nash, June. 1970. *In the Eyes of the Ancestors: Belief and Behavior in a Mayan Community*. New Haven, Conn.: Yale University Press.

Nash, Manning. 1967 [1958]. *Machine Age Maya: The Industrialization of a Guatemalan Community*. Chicago: University of Chicago Press.

———. 1970. The Impact of Mid–Nineteenth Century Economic Change upon the Indians of Middle America. In *Race and Class in Latin America*, ed. Magnus Mörner, pp. 170–183. New York: Columbia University Press.

Neuenswander, Helen L., and Shirley D. Souder. 1977. The Hot-Cold Wet-Dry Syndrome and the Quiché of Joyabaj: Two Alternative Cognitive Models. In *Cognitive Studies of Southern Mesoamerica*, ed. Helen L. Neuenswander and Dean E. Arnold, pp. 94–125. SIL Museum of Anthropology, pub. 3. Dallas: Summer Institute of Linguistics, Inc.

Oakes, Maud. 1951. *The Two Crosses of Todos Santos: Survivals of Mayan*

Religious Ritual. Bollingen Series, no. 27. Princeton, N.J.: Princeton University Press.

Olaverreta, José de. 1935. Relación geográfica del partido de Huehuetenango, 1740. *Boletín del Archivo General del Gobierno* (Guatemala City) 1(1) 16–24.

Oss, Adriaan C. van. 1986. *Catholic Colonialism: A Parish History of Guatemala, 1524–1821*. Cambridge Latin American Studies, no. 57. Cambridge: Cambridge University Press.

Pagden, Anthony, trans. and ed. 1986. *Hernán Cortés: Letters from Mexico*. New Haven, Conn.: Yale University Press.

Pansini, J. Jude. 1980. La situación de la salud de los trabajadores de las fincas en Guatemala. *Mesoamérica* 1(1): 188–217.

Paul, Benjamin D., and William J. Demarest. 1988. The Operation of a Death Squad in San Pedro la Laguna. In *Harvest of Violence: The Maya Indians and the Guatemalan Crisis*, ed. Robert M. Carmack, pp. 119–154. Norman: University of Oklahoma Press.

Pye, Clifton. 1986. Quiché Mayan speech to children. *Journal of Child Language* 13(1): 85–100.

Rappaport, Roy A. 1979a. The Obvious Aspects of Ritual. In *Ecology, Meaning, and Religion*, pp. 173–221. Richmond, Calif.: North Atlantic Books.

———. 1979b. Sanctity and Lies in Evolution. In *Ecology, Meaning, and Religion*, pp. 223–246. Richmond, Calif.: North Atlantic Books.

Recinos, Adrián. 1954. *Monografía del departamento de Huehuetenango*. 2d ed. Guatemala City: Editorial del Ministro de Educación Pública.

———, and D. Goetz. 1953. *The Annals of the Cakchiquels*. Norman: University of Oklahoma Press.

Redfield, Robert. 1941. *The Folk Culture of Yucatan*. Chicago: University of Chicago Press.

———. 1962a [1947]. The Folk Society. Reprinted in *Human Nature and the Study of Society: The Papers of Robert Redfield*, vol. 1, ed. Margaret Park Redfield, pp. 231–253. Chicago: University of Chicago Press.

———. 1962b [1935]. Folkways and City Ways. Reprinted in *Human Nature and the Study of Society: The Papers of Robert Redfield*, vol. 1, ed. Margaret Park Redfield, pp. 172–182. Chicago: University of Chicago Press.

———, and Alfonso Villa Rojas. 1934. *Chan Kom: A Maya Village*. Carnegie Institution of Washington, pub. 448. Washington, D.C.: Carnegie Institution.

Reina, Rubin E. 1966. *The Law of the Saints: A Pokomam Pueblo and Its Community Culture*. New York: Bobbs-Merrill Company, Inc.

Remesal, Fray Antonio de, O.P. 1932 [1619]. *Historia general de las Indias Occidentales, y particular de la gobernación de Chiapa y Guatemala*. Biblioteca "Goathemala" de la Sociedad de Geografía é Historia, vol. 5. Guatemala City: Tipografía Nacional.

Robertson, John S., John P. Hawkins, and Andrés Maldonado. n.d. *Mam Basic Course*. 2 vols. Guatemala City: U.S. Peace Corps.

Rubel, Arthur J., Carl W. O'Nell, and Rolando Collado-Ardón. 1984. *Susto, a Folk Illness*. Berkeley and Los Angeles: University of California Press.

Rus, Jan, and Robert Wasserstrom. 1980. Civil-religious hierarchies in central Chiapas: A critical perspective. *American Ethnologist* 7(3): 466–478.

Sahlins, Marshall. 1972. The Domestic Mode of Production: The Structure of Underproduction. In *Stone Age Economics*, pp. 41–99. New York: Aldine Publishing Company.

Saler, Benson. 1964. Nagual, witch and sorcerer in a Quiché village. *Ethnology* 3(3): 305–328.

Scott, James C. 1976. *The Moral Economy of the Peasant: Rebellion and Subsistence in Southeast Asia*. New Haven, Conn.: Yale University Press.

Sherman, William L. 1979. *Forced Native Labor in Sixteenth-Century Central America*. Lincoln: University of Nebraska Press.

Simon, Jean-Marie. 1987. *Guatemala: Eternal Spring, Eternal Tyranny*. New York: W. W. Norton and Company.

Smith, Carol A. 1978. Beyond dependency theory: National and regional patterns of underdevelopment in Guatemala. *American Ethnologist* 5(3): 574–617.

———. 1984a. Does a commodity economy enrich the few while ruining the masses? Differentiation among petty commodity producers in Guatemala. *Journal of Peasant Studies* 11(3): 60–95.

———. 1984b. Local history in global context: Social and economic transitions in western Guatemala. *Comparative Studies in Society and History* 26(2): 193–228.

———. 1987. Culture and Community: The Language of Class in Guatemala. In *The Year Left: An American Socialist Yearbook*, vol. 2, ed. Mike Davis, Manning Marable, Fred Pfeil, and Michael Sprinker, pp. 197–217. London: Verso.

———. 1990a. Class position and class consciousness in an Indian community: Totonicapán in the 1970s. In *Guatemalan Indians and the State: 1540 to 1988*, ed. Carol A. Smith, pp. 205–229. Austin: University of Texas Press.

———, ed. 1990b. *Guatemalan Indians and the State: 1540 to 1988*. Austin: University of Texas Press.

Smith, Waldemar R. 1975. Beyond the plural society: Economics and ethnicity in Middle American towns. *Ethnology* 14(3): 225–243.

———. 1977. *The Fiesta System and Economic Change*. New York: Columbia University Press.

Sociedad Bíblica en Guatemala. 1968. *Ju ac'aj tu'jil: El nuevo testamento de Nuestro Señor Jesucristo en Mam de Huehuetenango y en Español (versión popular)*. Guatemala City: Sociedad Bíblica en Guatemala.

Sperber, Dan. 1975. *Rethinking Symbolism*. Trans. Alice L. Morton. Cambridge: Cambridge University Press.

Stadelman, Raymond. 1940. *Maize Cultivation in Northwestern Guatemala*. Contributions to American Anthropology and History, no. 33. Washington, D.C.: Carnegie Institution.

Stavenhagen, Rudolfo. 1968. Classes, Colonialism, and Acculturation. In *Comparative Perspectives on Stratification: Mexico, Great Britain, Japan*, ed. Joseph A. Kahl, pp. 31–63. Boston: Little, Brown, and Company.

266   *Maya Saints and Souls in a Changing World*

Stephens, John L. 1969 [1841]. *Incidents of Travel in Central America, Chiapas, and Yucatan*, vol. 2. New York: Dover Publications, Inc.

Sywulka, Edward. 1966. Mam Grammar. In *Languages of Guatemala*, ed. Marvin K. Mayers, pp. 178–195. Janua Linguarum, Series Practica, no. 23. The Hague: Editions Mouton and Co.

Tarn, Nathaniel, and Martín Prechtel. 1990. "Comiendose la fruta": Metáforas sexuales e iniciaciones en Santiago Atitlán. *Mesoamérica* 11(19): 73–82.

Taussig, Michael T. 1980. *The Devil and Commodity Fetishism in South America*. Chapel Hill: University of North Carolina Press.

Tax, Sol. 1937. The municipios of the midwestern highlands of Guatemala. *American Anthropologist* 39(3): 423–444.

———. 1941. World view and social relations in Guatemala. *American Anthropologist* 43(1): 27–42.

———. 1953. *Penny Capitalism: A Guatemalan Indian Economy*. Smithsonian Institute of Social Anthropology, pub. 16. Washington, D.C.: Smithsonian Institution.

Taylor, William B. 1979. *Drinking, Homicide, and Rebellion in Colonial Mexican Villages*. Stanford, Calif.: Stanford University Press.

Tedlock, Barbara. 1982. *Time and the Highland Maya*. Albuquerque: University of New Mexico Press.

———. 1987. An interpretive solution to the problem of humoral medicine in Latin America. *Social Science and Medicine* 24(12): 1069–1083.

Tedlock, Dennis, trans. 1985. *Popol Vuh: The Definitive Edition of the Maya Book of the Dawn of Life and the Glories of Gods and Kings*. New York: Simon and Schuster.

Thompson, J. Eric S. 1970. *Maya History and Religion*. The Civilization of the American Indian Series, vol. 99. Norman: University of Oklahoma Press.

Valladares, León A. 1957. *El hombre y el maíz: Etnografía y etnopsicología de Colotenango*. Mexico City: Editorial B. Costa-Amic.

Veblen, Thomas T. 1982. Native Population Decline in Totonicapan, Guatemala. In *The Historical Demography of Highland Guatemala*, ed. Robert M. Carmack, John Early, and Christopher Lutz, pp. 81–102. Institute for Mesoamerican Studies, pub. 6. Albany: Institute for Mesoamerican Studies, State University of New York.

Vogt, Evon Z. 1969. *Zinacantan: A Maya Community in the Highlands of Chiapas*. Cambridge: Belknap Press of Harvard University Press.

———. 1970. Human Souls and Animal Spirits in Zinacantan. In *Echanges et communications: Mélanges offerts à Claude Lévi-Strauss à l'occasion de son 60ème anniversaire*, ed. Jean Pouillon and Pierre Maranda, pp. 1148–1167. The Hague: Editions Mouton and Co.

———. 1976. *Tortillas for the Gods: A Symbolic Analysis of Zinacanteco Rituals*. Cambridge: Harvard University Press.

Wagley, Charles. 1941. *Economics of a Guatemalan Village*. Memoirs of the American Anthropological Association, no. 58. Menasha, Wis.: American Anthropological Association.

―――. 1949. *The Social and Religious Life of a Guatemalan Village*. Memoirs of the American Anthropological Association, no. 71. Menasha, Wis.: American Anthropological Association.

―――. 1957. *Santiago Chimaltenango: Estudio antropológico-social de una comunidad indígena de Huehuetenango*. Seminario de Integración Social Guatemalteca, pub. 4. Guatemala City: Tipografía Nacional.

Wagner, Roy. 1981. *The Invention of Culture*. Revised and expanded edition. Chicago: University of Chicago Press.

Warren, Kay B. 1978. *The Symbolism of Subordination: Indian Identity in a Guatemalan Town*. Austin: University of Texas Press.

Wasserstrom, Robert. 1978. The exchange of saints in Zinacantán: The socioeconomic bases of religious change in southern Mexico. *Ethnology* 17(2): 197–210.

―――. 1983. *Class and Society in Central Chiapas*. Berkeley and Los Angeles: University of California Press.

Watanabe, John M. 1981a. Cambios económicos en Santiago Chimaltenango, Guatemala. *Mesoamérica* 1(2): 20–41.

―――. 1981b. Illness and essence: The conceptualization of sickness in a Guatemalan Indian town. Paper read at the 80th Annual Meeting of the American Anthropological Association, Los Angeles, Calif.

―――. 1983. In the world of the sun: A cognitive model of Mayan cosmology. *Man* n.s. 18(4): 710–728.

―――. 1989. Elusive Essences: Souls and Social Identity in Two Highland Maya Communities. In *Ethnographic Encounters in Southern Mesoamerica: Essays in Honor of Evon Zartman Vogt, Jr.*, ed. Victoria R. Bricker and Gary H. Gossen, pp. 263–274. Albany: Institute for Mesoamerican Studies, State University of New York.

―――. 1990. From saints to shibboleths: Image, structure, and identity in Maya religious syncretism. *American Ethnologist* 17(1): 129–148.

Whetten, Nathan L. 1961. *Guatemala: The Land and the People*. New Haven, Conn.: Yale University Press.

Wolf, Eric R. 1955. Types of Latin American peasantry: A preliminary discussion. *American Anthropologist* 57(3): 452–471.

―――. 1957. Closed corporate peasant communities in Mesoamerica and central Java. *Southwestern Journal of Anthropology* 13(1): 1–18.

―――. 1959. *Sons of the Shaking Earth*. Chicago: University of Chicago.

―――. 1986. The vicissitudes of the closed corporate peasant community. *American Ethnologist* 13(2): 325–329.

✛ Index ✛